Myth-Building
in Modern Media

Myth-Building in Modern Media

The Role of the Mytharc in Imagined Worlds

A. J. Black

McFarland & Company, Inc., Publishers
Jefferson, North Carolina

LIBRARY OF CONGRESS CATALOGUING-IN-PUBLICATION DATA

Names: Black, A. J., 1982– author.
Title: Myth-building in modern media : the role of the mytharc in imagined worlds / A. J. Black.
Description: Jefferson : McFarland & Company, Inc., Publishers, 2020. | Includes bibliographical references and index.
Identifiers: LCCN 2020022987 | ISBN 9781476675633 (paperback) ∞
ISBN 9781476637556 (ebook)
Subjects: LCSH: Myth in mass media.
Classification: LCC P96.M94 B53 2020 | DDC 809.3/937—dc23
LC record available at https://lccn.loc.gov/2020022987

BRITISH LIBRARY CATALOGUING DATA ARE AVAILABLE

ISBN (print) 978-1-4766-7563-3
ISBN (ebook) 978-1-4766-3755-6

© 2020 A. J. Black. All rights reserved

No part of this book may be reproduced or transmitted in any form or by any means, electronic or mechanical, including photocopying or recording, or by any information storage and retrieval system, without permission in writing from the publisher.

Front cover image © 2020 Shutterstock

Printed in the United States of America

McFarland & Company, Inc., Publishers
Box 611, Jefferson, North Carolina 28640
www.mcfarlandpub.com

For my wife, Steph.
She helps me dream.

Acknowledgments

I would like to thank my family and friends for their unending encouragement in this, my first published work.

My sincerest thanks to Darren Mooney. This book would likely not exist without him.

My deepest thanks to Frank Spotnitz for giving up his time to answer questions, and to Duncan Barrett for support and structural book advice.

Finally, I'd like to thank my endlessly supportive wife Steph, who has the patience of a saint.

Table of Contents

Acknowledgments   vi

Preface: What Is the Mytharc?   1

1. Before the Mytharc   7
2. The Monomytharc   22
3. The Divine Mytharc   56
4. The Cultural Mytharc   90
5. Mytharcs That Never Were   121
6. The Future of the Mytharc   131
7. Finding the Mytharc   156

Chapter Notes   159

Bibliography   193

Index   199

Preface:
What Is the Mytharc?

There has long been a certain amount of debate as to where the term "Mytharc" came from.

We know it came from somewhere on the proliferation of message boards which popped up to discuss the hit television series of the 1990s, *The X-Files*, but no one is quite sure who coined the term. It eventually slipped into the language used to describe the show from its third season onwards. *The X-Files* came to define the decade in which it was made from a pop-culture perspective.[1]

Stan Carey believes people were using the term "mythology" or "mythos" in connection with TV drama series *Twin Peaks* in the early 1990s.[2] A poster named "Devious Weasel" on the alt.tv.x-files.analysis forum edges closer to the mid–'90s as the origin of this terminology:

> Just dug out an old issue of *Cinescape* from the end of the third season [1996] where [Chris Carter] is referring to the fact that [Gillian Anderson's] pregnancy forced 1013 to develop the mythology a little faster in the second season than they would have liked. For some reason I don't think this is the earliest reference I've seen to the term, but it is the earliest I have available to me.[3]

We may never know for sure who first uttered or typed "Mytharc" but it started somewhere in the ether of fandom. What we do know is that from around the year 1995, the term was officially in circulation. It went on to define storytelling over the next two decades, on both the big and small screen.

To understand the derivation of "Mytharc" and the context in which it will be explored in this book, we need to know how and why the two words "Myth" and "Arc" were joined. What alchemy stitched together two pointedly diffuse terms which mean very different things? We've all heard of myths. We've likely all heard of an arc in fiction. How do you get from those positions to a word such as "Mytharc"?

Let's start with Myth. If someone was to say the word "mythology"

Preface

to you, what would be the first thing that came to mind? Would it be the Greeks? Ancient and wise, with their bearded gods atop towering mountains, or famous heroes riding legendary creatures? Impassable, intractable mazes and labyrinths in cities lost to history? Or even the Romans, with their pantheon of deities, all sporting powers that exist far beyond the mortal? Chances are, Mythology (with a capital M) has embedded itself within your mind as intrinsically defined by a specific set of images, and a very precise collection of stories.

That is all myths *are*, remember. Stories.

Indeed, part of the very definition of "Mythology" in the *Oxford English Dictionary* is: "A set of stories or beliefs about a particular person, institution, or situation, especially when exaggerated or fictitious."[4]

Stories. Beliefs. Two words that are crucial to this book, and how it will define, or perhaps *redefine*, the meaning of Mythology in a modern context—certainly when it comes to pop-culture entertainment and 21st century media.

A term that has been popular since the 1930s, "mythopoeia," also known as "mythopoesis," stems from the Hellenistic Greek. It literally translates as "myth-making" and corresponds directly to the act of creating an artificial mythology within fiction. The word first re-entered the cultural conversation thanks to perhaps the greatest mythmaker of all, J.R.R. Tolkien, creator of the *Lord of the Rings* series. He went on to write a poem using it.[5]

E.E. Stokely described "mythopoeia" as

> purely about the archetypes of the psyche that exist in the self. Mythopoetic writing is about constructing the larger themes of life and living life on the page, of grandiose tragedy, redemption, determinism vs. freewill, of the divine nature of the individual vs. the Gods, being and non-being, and of the greater themes of the unconscious mind that holds meaning in mythic symbols and imagery hidden in the lower brain. It is existential and profound, played out via characters in story, yet driven by a greater plan beyond a single protagonist or story arc.[6]

John Adcox describes Tolkien's definition of it as "sub-creation, the act of the artist reflecting the creation of the world—the very essence of myth—in art."[7] The concept of mythopoesis presents modern storytelling as a way of constructing the kind of mythology that our ancient forefathers used to give context and emphasis to their world, in order to understand ours.

This is nothing new. Storytellers have been doing this, many consciously, for decades. You only have to look at the comic-book as a key exemplar of archetypal mythology at work. Superman, the last son of

What Is the Mytharc?

Krypton, sent to Earth as the sole survivor of an apocalyptic world, is as pure a metaphorical Jesus Christ, with his super-heroic story an equivalent Second Coming, as fiction could imagine. Writers like Bob Kane, Jack Kirby and Stan Lee are the latter day Homer, Aeschylus and Sophocles, their tales serving as parables which often redefine tenets of ancient mythology for a modern audience, in some cases quite literally, such as the Asgardian mythology of Thor.

Given the recent prevalence of comic-book fiction in cinema, many of these stories have begun to reach a much wider audience. The entire Marvel Cinematic Universe provides a "who's who" roster of archetypal heroes and villains, many of whom match their mythological antecedents. Yet this is often where the confusion exists between what we would consider mythological characters and archetypes and mythopoetic storytelling. In recent years, pop culture has begun to rely more and more on wider, mythological storytelling in which characters aren't simply representative of bigger concepts, they are part of stories and worlds which allow us to contextualize our lives and meaning.

A key example: Middle-Earth, first represented in a collection of books and now award-winning films thanks to the talents of (principally) Peter Jackson. Tolkien was constructing a vast, natural ecosystem within which his parable about the danger of war, and nuclear power before the A-bomb was invented, could exist.[8] An example which many would consider comes close to matching Tolkien's reach is *A Song of Ice and Fire*, writer George R.R. Martin's saga, which led to HBO's TV phenomenon *Game of Thrones*, arguably the most popular and successful television show of the 2010s. These are worlds which carry dense, mythic themes and a level of self-aware referentiality which spread across various kinds of media.

Myth then exists as part of these wider and deeper forces built inside legends passed down from hundreds of cultures, which embedded themselves into the first proliferation of published fictional literature from around the 18th century onwards, and eventually found their way into comic-book serials, audio plays, movies and television dramas.

What though of the Arc, or more specifically the "Story Arc," from which the derivation "Arc" in the word "Mytharc" originates?

In simple terms, a Story Arc is a continuing narrative across whatever medium the story is being told. In a TV series, it may be the underlying, recurring plot beats that constitute a particular "season" of storytelling; Buffy Summers' battle against the Mayor in Season 3 of *Buffy the Vampire Slayer*, for instance.[9] The aforementioned Marvel Cinematic Universe is perhaps the most central example of a Story Arc playing out in cinematic

Preface

terms, given movies have traditionally operated in the manner of sequels; one story informs a follow-up featuring many of the same characters, but with a new situation and new point of dramatic conflict. This is different from an Arc which directly continues narrative beats and character points, as opposed to revisiting characters and ideas.

A key example of the Story Arc and how it informed television brings us back to *The X-Files* and what became known as the "alien mythology" or, later, the Mytharc. Due to circumstances outside of the control of the show and its writers,[10] the series naturally developed an ongoing narrative concerning a global government conspiracy to cover up not just the existence of extraterrestrial life, but their complicity in a massive plot by those aliens to colonize the Earth. Woven within this overarching story, which would be revisited from various different angles in six to eight episodes per season, were the character Arcs of protagonists Fox Mulder and Dana Scully and their involvement in exposing the truth behind this grand conspiracy.

The Arc of those characters in particular serves as the core of not just drama but also Myth. In his seminal comparative mythology text *The Hero with a Thousand Faces* (1948), Joseph Campbell, the landmark human anthropologist of mythmaking of the 20th century, describes what he terms the "Monomyth" as the Arc of the hero undergoing a transformative process, a.k.a. "the hero's journey": "A hero ventures forth from the world of common day into a region of supernatural wonder: fabulous forces are there encountered and a decisive victory is won: the hero comes back from this mysterious adventure with the power to bestow boons on his fellow man."[11]

At this point, it is worth defining the word "hero" in the Campbellian term as he describes it. The etymology of the word hero is described variously as a "man of superhuman strength or physical courage," or a "hero, demigod, illustrious man" as it comes from the Ancient Greek.[12] In mythological terms, that is how we consider the Hero: Hercules and his rippling muscles battling creatures in the labyrinth, Leonidas and his small force of Spartans fighting off an entire empire. They are often, as the term demigod suggests, born of both God and mortal. They are more than man. Hence why the term has prevailed into the modern-day lexicon. Our modern heroes are James Bond or Indiana Jones on the cinema screen, or men like Martin Luther King, Jr., in the arena of social change. Heroes are now, contrary to historic mythology, as much women as men.

Yet the hero of Campbell's Monomyth is different. His hero undertakes a journey, or quest, which may often involve a reward or a deed

What Is the Mytharc?

which protects others or saves a particular situation from destruction. But the true journey in Campbellian myth is *inward*. Campbell's comparative study arranges hundreds of examples across historical mythology, from dozens of civilizations, which all describe a heroic quest in which the hero returns having not just changed the world around them, but having *been* changed by their experience. James Bond may stop the super-villain from destroying the world from their underwater base, and in doing so he may "get the girl" once the credits roll, but he rarely changes himself from this experience.[13] The Monomythical journey is one, fundamentally, in which the heroism of the character is counterbalanced by what they learn about themselves, and how they take that into their future.

We will find, across this book, that many examples of the Mytharc are driven, principally, by some aspect of the Monomythical Hero's Journey.

Story Arc and Character Arc in modern fiction are therefore one and the same. The conspiracy to expose the truth about alien life in *The X-Files* is meaningless unless it informs and illuminates Mulder's own internal search for closure regarding his missing sister Samantha. This is just one of countless examples which feed into our own search for what became known as the Mytharc in popular culture entertainment, or by degrees simply the "mythology" of a given piece of work, particularly in the medium of television.

The Mytharc serves as the perfect confluence between these two distinct aspects: myth, whereby legend, theme and our basic understanding of the human condition exists through a tapestry of interconnected stories and characters who serve to illuminate knowledge. Story, which takes characters on a journey inside an established universe designed to make a spiritual, political or sociological point about who we are and where we are as people. And the Arc, be it Story or in particular Character, in which the protagonists we follow intersect with these mythic archetypes and world-building constructs to undergo a journey of self-fulfillment and understanding, while often affecting (and in the hero's journey, saving) the world around them.

In this book, we will explore the Mytharc as a concept in modern storytelling and how it has influenced cinema, television, literature and popular culture. We will investigate the genesis of narrative that would breed the kind of storytelling that led to the popularization of the term. We will examine the properties, beyond simply *The X-Files*, which propagated the concept of a mythological underpinning to their storytelling. We will look at how the Mytharc has evolved beyond these first examples and how it informs narrative in a multitude of media into the present day. And

Preface

we will consider where the Mytharc may be headed as storytelling evolves, and with the continuing advent of technology, what forms it could take in the future.

Though we will discuss and dissect several mythologies from across television and cinema, this is by no means an exhaustive list, and there will almost certainly be examples that people will consider key omissions; for example, David Lynch and Mark Frost's *Twin Peaks*, which many regard as the formative, early television mythology which directly inspired *The X-Files*.[14] Ronald D. Moore's *Battlestar Galactica* remake, which tells a human and technological story of scope and brevity across space and indeed time, as does the space-opera of J. Michael Stracyznski's *Babylon 5*, both of which also tap into wells of mythological antiquity to tell their stories.[15] In cinematic terms, the *Harry Potter* franchise cleaves to the same heroes' journey we will see repeat time and time again, with behind it a keen sense of mythology and backstory. To best help explore and understand the concept of the Mytharc, this author has chosen the worlds, characters and storylines he knows and has studied the most over years of consuming this medium.

What will become clear, as we undertake this quest to understand the core principles of the Mytharc and how it has become central to our modern mythology as audiences in the early 21st century, is how frequently many of the key texts we have enjoyed across the last quarter century cover the same basic Monomythical and mythopoetic journeys. The quest to understand the Island in *Lost* is no different from the arcane apocrypha of the Rambaldi mystery in *Alias*. The ancient battle against shadowy dark forces from antiquity is repeated, cyclically, in the operatic fantasy trappings of *Game of Thrones*.

This list goes on. The comparisons continue. While each Mytharc is different and unique and in its own way complex, all of them return again to the same basic fundamental human questions we have been asking since the Greeks and Romans framed their lives in the context of their pantheon of deities.

Who are we, and where are we going?

Those questions are central in our Quest for the Mytharc.

1

Before the Mytharc

Long before the word "Mytharc" was popularized in the cultural lexicon, there existed another associated word which suggested a similar fusion of idea, theme and narrative: "Mythos."

In 1917, in Providence, Rhode Island, there lived a 27-year-old man named H.P. Lovecraft. Though it would not be published until 1922, he would write a short story called "The Tomb," in which a young man becomes obsessed with the secrets that lie inside a mausoleum. It was the first of dozens of similar, concise tales, all of which spoke to an incredibly dark (some might say nihilistic) approach to humanity and its place in the cosmos. They became known, in time, as the "Cthulhu Mythos," and serve as one of the earliest examples of a fictional, artificial, mythopoetic shared universe. The word Mythos was attributed to Lovecraft long after he wrote stories like "The Tomb," indeed long after his death at the relatively young age of 47 from cancer of the small intestine and malnutrition.[1]

"Mythos" comes from the Ancient Greek meaning "tale" or "story," which naturally connects it as a definition to the work of Lovecraft, and the many other creators whose work this book will discuss. A deeper definition: "A story or set of stories relevant to or having a significant truth or meaning for a particular culture, religion, society or other group."[2] This cuts to the very heart of narrative mythology—the greater meaning behind the storytelling.

Where the definition resonates with Lovecraft and the body of work he created is in Mythos being described as "a tale, story or narrative, usually verbally transmitted, or otherwise recorded into the written form from an alleged secondary source."[3] One of the key, recurring elements in Lovecraft's work, and the Cthulhu Mythos in particular, is the description and recounting of events being transmitted verbally, or via some kind of diarized recount, events which often defy characterization and even meaning. Many of Lovecraft's descriptors are primary sources, as in they experienced these events first hand, but all of them pass down information which swiftly is questioned by those around them. The reader is being brought in on sacred, mythical knowledge acquired by these protagonists who have peered behind the veil.

While we have already touched on the meaning of Myth, it has also been described in its broadest essence thusly: "a traditional story, especially one concerning the early history of a people or explaining a natural or social phenomenon, and typically involving supernatural beings or events."[4] Myth therefore seems to suggest an ancient world, one that existed outside of our reach of natural history or accepted timeline of events on our planet or in our universe (using that term in more of the philosophical sense rather than the cosmic). Lovecraft's work, the "Mythos" which grew to encompass his lexicon, is firmly rooted in the concept of not just myth, but the idea that everything we *consider* to be myth, to be fiction, to be nothing more than legend or a childish whimsy, is in fact a reality we simply cannot either see or understand.

Lovecraft's aforementioned primary sources are not just frequent descriptors of these unfathomable happenings, but they are almost always people who deserve some level of terrible judgment. They could be the German U-boat officer in "The Temple," who believes in the teutonic righteousness and superiority of the German race in the midst of the Great War,[5] and who shoots most of his crew members for madness, before being consumed by a strange ancient city below the ocean. Then there are the three robbers in "The Terrible Old Man" who conspire to rob and possibly murder a seemingly frail old sea dog in the town of Kingsport, only to suffer a bloody fate at the hands of that same man, a man with a great deal more power than they could conceive. There are many such examples across Lovecraft's episodes and greater stories, which almost always see men coming face to face with forces utterly beyond the limits of human understanding. Many of them have a supernatural source.[6]

Thematically, Lovecraft's canon ties together on numerous fronts. The writer rarely seems interested in "character" as most fiction would place as primary importance to any text—his protagonists are rarely people to care about or invest in, even if they're not loathsome, selfish individuals. They are ciphers bearing witness to bigger and darker cosmological forces. Lovecraft often displays anti–Semitic or deeply negative racial epithets in his work, particularly in his early stories.[7]

His tales are also frequently set in his native New England, in a manner one of his spiritual narrative descendants Stephen King employed himself.[8] Not all of them, however, conform to the in-world "Mythos" which characterizes the shared-world mythology inside Lovecraft's work. They all prescribe to the author's determined nihilistic belief than humans are

1. Before the Mytharc

dwarfed by the unknowable forces of the cosmos, obsessive about death, about the power of dreams, and the futility of existence. Everything does not connect in a straight line. Nonetheless, Lovecraft's work certainly prescribes to an internal mythology which would inspire writers and creators over the next century, consciously or not.

The central concept of the Mythos runs something like this. In a time long before antiquity, quite literally millions of years in the past, there existed the Old Ones, a race of extraterrestrial beings who came to Earth and ruled. The arrival and rise of mankind coincided with their banishment to another inter-dimensional realm from which they sometimes, through the dreamscape of individuals tuned into their position or via ritual incantations from arcane lore, can be made visible. They are spearheaded by the great sea creature Cthulhu, a "priest" of the Old Ones. It is prophesied that these ancient creatures will eventually rise up again, wipe humanity from the face of the Earth, and re-assume their place as rulers of the planet.

That is the basic underpinning of the Mythos, but there is a deeper level of complexity which Lovecraft suggests in ambiguous terms. "The Call of Cthulhu," perhaps his signature story, lays out this essential overarching mythology to stories which aren't precisely connected, but serve a greater mythological purpose. In this story, Lovecraft suggests that the Old Ones must be freed from their eternal resting place "inside the earth and under the sea" by men. This is why Cthulhu, using dreams, has created his own cult of devoted worshippers committed to doing his bidding. These creatures may be all-powerful but they are hampered in their dominance by the cosmic forces of the stars needing to be in alignment, and the spell incantations which have seen them locked away need to be removed. The story also suggests that the Old Ones wouldn't destroy humanity at all—contradicted by "The Dunwich Horror" later—but usher in a new age whereby humanity are shorn of laws and morals and given "freedom" to behave like animalistic savages. From a psychological and sociological standpoint, this makes the Old Ones even more interesting as a mythological concept.

You see, the Old Ones never had any direct overlap with humanity. They had long descended into the secret places of the earth before human beings arrived on the scene, and consequently, in almost all of his stories Lovecraft treats them as purely and powerfully unknowable. This in many ways represents the writers' terrible fear and suspicion of the "other," hence the visible racism and even anti–Semitism in certain parts of Lovecraft's work. He didn't seem to trust or understand people not of his color or creed and hence he pivots this entire mythology around creatures who,

Myth-Building in Modern Media

if we were able to glimpse them, would send a human being into the veritable pit of madness and despair. Such was the fate of Abdul Alhazared, a.k.a. "the mad Arab." He was the writer of the Necronomicon, a fictional book created by Lovecraft and referenced in many stories connected to the Mythos of the Old Ones. It serves as a unifying MacGuffin of sorts for characters in many of his stories to utilize where necessary to aid or combat the agenda of the Cyclopean beasts. This idea of sacred knowledge in text or tome would carry through across fiction throughout the 20th century and beyond; the Necronomicon became so iconic in occult circles that many believed for a time that it could be a real book. It later plays a key part in Sam Raimi's classic *Evil Dead* movie series.

Lovecraft was a man obsessed not just with death but equally the powerlessness and smallness of mankind in the face of a universe filled with unfathomable truths. Many writers before and since characterize these ideas in their own mythologies as positives or factors to strive for—look at Gene Roddenberry's *Star Trek*, a franchise all about the wonder of seeking out new worlds and new life. But Roddenberry's vision was a different outlook for an entirely different age. Lovecraft doesn't believe the universe holds wonder, only terror. He believes that, should humanity glimpse those civilizations or worlds or cosmic imaginings, we should run away screaming, lest we become consumed by our own mania. He's a writer who doesn't believe in the human condition and this is perhaps understandable given the fact that he started writing during the Great War, a time filled with a nihilistic despair as to why millions of young men were fighting and dying on foreign fields. Mythologies within fiction are formed either thanks to the worldview of their creator, or the political and sociological realities of their age, and Lovecraft is a pointed example of the former being influenced, to an extent, by the latter.

Most interestingly, Lovecraft's Mythos didn't die with the writer in 1937. Numerous contemporaries took Lovecraft's style and sense of world-building and added foundations across the rest of the 20th century: Robert E. Howard, Frank Bellknap Long and principally August Derleth, who took the interconnected world of stories Lovecraft created[9] and helped birth what subsequently was referred to as the "Cthulhu Mythos."[10] Aside from works written before the age of copyright law, such as the science fiction, utopian escapism of the Victorian age of Jules Verne, H.G. Wells and Arthur Conan Doyle, etc., rarely has any interconnected "universe" in fiction been canonically continued by other writers without some level of express permission or consent from the estate of the writer in question. This isn't Brian Herbert continuing his father's *Dune* saga. In

1. Before the Mytharc

many ways, the Mythos born out of Lovecraft's unique and underappreciated work can be seen as an early example of fan fiction, which would much later emerge as a mode of expression amongst fandom communities which came together from the 1960s onwards, in the wake of new worlds and mythologies for more of a socially mobile era.

Lovecraft may not be a household name like Conan Doyle or Verne or even contemporaries of his age, principally because his niche corner of "weird fiction" frankly has never stopped being unerringly strange almost a century on; if anything, it gets stranger and harder to classify. But his purple prose, lack of humor and mordant narrative style have arguably inspired modern fictional mythology in a great many ways. From the authors inspired by him, to the authors who *still* add to the ever-growing and developing "Cthulhu Mythos," through to filmmakers such as the aforementioned Raimi, John Carpenter and Guillermo del Toro who heavily were influenced by his Gothic tales in their own unique work,[11] to modern-day endeavors such as the hit Netflix series *Stranger Things*, with its Cthulhu-like demi-gorgon in the Upside Down, an inverted hell dimension of the 1980s. A huge amount of storytelling over the last century has been inspired, consciously or unconsciously, by the short stories and creeping novellas put forth by the inimitable Lovecraft.

At the same time that Lovecraft churned out his strange tales in his Providence attic, over in midtown Manhattan, another man launched an entirely different world in an entirely different medium which came to define modern storytelling and modern mythology...

While he cannot be credited with inventing the comic book itself, Major Malcolm Wheeler-Nicholson will go down in history as one of the most important men in the history of the medium and of the nascent concept of the Mytharc in modern narrative. In the autumn of 1934, Wheeler-Nicholson founded National Allied Publications, a company which, decades later, became known by the moniker that staff members had used for many years: DC Comics.

In recent years, DC Comics' motion picture arm has attempted to launch what became known as the DC Extended Universe, the latest salvo in their half-century rivalry with the publishing house that, from the 1960s onwards, became their greatest competition: Marvel Comics. Fans of the artful medium often line up to declare themselves, on modern social media, as either "Marvel or DC."[12]

In the spring of 2016, DC launched their much-hyped *Batman vs. Superman: Dawn of Justice* movie while Marvel debuted *Captain America: Civil War*, the latest in their pre-established and much venerated Marvel

Myth-Building in Modern Media

Cinematic Universe, going strong since 2008's *Iron Man*. This conflict, much like the superhero and the super-villain, shows no sign of abating.

When it comes to a fictional, mythological standpoint, both of these comic-book institutions share a common thread: Their worlds, characters and narratives all are encapsulated within the same overarching universe. Arguably DC and Marvel were among the first publishers of fiction across the mid–20th century and beyond to popularize the idea of characters and stories interweaving their way through multiple-run issues over months and sometimes years of ongoing storytelling. (On a technical level, the crossover has its narrative roots as far back as Greek myth.[13])

This approach to layered, ongoing storytelling differed substantially from Lovecraft's formative, indeed unformed approach to the shared universe; he fell into a Mythos not by design but almost by accident, building and expanding on his strange short stories. DC and Marvel were a different beast. They very much knew they desired a shared continuity.

More perhaps than any other strand of storytelling we will discuss in this book, the comic book can trace its roots back to the mythological. Paul Levitz has described this pre-comic history as "The Stone Age."[14] Some may even suggest that Superman stems, in part, from Friedrich Nietzsche's theories about racial and hegemonic superiority and the "Ubermensch."[15] Comic-book characters, therefore, have always been with us.

How does this connect to either DC or Marvel, and their world of a connected Mythos? Superman and Batman's solo comic success gave us new creations such as the Atom (in 1940) and Green Lantern (in 1941). In 1941, DC Comics writers Shelly Mayer and Gardner Fox came up with this simple but rather revolutionary idea: What if the heroes featured in *All-Star Comics* became part of each other's stories? Paul Levitz wrote,

> In popular culture today, the idea of a crossover permeates television, film and novels, and is one of the great engines of comics.... But in 1941, the idea of mixing separate properties together was radical, and an enduring enough hit that Justice Society of America (JSA) ran to the end of the Golden Age (even, by some scholars' logic, defining the end of the Golden Age when it stopped)."[16]

The Golden Age is recognized as the era in the late 1930s in which the major heroes in comic-book history were born. It was the crossover, the concept of a shared universe, which changed the paradigm of comic-book storytelling forever.[17]

Robert Overstreet described the first superhero team-up as "a breakthrough concept, second in importance only to [their] creation [itself],"[18] and this speaks to the immediate importance of placing these characters

1. Before the Mytharc

within the same storyline. This goes beyond Lovecraft's perhaps unintentional references to broader characters and monsters within his loosely connected narratives. Comic books were the first medium to place characters with their own titles, particularly Superman and Batman, into stories where both characters were central to the outcome, and whose battles would directly influence future narratives. The storytelling, for the first time, did not end with the conclusion of the issue or comic-strip. The idea of the shared universe had truly been born.

Batman was featured in two cheap cinematic productions in the 1940s and later in the colorful and camp TV series of the 1960s. TV's *The Adventures of Superman* starring George Reeves in the 1950s saw Clark Kent's world realized on screen for the first time. But neither of these series cleaved to any sense of shared, unified, mythological continuity.[19] They don't exhibit the growing narrative complexity or scope that the comic-book medium does. The comic-book, first from DC Comics and later Marvel Comics, truly spearheaded the road toward the deeper mythological worlds we would see across fiction of all media over the last 50 years.

One element that would presage the development and growth of mythological world-building on screen is how the comic-book industry, in the 1970s and particularly the 1980s, began to craft their characters and titles around creative "names." Jack Kirby returned to DC with an ambitious, trumpeted internal mythology he was keen to create, while Frank Miller powerfully revived Daredevil for Marvel and developed *The Dark Knight Returns* for DC. Alan Moore cast his spell over DC with titles such as *Swamp Thing* and players such as John Constantine, as did Neil Gaiman with *Sandman*.

All of them brought with them their own styles and sensibilities, and their own belief systems and ideals which would become part of the comic-book runs they developed. These creators would take well-known, beloved characters and internal mythologies and recast them with their own cultural commentary, on everything from race to sex to politics and beyond. The power of the auteur behind such world-building took a great step forward in the comic-book world.

While the comics medium has undergone, and continues to undergo, a great deal of reimagining from various different creatives, often reflecting the social and historical realities of their age,[20] there is no question that the broadened scope of the comic-book world in the 1950s and especially the 1960s bled into the cultural changes emerging thanks to the counter-cultural revolution of the postwar decades.

Myth-Building in Modern Media

Without people like Stan Lee, Jack Kirby, Bill Finger, Jerry Siegel and Joe Schuster, we may never have begun to witness the dawn of escapist entertainment in the visual medium which started to transform the way we read entertainment and the way we watch it, and engage with mythological, fictional worlds in the manner we do today.

If the province of fictional universes and artificial Mythos had heretofore lain in the world of literature, it was the 1960s which truly saw its evolution into the domain of cinema and the burgeoning realm of television, as well as its aforementioned blossoming in the comic book world with Marvel as well as DC.

Cinema had touched upon these areas previously, perhaps most principally in *The Wizard of Oz* (1939), adapting L. Frank Baum's successful series of fantasy tales. But in truth the picture angled itself far more toward being a vehicle for Judy Garland's musical talents and as a vibrant expression of Technicolor at the end of the first decade of talking pictures. The mythology and world-building behind the fantasy was slim. The 1940s gave way to a Hollywood consumed by the Second World War, with propaganda pictures designed to rouse the American spirit; a surfeit of Westerns which explored the cultural and historical identity of American life and American exceptionalism,[21] and MGM musicals with Garland, Gene Kelly *et al*. Then, too, there was the detective noir of Humphrey Bogart. The picture in the British film industry was much the same. War and nationalism allowed no place for the fantastical. What the world was going through felt fantastical enough, akin to the great struggles many a science fiction or fantasy drama would later convey.

By the 1950s, the landscape had started to change. Though never truly embracing any sense of mythological world-building, Hollywood began allowing escapism to start creeping into the system. The now revered B-movie science fiction films of that decade, many adapted from pulp novels by some of the most recognized authors in the business, started to embrace the kind of storytelling which would later evolve into deeper mythological worlds: alien invasions such as *Invasion of the Body Snatchers*, battles with Lovecraftian sea beasts in *It Came from Beneath the Sea*, and even claustrophobic adventure stories such as *The Thing from Another World*. (In 1982, the latter was memorably remade, and arguably improved upon, by John Carpenter as *The Thing*.) These examples serve as establishing templates for genre-based fiction that would truly be embraced over subsequent decades.

In the same decade, television became an innovation that, following particularly the 1953 broadcast of Queen Elizabeth II's coronation, found

1. Before the Mytharc

itself inside the living rooms of millions of British families. The same was happening across the pond in America. In this decade, we were graced with the first significant TV dramas and situation comedies—Westerns such as *Rawhide* and comedies like *I Love Lucy* in the U.S., while U.K. viewers were graced with romps such as *The Army Game* and dramas like *Dixon of Dock Green* and *Z-Cars*. Escapism was, equally, a growing concern. Take a young Roger Moore in *Ivanhoe*, for example, and as a genre unto itself these would sow the seeds for a varied range of colorful shows in the 1960s. Depth and mythology start emerging nonetheless in projects such as the seminal *Twilight Zone* in the U.S. from Rod Serling, and in the U.K. Nigel Kneale's *The Quatermass Experiment*.

Quatermass feels important because it sits on that border between the emergence of counter-cultural escapism and the austere rigidity of postwar Britain evident in the 1950s. Kneale's writing, particularly in the original live 1953 serialized broadcast,[22] is frequently quite stiff and formal, but there are broad, deep-rooted science fiction ideas at the heart of his narrative which evoke Lovecraft, evoke the B-movie aesthetic that American cinema was developing in the same decade. They suggest a bigger sense of a Mythos behind the events of the manned test rocket which crashes in London and unleashes an alien force, even if Kneale's series—and Hammer's subsequent film series—never quite dig as deeply into it as later television projects would.

As the 1960s dawned, and the counter-cultural revolution began on both sides of the pond, TV science fiction began to emerge as a major cultural force, in particular for viewers looking for a colorful escapism from postwar hardship, in line with the economic upturn the Baby Boomer generation were enjoying, not to mention the musical revolution of the Beatles, the Rolling Stones, and the true birth of rock'n'roll as a populist medium.

In America, Batman staked a claim on an entire generation with his TV presentation in several seasons of half-hour, camp and colorful comic romps. There was also a wonderfully kitsch big-screen version which immortalized Adam West and Burt Ward on the psyches of millions as Batman and Robin until 1989 when Tim Burton's blockbuster movie adaptation returned the characters to their DC comic-book roots. At the same time, *Star Trek*—which will be discussed in greater detail elsewhere in this book—presented an optimism and allegorical lightness in its storytelling which captivated an entire generation in a different way.

One of the major cultural touchstones which emerged from the U.K. on television, just a year after James Bond debuted on the big screen, was

Myth-Building in Modern Media

Doctor Who. These two wildly different characters are positioned in parallel because both of them have survived into the present day, and within just a year of each other celebrated half a century of success in popular culture in 2012 and 2013 respectively, with two of their biggest and most applauded storylines yet.[23] Though Bond avoided a sense of underpinning mythology and was always positioned as more of a post-colonial British escapist archetype, the Doctor is a character who epitomizes how British writers present science fiction through the nation's unique lens. Though he may be a time-traveling alien with two hearts, the Doctor has a metamorphosing humanity which alters and adapts with each "regeneration," allowing him to become a new man every time the lead actor plans to leave the series.

Steven Moffat's tenure in charge of the series from 2010 to 2017 arguably explored the Doctor's literal and psychological origins in far greater detail than any writer since 1963's "An Unearthly Child,"[24] but beyond the Doctor's role as a cyclical, archetypal hero, over decades of storytelling there has never truly been a key sense of mystery and consistent world-building in the same manner as we have seen in the *Star Trek* universe or the DC–Marvel comic universes. *Doctor Who* has always been about forward movement as opposed to consolidation, which is perhaps a result of being a series all about time travel and exploring different time zones as well as space. There is no unified galactic framework of rules beneath the Doctor's adventures. There *is* a sense that if there are any rules, most of them can eventually be rewritten. To this day, it is in many ways the ultimate example of escapist genre television.

That doesn't make it any less important to the development of mythological storytelling on the modern-day world. *Doctor Who* has its place in the continued development of fictional properties which have brought us to a type of storytelling where internal world-building and mythology often underpin the most powerful examples of popular culture. Without *Doctor Who*, or *Quatermass* and *Twilight Zone*, without even James Bond, we may not have ended up with a seminal, nay crucial, example of when escapism and television come together to make something truly mythologically groundbreaking.

We may never have ended up with *The Prisoner*.

At first glance, ITV's *The Prisoner* feels very much like a vestige of the 1950s, a decade its position toward the tail end of a vibrant, radically different '60s proved had been left behind.

The Prisoner can be seen as a significant breakthrough in the presentation and realization of an internal narrative mythology on television.[25]

1. Before the Mytharc

The Avengers before it had combined a level of British eccentricity and surrealism alongside the kind of populist James Bond theatrics also seen in its contemporary *The Man from U.N.C.L.E.* But the ITV series developed by journalist George Markstein and star Patrick McGoohan rapidly carved its own unique niche not just in British television history, but genre storytelling as a whole. You can point to dozens of shows influenced by *The Prisoner*—for example, the American dramas *Lost* and *Alias*—due to a scope and intellectual reach decades ahead of its time.[26]

The series presents a fairly simple set-up and then constructs a fascinating, fantastical world around it. McGoohan, a government intelligence agent, decides to resign for undisclosed reasons and is subsequently gassed in his London home and abducted. He awakens in "The Village," a self-sustained community in an unknown location. Here dubbed Number Six, McGoohan swiftly realizes that, despite the Village's charming old–English atmosphere and all the amenities he could want, the place is his prison. His unknown captors, driven by a man known as Number Two, want to know why Number Six resigned, and they undertake a number of complicated, unorthodox methods to get the information. *The Prisoner*, at least early on, is concerned with Number Six fighting back against these attempts to get him to talk while seeking any opportunity to either escape or understand where he is, and who the unseen, enigmatic Number One pulling the strings is.

Immediately, *The Prisoner* immerses you in its setting, in its the sense of place. The Village is a fascinating location for a power play between free will, individualism and totalitarian surveillance. It has all the affectations of a traditional, courtly English seaside town—friendly locals who unnervingly say "Be seeing you...," shops, social events and gatherings. In "Many Happy Returns," in which Number Six manages to escape the Village, we discover the location of this strange place is most likely an island off the North African coast. English quaintness has been replicated and staged in a very different clime for the purposes of strategic effect.

As you dig further, the Village has elements which both defy clear explanation and speak to an advanced level of control and technology. Doors electronically open and close. An ever-present speaker system communicates into both homes and across the Village. Number Two and the controllers of the Village occupy underground, advanced surveillance bases with cameras linked into every part of the location, inside homes and outside—they even use cordless telephones, many years before the first cell phones began to appear in cinema and television productions

Myth-Building in Modern Media

(and of course became a staple of modern life). The strangest element is "Rover": A large white ball which emits a sound like a whistling siren, it appears whenever Number Six or anyone else looking to either escape the Village or venture somewhere they shouldn't. It has no visible means of control, perhaps its own sense of intelligence. In "Arrival," it smothers a Villager to death. It is terrifying in its aberrance, and no explanation is ever ventured and to what it is, or even who controls it. It is simply *there*.

A key element to mythology in pop-culture media often lies in the *why* behind the *what* when it comes to the establishment of a place and setting. *The Prisoner* is an early example of a property where the why is never on the table. The more McGoohan exerted creative control over the series, the more he took it into absurdist, surrealist and esoteric territory, delivering a final episode ("Fall Out") which by today's standards would be judged as utterly maddening; McGoohan said that he had to go into hiding[27] after the episode aired.[28] People were used to explanations and understanding the basis of the world they had invested in. Why did Number Six resign? Who controls the Village and who created it? Who is Number One and what side is he on? Information (a word key to *The Prisoner*) was something which audiences didn't just expect, but demanded. Information they were never conclusively given. As bizarre a viewing experience *The Prisoner* can be 50 years removed, there is no denying that the fact that it encouraged viewers to infer, question and make up their own minds about what it all meant is the primary reason it has endured as a seminal piece of 1960s culture, moving beyond the reach of pure escapism into the kind of mythological world-building and thematic commentary many series lack the inventiveness or intelligence to reach.[29]

Looking back on each of these examples we have discussed, covering a multitude of different types of media, all of them share this commonality in how they struck a chord in popular culture across the many decades they were created, and why these examples have endured and inspired many of the pieces of entertainment we will discuss throughout this book—and beyond.

Every one of them has a voice, whether it's Lovecraft's terror of death and the unknown abyss of creation, minds such as Lee, Kirby and Roddenberry and even arguably McGoohan, using their escapist worlds to engage readers and viewers with potent examples of counter-cultural allegory. Whenever these creatives build a world around their characters and ideas, their mythologies frequently come from an anxiety or personal outlook which drives their storytelling. This is a trend which continued long after

1. Before the Mytharc

the 1960s saw the embrace of mythological construction beyond the pages of written texts and onto the big and small screens.

Therefore, the construction of the Mythos was key to some of the most important creative, resonant and dramatic texts in popular culture of the first half of the 20th century.

From the terrifying parables of Lovecraft, to the heroic mythological retelling of ancient stories through DC and Marvel's colorful texts, through to the allegorical subtext and cautionary tales of writers such as Roddenberry, Kneale, Serling and McGoohan, we have seen the formative examples of the Mythos in everything from literature to television. We have seen the groundwork laid for what we will come to know as the Mytharc, or mythology, in modern storytelling.

What happens next is critical. Cinema begins to evolve across the 1960s as Hollywood edges out of the Golden Age studio system of contracted stars, replicated sets and storylines. True auteurs begin to emerge as the New Wave of storytellers start to make their mark. Stanley Kubrick, Robert Altman, William Friedkin, Francis Ford Coppola, Martin Scorsese, George Lucas, Steven Spielberg—these are the men who will dominate the popular consciousness with motion pictures that encompass everything from the birth of man to the farthest reaches of outer space. These are the creatives who pave the way for the intersection of storytelling and culture, of the proliferation of dedicated fandom, and push the burgeoning advent of camera technology to show what cinema can truly achieve.

The renaissance of television would be a slower process. The 1970s would see shows such as *M*A*S*H*, based on Altman's 1970 movie, that would fuse the traditionally stark and divided genres of drama and comedy. Jeff Rice's *Kolchak: The Night Stalker* served as a major influence on *The X-Files*—the first major key text of the Mytharc—combining the traditional "cop show" format with aspects of the paranormal.[30] Escapism would evolve with creators such as Aaron Spelling and Stephen J. Cannell, who created a legion of shows (from *Charlie's Angels* to *The A-Team* and *Knight Rider*) that captured the tides and trends of their eras but all lacked that crucial component central to the Mythos. None of them truly married story and character to a mythic archetype strongly enough to truly create what we would consider a Mytharc by modern standards.

What these cinematic auteurs and television pioneers did do, however, was pave the way for the right circumstances for the two key creatives in the 1990s who did the most to create what we understand as the first true examples of the Mytharc in modern storytelling. Two men who created shows vibrantly different from one another, with wildly separate production design. But both men tapped into what we understand as Mythos in a way no creatives had truly done before.

Those two men were Chris Carter and J. Michael Stracyznski.

Carter's *The X-Files* and Stracyznski's *Babylon 5* arrived in the same year, 1993. The year previous had seen the debut of another important text to the early Mytharc, *Star Trek: Deep Space Nine*, but that was a series which lacked the pull of an initial creative auteur with a vision guiding the scenes. *Deep Space Nine*'s contribution to the birth of the Mytharc comes in the comet tail's wake of both *The X-Files* and *Babylon 5*.

The X-Files was an evolution of the Kolchak idea—a supernatural "cop show," with FBI agents traveling spooky modern America investigating aliens and monsters. *Babylon 5* was the biggest and broadest space opera ever committed to television (a mantle it may still wear to this day), with an ensemble cast of humans and aliens with the kind of colorful makeup that would make the artists on *Star Trek*'s various series blush. They could not be further apart as entities and yet, while they approached the concept from different angles, only one would coin the term Mytharc. Carter and Stracyznski became the dominant fathers of a new age of television.

The Mytharc as we know it today was born from television. Around the advent of the series that fomented modern narrative mythology, television underwent a remarkable renaissance.

The early 1990s saw the true emergence and development of science fiction and what would be termed "genre" on the TV landscape. Across the '80s, as we have previously discussed, television drama was dominated by either the groundbreaking cop show (*Homicide: Life on the Street*, *Law and Order*), the soap opera (*The Colbys*) or purely escapist offerings (*Knight Rider*, *The A-Team*, *Airwolf*, *Manimal*). Despite the emergence of the cinematic auteur during the 1970s, the same did not happen on the small screen. The super-producer (such as Donald P. Bellisario) came to prominence behind fare such as *Quantum Leap*, but the televisual auteur didn't arrive until 1991 and a show we have already mentioned: *Twin Peaks*.

Joint writers and show runners David Lynch and Mark Frost may not have given birth to the Mytharc, but *Twin Peaks* was a forerunner for what television as a medium was developing into. As opposed to many of the aforementioned shows which took a concept, often a high-concept, and developed a succession of 24 or 26-episode seasons with variations on a theme, *Twin Peaks* was a curated story with a beginning, middle and end. The strange death of Laura Palmer in the titular Colorado town allowed Lynch to bring many of his trademark quirks as an eccentric, well-established cinematic auteur to a two-season, longer form narrative

1. Before the Mytharc

which concluded in the TV movie *Twin Peaks: Fire Walk with Me*. (Then came 2017's critically divisive third season, but that operates in a very different space.)

Television just did not tell stories like these in this kind of way before *Twin Peaks*. It opened the door for the kind of storytelling which indulged what will become known as the Mytharc, and arguably displayed the possibility that television had to be more than just throwaway escapism. This was the baton picked up by creatives such as Chris Carter and J. Michael Straczynski, who paved the way for the television (and the cinematic franchise) that we know today.

In the 1990s, the Mytharc was born out of a need to respond to the latent tides of history across the 20th century and the need for a unified narrative across shows as diverse as *The X-Files* and *Babylon 5*, to explore the hopes and fears of the century to come. Serialization almost came as a consequence of drama, both in television and cinema, embracing the mythological to tell long-form narratives which gave viewers some level of catharsis—whether seeing the Federation overcome the Dominion, seeing Sheridan and Delenn move beyond the Rim, or cheering on Mulder in his never-ending search for the Truth.

As a result, the Mytharc became a construct of narrative in modern fiction, across numerous aspects of media, as a way of culturally and socially exploring the world around us, and confronting not just the ghosts of our past, but the looming specter of our futures.

It also works seamlessly alongside one of the most primal, recurring features in storytelling across human history: the Hero's Journey.

2

The Monomytharc

One of the best-known advocates of Joseph Campbell's Monomyth in recent years, and someone who helped reintroduce it out of the realms of comparative anthropology into popular culture, was George Lucas, the writer-director of perhaps the most influential motion picture of the last half-century: *Star Wars*.

Lucas is on record about how important studying Campbell's mythological treatise was to crafting the hero's journey of his protagonist Luke Skywalker, taking him from an eager, simple farm boy filled with wonder at the universe through a spiritual journey into the cosmos where, to fulfill his sacred destiny, he must slay his own father. It is almost Oedipal in overtone, certainly Campbellian in delivery, and layers what is otherwise a colorful, escapist, blockbuster space opera with a philosophical and mythological undertone. If the original *Star Wars* trilogy has a Mytharc, it belongs to Luke Skywalker.

But to use the Mytharc term in conjunction with *Star Wars* is to misinterpret the reach of what this fusion of story and character means. In recent years, movie franchises—including *Star Wars*—have started to embrace the Mytharc in much keener terms, but since the advent of the aforementioned TV series at the beginning of the 1990s that led to the term being coined, the Mytharc has largely been a phenomenon of long-form storytelling on television.

What may not immediately be as clear is how the Monomyth also has been utilized frequently within these television series to add an extra dimension to the Mytharc being constructed by many of these creatives and auteurs.

This Monomytharc concerns a protagonist whose journey, traversing the Campbellian constructs of initiation, rebirth and transformation, is internalized through external forces. The narratives that weave around this primal hero's journey, often complex and multi-faceted, covering many of the Divine and Cultural examples this book will discuss, serve to illuminate a wider sociological and humanistic viewpoint around the character in which we have invested.

2. The Monomytharc

In this section, we will explore this journey through three examples: Fox Mulder from *The X-Files*, Jack Shephard from *Lost* and Frank Black from *Millennium*. They may exist in very different worlds but their Monomytharcs tread similar ground.

All of them, in the long run, are heading in the same direction.

The Call to Adventure

For a character as outwardly handsome and innately witty and erudite as Fox Mulder, there exists an equal aura of incredible tragedy about him.

Though there is a strong argument that *The X-Files*, Chris Carter's cultural phenomenon of the 1990s, is the story of FBI Special Agent Dana Scully, there is no question that without her partner Mulder, there would be no X-Files and there would be no show. While Scully may be *us*, the rational-minded natural scientist approaching with logical skepticism the paranormal and supernatural forces Mulder throws at her, Mulder is the series' Monomythical "hero." This is his journey, his quest. And the Mytharc of *The X-Files*, as multi-faceted as it is, pivots around that journey.

Mulder's quest may appear to be about proving the existence of extraterrestrial life and, as a byproduct, a nefarious global government conspiracy to cover up that existence from the human race. But this disguises his true mission: finding his sister Samantha, abducted from the family home when he was 12 and she was 8. Samantha's disappearance is at the core of Mulder's existence. Finding her helped shape the man he became, the man who did well enough at school to study at Oxford University, the man who went on to become one of the keenest violent crime profilers in the Federal Bureau of Investigation,[1] and who later discovered a long-forgotten set of cases in a drawer marked "X," buried in the basement of the J. Edgar Hoover Building,[2] and saw in them the key to his life's work: the search for Samantha.

At times, *The X-Files* plays fast and loose with Mulder's history, both in terms of his family and particularly his career, with Carter allowing multiple interpretations of what happened to Mulder in his formative years. "Little Green Men" suggests he witnessed a bright light lift Samantha out of the window of their living room, before seeing a haunting alien silhouette at the door. He later sees the same silhouette while seeking to make contact with alien life at a Puerto Rican radio observatory, an experience he recounts throughout his life in regression hypnotherapy sessions, as we learn in the episode "Conduit."

Season 4's "Paper Hearts" suggests a different interpretation of that same event: that it was a child killer named John Lee Roche, whom Mulder helped capture in his early FBI years, who as a traveling Hoover salesman abducted and murdered Samantha.[3] Roche is convincing enough to make Mulder question his long-held belief that his sister was taken by alien forces, forces who tease him (in episodes such as "End Game" and "Redux II") that Samantha may still be alive somewhere. Later in Season 4, "Demons" sees Mulder undergo an extreme form of cranial treatment to unlock memories of his father Bill Mulder's relationship with the sinister Cigarette-Smoking Man, the grand master at least in the early seasons of the hegemonic conspiracy. Season 5's "Unusual Suspects" suggests an alternative explanation for how Mulder became obsessed with the X-Files and ostracized himself from his FBI colleagues, in his exposure to an experimental chemical gas that the conspirators were indiscriminately testing on innocent citizens.[4]

The point is that Mulder's own past is clouded and at times shrouded in mystery which the character never seems inclined to reveal, even to Scully, and which Carter enjoys keeping from his audience.[5] But the event we know *did* happen—Samantha's disappearance—serves as the first step on Mulder's own Monomytharc: the Call to Adventure.

This is also the first step on Campbell's journey of the hero, whereby the hero leaves the mundanity of his normal existence to head off into the unknown on a quest, figuratively or not taking up arms to face a challenge or problem. Psychologically, the Call for Mulder comes at a very young age with Samantha's disappearance and how it leaves him with a hole in both his life and his heart. Campbell describes the ultimate goal of the adventure as the "treasure" to be attained at the end of the quest:

> This first stage of the mythological journey signifies that destiny has summoned the hero and transferred his spiritual centre of gravity from within the pale of his society into the zone unknown. This fateful region of both treasure and danger may be variously represented: as a distant land, a forest, a kingdom underground, beneath the waves or above the sky, but it is always a place of strangely fluid and polymorphous beings, unimaginable torments, superhuman deeds and impossible delight.[6]

That treasure, for Mulder, is his sister. Not the exposure of extraterrestrial life to the public nor the destruction of the conspiracy to hide it, but the recovery of Samantha. That "fateful region," in parallel, is his ever-present analogous search for the Truth with a capital T. *The X-Files*,

2. The Monomytharc

as a show more concerned with the construction of a devastating future event rather than depicting the event itself, never really sees Mulder examine what he would do with a literal, concrete Truth. The series' most infamous moniker became "The Truth Is Out There," seen in every credit sequence[7] and voiced by Mulder on numerous occasions, but there is never a sense that Mulder's treasure is a literalized Truth. It is never standing on the steps of the White House next to the president and an alien life form, or standing in courts of law presiding over the justice of mysterious government officials. His treasure, his goal is to literalize that which he never had: his sister and, by extension, a traditional family structure.

This quest is central not just to Mulder's character arc, but the entire Mytharc of *The X-Files*. Early episodes hint that Mulder has far more of a dysfunctional family background than his partner Dana Scully. Though she suddenly loses her father early on in "Beyond the Sea," she has a loving mother and two brothers[8] who are uncomplicated by the dark histories of the larger conspiracy in the manner of the Mulder family. When we finally do meet Mulder's parents Bill and Teena in "Colony," they are long estranged and haunted by secrets. Neither seems particularly stunned at Samantha's sudden reappearance as a young woman after almost 20 years, nor at learning that Mulder "lost" her.[9] The treasure, in this instance, is false. Mulder is heartbroken but Bill stoic, a clear gulf between them that will never be overcome.

It takes the end of "Paper Clip," following Bill's murder in the Season 2 finale "Anasazi" and revelations in the Season 3 premiere "The Blessing Way," for Mulder to understand the role Bill played in everything he has been investigating to date. He was not just one of the chief architects of a conspiracy against the American people going back over 50 years but he made a choice that directly affected Mulder's entire life: He *chose* for Samantha to be taken by the Syndicate, the conspirators working with alien forces, as insurance in case Bill ever exposed their work, over Mulder—who was originally to be sacrificed.

This is a remarkable personal revelation to Mulder, especially given that his mother Teena was party to Bill's decision. "I couldn't choose. It was your father's choice. And I hated him for it. Even in his grave, I hate him still,"[10] Teena admits when Mulder questions her about whether Bill made her choose Samantha over him. It comes back to Bill's presumed desire to see his son survive, endure, perhaps even one day take on the Campbellian Call to Adventure in finding Samantha and, by proxy, take on the conspirators and shadowy alien forces responsible for her disappearance.

Myth-Building in Modern Media

In what could be construed as a latent level of sexism, did Bill not believe Samantha would serve the same function had her brother been taken? This remains a question Mulder will never answer, given Bill is dead and gone before he can fully become another Campbellian trope on Mulder's journey: the Supernatural Aid.

This often comes in the form of support for the hero, after taking up the quest, either as a "talisman," "map" or sacred object, frequently through a wise figure capable of providing key skills or knowledge.

> What such a figure represents is the benign, protecting power of destiny. One only has to know and trust, and the ageless guardians will appear. Having responded to his own call, and continuing to follow courageously as the consequences unfold, the hero finds all the forces of the unconscious at his side. Not infrequently, the supernatural helper is masculine in form. The higher mythologies develop the role in the great figure of the guide, the teacher, the ferryman, the conductor of souls to the underworld. Protective and dangerous, motherly and fatherly at the same time, this supernatural principle of guardianship and direction unites itself in all the ambiguities of the unconscious.[11]

One of the most signature examples of the Supernatural Aid is present in *Star Wars: A New Hope*: Obi-Wan Kenobi, the aged, wizened Jedi (read: wizard) who re-enters society from isolation to guide Luke Skywalker on his journey to understand and channel the Force, dying or sacrificing himself to ensure that the hero completes the first key part of his quest. While there may be no Jedi or wizards in the world of *The X-Files*, there certainly exist analogous Obi-Wan figures. Bill is murdered before he can provide Mulder with the answers he seeks in "Anasazi." Some of the last words he speaks to his son are prophetic: "You're going to learn of things, Fox. You're going to hear 'the words' … and they'll come to make sense to you."[12]

Mulder already found and lost a previous Aid figure in Season 1: his enigmatic informant Deep Throat, who gives Mulder the equivalent of the Campbellian map in the information he discloses in numerous episodes about facets of the conspiracy, chiefly the same nefarious grand plan that connects directly to what happened to Samantha. "Paper Clip" confirms that Deep Throat was part of the same Syndicate and would have known Bill Mulder, not to mention the Cigarette-Smoking Man. Deep Throat more directly sacrifices himself, in the vein of Obi-Wan, in "The Erlenmeyer Flask" as part of a trade to save Mulder's life, fulfilling his function on Mulder's journey. It is a function that later informants such as Mr. X (who suffers a similar sacrificial fate) and Marita Covarrubias continue, providing that Supernatural Aid to Mulder in the form of sacred knowledge to help him on the adventure.

2. The Monomytharc

Once Mulder understands the key links between his family history, his childhood and the disappearance of Samantha, to the work he has pursued in *The X-Files* for many years, it galvanizes him and pushes him into the next phase of the journey: crossing the First Threshold.

> With the personifications of his destiny to guide and aid him, the hero goes forward on his journey until he comes to the "threshold guardian" at the entrance to the zone of magnified power. Beyond them is darkness, the unknown, and danger; just as beyond the parental watch is danger to the infant and beyond the protection of his society danger to the member of the tribe.[13]

This is the point of no return for the hero. Mulder accepted the Call long ago when he resolved to find his sister, but the revelations about the choice, about his father's misdeeds, serve to focus the Mytharc in play as Season 3 of the series begins. It is equivalent to a rite of passage, a rebirth of the like he undergoes in "The Blessing Way" thanks to the Native American tribesmen with their own sacred knowledge; Albert Hosteen, the Navajo code talker, is yet another Aid, a ferryman who helps Mulder cross from the living to the dead and back again, his tribal rituals allowing Mulder to essentially finish the conversation with Bill that was cut short in "Anasazi" on a spiritual plane, and receive wisdom from his other surrogate father figure Deep Throat. Bill confesses to him:

> The lies I told you were a pox and poison to my soul and now you are here because of them. Lies I thought might bury forever a truth I could not live with. I stand here, ashamed of the choices I made so long ago, when you were just a boy. You are the memory, Fox. It lives in you. If you were to die now, the truth will die. And only the lies survive us.[14]

It allows Mulder his first point of closure. Much as the Anasazi trilogy feels like an ending to the first phase and incarnation of *The X-Files* as a series, ushering in a bold new season and the true advent of the Mytharc, Mulder is never quite the same after these three episodes. He crosses the threshold of his journey, steps boldly into a new world, and survives the monsters "within and without" as *The X-Files* takes an equally bold step into a new phase of storytelling.

Threads which have dangled over the first two seasons begin stringing and connecting together as Mulder discovers new facets of the conspiracy and extensions of what he learned, particularly in the Anasazi trilogy. Scully's abduction in Season 2 connects to women dying of cancer and possible alien technology being implanted in abductees in "Nisei" and "731." In those same episodes, Mulder discovers the existence of dark misdeeds still in effect that play off the American collaboration with former

Myth-Building in Modern Media

Nazi scientists on secret experiments following the Second World War. That theme continues all the way through to the Season 3 finale "Talitha Cumi," which further contextualizes the revelations key to the Mytharc and Mulder's quest, leading him to the next Monomythical stage.

Both the Season 3 finale "Talitha Cumi" and the Season 4 premiere "Herrenvolk" serve as key points on Mulder's quest and establish significant Mytharc components the series will later revisit. They also seed a key question at the heart of Mulder's journey: the true nature of his parentage. "Talitha Cumi" is the first episode to specifically suggest that the Cigarette-Smoking Man is the true biological father of Mulder. "Musings of a Cigarette-Smoking Man" and "Demons" in Season 4, plus "Redux II" in Season 5, suggest that he may also have sired Samantha. This is key because the Smoking Man has already been established in concrete terms as the primary antagonist of the entire Mytharc: While Season 3 explicitly shows him to be a cog in a bigger conspiratorial machine as part of the Syndicate, "Talitha Cumi" in particular re-establishes him as the villain incarnate. This is the man who took Mulder's sister away, and who stands as the guardian of the Truth he seeks.

A key stage described by Campbell is the Meeting of the Goddess, in which the hero bonds with mystical feminine figure and she provides support as his quest continues. Logically, in the broad scheme of *The X-Files*, that goddess is the character of Scully; she is the constant (as he describes her much later in "The Sixth Extinction II: Amor Fati") who often furnishes him with the will to go on, but she doesn't quite fit the Campbellian model of this stage in the journey.

> Woman, in the picture language of mythology, represents the totality of what can be known. The hero is the one who comes to know. As he progresses in the slow initiation which is life, the form of the goddess undergoes for him a series of transformations; she can never be greater than himself, though she can always promise more than he is yet capable of comprehending.[15]

For me, a better example of the Goddess is the character of Jeremiah Smith. Introduced in "Talitha Cumi," he becomes the MacGuffin[16] of Mulder's search for the Truth. A shapeshifting alien being who can heal with the palm of his hand, Jeremiah also serves as the Campbellian Woman as Temptress figure, given that he promises Mulder he can reveal the Truth and can take him to his sister. Jeremiah is the manifestation and actualization of everything Mulder has been seeking so far, hence why he is at one point captured and brought in parallel to the Cigarette-Smoking Man, who attempts in grand mythological scenes to reduce Jeremiah's apparent God-like apostle to little more than a cog in

2. The Monomytharc

a machine bigger than his own.[17] "You think you're God. You're a drone, a cataloger, chattel!"[18]

The Smoking Man fears Jeremiah: Jeremiah defines everything the Smoking Man strives to prevent Mulder from finding. This becomes even more apparent as Mulder has to discover a sacred, arcane and near-mystical alien weapon in the stiletto in order to defend Jeremiah from the silent, monolithic Alien Bounty Hunter who comes to silence him. Mulder is shown a key piece of the puzzle by Jeremiah, chiefly that the conspiracy is not just to hide the existence of aliens but the fact they intend to wipe out the human race, a revelation which becomes clearer to Mulder through the Mytharc episodes in Seasons 4 and 5 before being confirmed in *Fight the Future*, the first motion picture (released between the fifth and sixth seasons). Mulder even is reunited, for the second time after "Colony" and "End Game," with Samantha, but again the treasure is false; the mute little girl, not aged since Mulder lost her, working a remote apiary to engineer an extraterrestrial virus in bee pollen, is every bit a science experiment and no more his sister than the woman he encountered previously.

The promise of Jeremiah ends up being a false hope, as Mulder is unable to save him from the Alien Bounty Hunter, nor indeed the clone Samantha who he attempts to rescue in a quasi-completion of his journey (however false). But it once again serves to provide Mulder with boons that spur him on in his journey. It had already happened in "End Game," before the threshold point where he started to wonder if his quest had meaning, and it happens again in "Herrenvolk," with the healing of Teena Mulder on her deathbed, after a conflict with Cigarette Smoking Man. Mulder receives both the gift of Teena's life, under the auspices of the Smoking Man who says of Mulder: "The fiercest enemy is the man who has nothing left to lose,"[19] plus while he loses one Supernatural Aid in X, he gains another in Marita. Mulder was told by the Bounty Hunter that his efforts were futile but Marita assures him: "Not everything dies."[20] In this case, both his mother and, indeed, his quest.

Seasons 4 and 5 provide what end up being Mulder's greatest challenges as he reaches a point of Campbellian Apotheosis in his journey. Having established key pieces of the Mytharc over his quest, putting together a concrete picture of the Syndicate's efforts to collude with an alien race and perhaps seek a vaccine against an apocalyptic plague, the forces against him attempt to engineer Mulder in "Gethsemane," "Redux" and "Redux II" toward his own downfall, chiefly by making him question and doubt everything he held sacred. He is engineered to believe the entire

Myth-Building in Modern Media

existence of extraterrestrial life and the conspiracy surrounding it has been a lie from the very beginning.

The Apotheosis of the hero is yet another point of no return but an even deeper transition, one where he finds a level of heretofore unachieved enlightenment. Apotheosis is defined as "the act of making someone into a God,"[21] and in Campbellian terms moving beyond one current state of being into another. In truth, the aforementioned trilogy of episodes which conclude Season 4 and begin Season 5 feel like the beginning of that journey for Mulder, given how Season 5 plays with the very notion of his faith in the Truth he believed for so long. By the end of "Redux II," in which he almost loses Scully to cancer before she receives a miracle cure, Mulder returns from faking his own demise to the events of the "Anasazi" trilogy on his journey. There, he faced literal death and crossed briefly into another realm to receive wisdom that spurred him on. Here, he engineers his own demise to go to a different underworld, one where (in "Redux") he meets another ferryman who changes the nature of his journey and quest.

Put simply, Mulder loses his faith in what he considers the spiritual side of the Truth, his belief in aliens, and channels it into a more rational side: A conspiracy of *men*, not otherworldly beings, are behind what happened to Samantha, or Scully, or all of the people who have so far died as part of his quest. The aforementioned ferryman is a Department of Defense employee, Michael Kritschgau, who we learn two seasons later "believed the lie" of what turns out to be a false conspiracy geared around Cold War apocrypha involving nefarious tests on the American people by a shadowy New World Order. These are ideas Carter would revisit in Season 10 and 11 (the 2016–2018 revival seasons), for reasons we will discuss later as they frame a different side to the Mytharc of *The X-Files*. But Mulder's own Apotheosis is in first believing that lie and later, when in "The Red and the Black" he glimpses the unassailable proof once again that cosmic forces do indeed exist, the faith he has carried for decades is born again as Season 5 races toward a conclusion.[22]

Carter swiftly puts Mulder back on course for the end of Season 5, the movie *Fight the Future* and Season 6 as, at last, he sets Mulder in the direction of the final part of his journey: the Ultimate Boon of Campbellian Monomyth.

"The End," *Fight the Future* and "The Beginning," which straddle Seasons 5 and 6, form a staccato overarching story in which Mulder sees his office and work burned to the ground but discovers the key puzzle pieces of the Truth being hidden from the people of the world. Season 6 lays the groundwork for, essentially, the end of Mulder's quest, even if the series

2. The Monomytharc

refuses to let the character go beyond it. *Fight the Future*, and particularly the Season 6 two-parter "Two Fathers" and "One Son," conclude the Mytharc of the first six seasons of *The X-Files*. Carter and his writing partner Frank Spotnitz, who had been a key influence in constructing the labyrinthian global conspiracy to hide alien life and the fact that the Syndicate has been colluding with them on their plans to both colonize Earth and destroy all human life, made a choice to no longer keep audiences waiting for answers about a conspiracy they had, in narrative terms, played out.[23]

What is surprising about such a key story for the Mytharc of *The X-Files* is how passive Mulder ends up being as the end of the world dawns, as colonization begins, and he is only stymied by the near-cosmic intervention of forces that destroy most of the conspirators. If the writers are tired of the mythology, then Mulder is tired of the fight. Time seems to have turned him into a weary, aging hero, despite how Scully (in the Season 6 conclusion "Biogenesis") reminds him he took these people down: "I mean, you've won. What more could you possibly hope to do or to find?" Mulder's reply is simple: "My sister."[24]

Even with all of the Mytharc threads and years worth of storytelling wrapped up, *The X-Files* comes back to Mulder's Monomytharc as it takes steps to ending it once and for all. There are three key trilogies in the larger narrative of the show; after the Anasazi and Redux trilogies, the Biogenesis trilogy is the final one and the true beginning of the end, in functional heroic terms, of Mulder's story arc. It even features a Campbellian step which often exists in advance of the Ultimate Boon in the Atonement with the Father. Campbell describes it thus:

> The ogre aspect of the father is a reflex of the victim's own ego—derived from the sensational nursery scene that has been left behind, but projected before; and the fixated idolatry of that pedagogical nothing is itself the fault that keeps one steeped in a sense of sin, sealing the potentially adult spirit from a better balance, more realistic view of the father, and therewith of the world. One must have faith that the father is merciful, and then a reliance on that mercy."[25]

Put simply, Atonement with the Father is the key point in which the hero on the journey confronts and defeats the "father figure," a person in high authority who he must overcome. While Mulder has numerous "father figures" across *The X-Files*, the most potent and controversial is the Cigarette-Smoking Man, and Season 7's second episode "The Sixth Extinction: Amor Fati" provides what feels like the culmination of their interaction; the Smoking Man, medically putting Mulder into a dream state, tempts him with a perfect alternate life away from his quest, away from the resolute, continued search for Samantha. While Mulder doesn't

Myth-Building in Modern Media

literally overcome the man until "The Truth" (and then "My Struggle IV"[26]), if you can ever overcome the Smoking Man, "Amor Fati" serves as the point in which the strength Scully imbues in Mulder more than anything else wills him to go on. That's the ultimate way in which Mulder defeats the Cigarette-Smoking Man—by enduring.

Season 7 is the point at which, arguably, Mulder's story arc ends. There is a sense that David Duchovny knew it, that Chris Carter knew it, hence why Mulder's abduction by aliens—mirroring his sister's fate—serves as the crux of a radically different Season 8, and when Mulder does reappear he shifts into a version of the Supernatural Aid figure, the veritable Obi-Wan Kenobi passing down his knowledge and virtue to the new heroes. When the series returned in the revival seasons, and the reset button on Mulder and Scully's circumstances was applied after how the original run of the series ended come the conclusion of Season 9, Mulder is more of an archetype than a hero on a journey. His quest is over. His quest ended the moment, in Season 7's mid-season episode "Closure," he received the Ultimate Boon at the end of Campbell's mythic journey: He finds his sister.

> The agony of breaking through personal limitations is the agony of spiritual growth. Art, literature, myth and cult, philosophy, and ascetic disciplines are instruments to help the individual past his limiting horizons into spheres of ever-expanding realisation. As he crosses threshold after threshold, conquering dragon after dragon, the stature of the divinity that he summons to the highest wish increases, until it subsumes the cosmos. Finally, the mind breaks the bounding sphere of the cosmos to a realisation transcending all experiences of form—all symbolizations, all divinities: a realisation of the ineluctable void.[27]

Mulder's Ultimate Boon is not finding the Ark of the Covenant like Indiana Jones, or dropping the bomb into the heart of the Death Star thanks to the power of the Force like Luke Skywalker, but appropriately for a show about knowledge and Truth, Mulder's boon is learning Samantha died long ago, after being taken as part of the Syndicate's deal with their alien overlords. But as a child, her soul was rescued by a spiritual concept called a "walk-in" and in one of *The X-Files*' most heart-wrenching scenes, Mulder on an open, near–Elysian field, embraces the ghostly child visage of Samantha and comes down the mountain unburdened. Scully asks if he's okay. "I'm fine," Mulder replies. "I'm free,"[28] he adds, heart in his mouth. Mulder's freedom is cathartic and emotional. It is here that he finds the Truth he spent a lifetime searching for; everything that happens to him after this is largely incidental. It matters less. It is telling, following "Closure," that *The X-Files*'s quest narrative shifts to Scully. In her case, she ends up searching *for* Mulder, whether having lost him or forced to be apart from him.

For a series often vilified for not having a concrete structure to the Mytharc or the character through line of its protagonists, Fox Mulder's Monomytharc is chartable and affecting. Though the show continues, the fight against the alien menace and the human conspirators continues, Mulder's quest for the Truth has a beginning and an end. What he learns in the unexpected way the mystery of Samantha's fate is concluded, is that the Truth he was searching for was always inside, rather than out.

When Mulder realizes this, he truly becomes free, he ascends, and cements his story into the lexicon of legendary sagas of the modern age of mythical storytelling.

Road of Trials

After three seasons of playing with a character like Fox Mulder, a dysfunctional genius from a home shattered by secrets and lies, Chris Carter chose to have his second series *Millennium* depict an altogether different kind of protagonist: Frank Black, a man looking inward for answers. A man with the strongest bond of family in contrast.

Frank's Monomythical journey is as interesting as *Millennium* is a TV series. Arriving in 1996, at the point *The X-Files* was on the cusp of becoming a decade-defining global small screen phenomenon, *Millennium* was designed as a direct counterpoint to the blockbuster pulp of Carter's hit show. If *The X-Files* updated and reinvented tropes and concepts first introduced in the 1960s, *Millennium* followed the lead of novelist Thomas Harris in the 1980s in creating Frank as a pseudo–Will Graham from *Red Dragon*,[29] a gifted (or alternatively cursed) middle-aged criminal profiler who sees "what the killer sees."[30]

Millennium actualized that horror. From the pilot episode, Frank works to stop the Frenchman, a serial killer of women who recites verbose, lurid poetry such as "I want to see you dance on the blood-dimmed tide,"[31] a man touched by anxiety and fear about the coming millennial apocalypse. We see Frank get inside the head of the man with a rush of violent, disturbing, connected images which allow him to estimate and predict the killer's motives, triggers and in many cases his backstory. To catch the worst of humanity, Frank has to think as they do, and early on there are more than a few suggestions that the "gift" is something he cannot simply turn on and off. "It's my gift. It's my curse,"[32] he tells friend and

Myth-Building in Modern Media

colleague, Bob Bletcher. What keeps Frank sane, and prevents *Millennium* from being so relentlessly dour it becomes unwatchable, is his family. He is happily married to younger, emotionally strong and supportive counselor Catherine, with whom he has a charming three-year-old daughter named Jordan.

Millennium begins in the wake of Frank having recovered from a nervous breakdown due to years of immersing himself in violent crime as an FBI agent,[33] moving to Seattle (where much of Season One takes place), into a symbolic yellow house where he and Catherine intend to start a new phase of their life free from the darkness outside.

Frank is in some senses a reluctant hero but in others quite the opposite. Described as the modern archetype of a Western sheriff, the noble, stoic figure who refuses to flee the bandits and killers,[34] Frank cannot simply run away from the "evil" in the modern world, as much as the yellow house provides a barrier, a safe zone in which he can feel the comfort of security most people in society enjoy. For Frank, the house is as much his own barrier to protect Catherine and Jordan as it is the salve for his own mental health problems. The yellow house is the rebound reaction to his near-descent into madness and there is a built-in hypocrisy to it, not to mention foreshadowing for events to come, in how the pilot ends with Frank still being haunted by the other reason they moved to Seattle: to escape an unknown stalker sending him pictures of Catherine, a stalker who seems to have followed them to their new home.

This won't be followed up until the season finale "Paper Dove," but it serves as the next step on a Monomytharc for Frank which Season 1 plays with in a fairly static way. The yellow house is the Campbellian Refusal of the Call:

> Refusal of the summons converts the adventure into its negative. Walled in boredom, hard work, or "culture," the subject loses the power of significant affirmative action and becomes a victim to be saved. His flowering world becomes a wasteland of dry stones and his life feels meaningless—even though, like King Minos, he may through titanic effort succeed in building an empire of renown. Whatever house he builds, it will be a house of death; a labyrinth of cyclopean walls to hide him from his Minotaur.[35]

Frank has already endured several of the points on the hero's journey at this stage, as much as the Monomyth, as it relates to him, does not work in a straight line. But having gained the Ultimate Boon (in many ways the gift of Jordan late in life, having not believed they could conceive), Frank is partly in a place of bliss after undergoing extreme trial and hardship battling the darkness. But the very concept of *Millennium* concerns this

2. The Monomytharc

battle-worn hero unable to turn away from those demons, both within and without. Refusal of the Call is layered with the idea that the hero simply cannot accept normal life and yearns for the adventure once again. Frank isn't yearning for the battle against the darkness but rather it calls to him, via the nature of what he describes as his "facility." This is what brings him into contact with the Millennium Group.

The Group is established in Season 1 as a criminal-profiling organization that consults with local law enforcement on extreme cases.[36] In the pilot, Frank is already working with the Group and across Season 1 he will work with a variety of partners and fellow former agents and experts recruited—principally Terry O'Quinn's equally stoic Peter Watts. Carter, as a writer and show runner, in Season 1 is less interested in Frank to some degree than in the forces he works against, in exploring the nature of evil in relation to modern Americana of the late 1990s. Episodes such as "The Well Worn Lock" (which is actually more of a rare showcase for Catherine) confronting child sexual abuse, "Wide Open" where murderers break into homes supposedly secured with modern alarm systems, or "Weeds," where a polite, civilized, gated community is confronted with the reality of murder. The list goes on.

As a character, Frank nonetheless remains the bulwark of morality and civility against this tide of violence and horror. He never carries a gun and he uses his powers of deduction and understanding of the killers' motivations to help catch them and save lives. Though the cases fluctuate and the nature of the crimes change, Season 1 does not hold to either a Mytharc or a Monomytharc to Frank. In Campbellian terms, the Millennium Group served to deliver him the Call to Adventure, following receiving the Ultimate Boon, and Season 1 sees Frank accepting this call.

Frank balances the protection of Catherine and Jordan in the symbolic yellow house with his own calling by the Group, who remain entirely in the background as the organization which licenses his "facility." This only begins to change when Carter layers in the first expressly supernatural element in the episodes "Lamentation" and "Powers, Principalities, Thrones and Dominions." This move serves to inform the Mytharc introduced in Season 2, and the bigger journey Frank undertakes across that season. In these episodes, the first loosely connected to each other across a season built on stand-alone parables about the monster within mankind in modern America, Carter introduces the idea of a demonic force which exists underneath the aforementioned exploration of the human monster, and the angelic spiritual counterbalance designed to combat it. In the process, Frank loses two of the people closest to him: his Seattle detective

Myth-Building in Modern Media

friend Bletcher, and Mike Atkins, the former profiler who brought him into the Millennium Group.[37]

Bletcher, played with a relatable sense of grounding by Bill Smitrovich, appears in the majority of Season 1 as the frequently exasperated, out-of-his-depth beat detective who barely understands Frank's ability, but respects him for his decency and professionalism. By "Lamentation," Bletcher is friendly with Catherine and Jordan, and close enough with Frank that they go hiking in the mountains in their spare time. When he is found hanging in the basement of the yellow house, his throat slit after protecting Catherine from the unknowable menace personified by the seemingly feminine and non-threatening Lucy Butler, it is the first indication of a change in Frank.

Not only has a powerful evil murdered his friend (and then another in swift succession), it killed Bletcher inside the protective barrier Frank had established to keep Catherine and Jordan safe, and keep his own monsters at bay. Lucy Butler proves the yellow house is an illusion, an illusion Frank can maintain for only so long before it collapses in on itself. While Lucy doesn't personify the core of the Mytharc or Frank's Monomythic journey, the deeper philosophical concept behind her is crucial to what becomes of his character in Season 2. "Paper Dove," just a few episodes later, instigates what we have always suspected was coming: the implosion of Frank's idealistic protection against the evil he seems destined to confront. The so-called Polaroid Man, established as a looming threat in the pilot, rears his head and abducts Catherine in the climactic moments of the season. Frank's greatest fear, that he might lose his family, becomes a reality.[38]

At this point, *Millennium*'s unique legacy is established as a show which, over its three short seasons, transforms radically depending on the creative forces in charge. Carter placed his stamp on Season 1, using the show and Frank to explore the kind of real world anxieties he could not get into in *The X-Files*, given its supernatural trappings, taking a cue from real-life inspirations inside the FBI and criminal profiling. But by 1997 he was forced to step away from the show in order to balance producing simultaneously the upcoming first *X-Files* feature film, *Fight the Future*, and the show's fifth season. In came replacements Glen Morgan and James Wong, esteemed writers who had already penned *Millennium* scripts as well as celebrated episodes of *The X-Files*, but whose own series *Space: Above and Beyond* had been cancelled after just one season. In taking charge of *Millennium*, they not only radically altered the series' course, but established a Mytharc and clear, concrete Campbellian journey for Frank to follow.

2. *The Monomytharc*

They jokingly described Season 2 as having the mission statement of "90 percent less serial killers" but they largely proved their words to not entirely be in jest, as they chose to re-focus on the underpinning notion in Carter's original idea that the impending arrival of the year 2000 and the 21st century, in relation to the moral decay of modern America, was something we should fear.[39] Season 1 episodes such as the aforementioned pilot and "Force Majeure," which relates a series of deaths to a future cosmological alignment people believe could serve as an apocalyptic trigger, hinted at a bigger theological and philosophical aspect to *Millennium*, not to mention a quasi-religious mythology which Carter seemed reluctant to truly explore. From the season premiere, Morgan and Wong frame Frank's story around the growing cultural unease about pre-millennial anxiety in tune with transforming the Millennium Group from a criminal-profiling organization into a powerful, ancient doomsday cult. The show never should have gotten away with it, but the lack of clarity on the Group in Season 1 allows this change to make sense, if at times be somewhat implausible.

Crucially, it continues a change in Frank which was seeded in "Lamentation" and carries through into "The Beginning and the End," whereby Frank rescues Catherine from the clutches of the Polaroid Man—turned from creeping stalker into a meditative pre-apocalyptic madman—by quite savagely murdering him in front of his wife. Frank previously had imagined the darkness in order to stop men like that, but when the threat is personalized, he lets the darkness in to save his family. This serves as the trigger for Catherine, afraid of what Frank might become while indulging his "facility," moving out with Jordan and Frank abandoning the yellow house. The barrier is gone. The security of the family has been shattered and, conversely, this begins Frank's Monomythical journey. His destination: to get *back* to that security, to get back to his family, to get back to the dream of the yellow house. This could also be described as another Crossing of the Threshold, a point of no return.

Subsequently, he is lent what Campbell describes as Supernatural Aid, as in wise forces providing him with help and talismans to increase his strength on the Call to Adventure. The Millennium Group becomes a deeper, more closely connected part of his life. Peter Watts, a pervasive partner across Season 1, transforms from a skilled Group profiler into Frank's closest friend and guide, a man deeply indoctrinated into the beliefs and arcane practices of the Group. Frank is also given a new partner, Lara Means, a gifted but troubled profiler who serves as a contrast to Frank when introduced in "Monster." Where Frank sees evil and darkness, Lara sees angels, but her own facility is not as clear-cut as mere good wrought against evil.

Alongside this, Frank begins to face his Road of Trials. The final shot of the season premiere sees Frank literally driving down a road in his symbolic, blood red people carrier toward an uncertain future, and Campbell's road is filled with tests and battles in which the hero, on the mythical journey, gains confidence and capability:

> Once having traversed the threshold, the hero moves in a dream landscape of curiously fluid, ambiguous forms, where he must survive a succession of trials. This is a favourite phase of the myth-adventure. The hero is covertly aided by the advice, amulets and secret agents of the supernatural helper he met before his entrance into this region. Or it may be that he here discovers for the first time that there is a benign power everywhere supporting him in his superhuman passage.[40]

Frank's road, once he separates from Catherine and Jordan, is toward the Millennium Group, as he is drawn further into their orbit and begins to peer behind the veil of their secret rituals and practices. In "Beware of the Dog," Frank is sent by the Group to a small town in the middle of nowhere being plagued by near-demonic, man-eating dogs. The townsfolk address him as Sheriff Black. This is not just simply actualizing the trope of Frank as the hero of a modern American neo-western,[41] it turns out to be a test of initiation by the Group which leads him to the Old Man, an enigmatic figure who lives in the woods outside of town, inside his own pastoral shack surrounded by ritual stones akin to markers protecting him from the evils without, akin to how a magic circle protected people from demons.[42] Frank later discovers that reaching the Old Man, nominally the detached leader of the Millennium Group, is a trial every initiate must face and have faced for decades, perhaps even centuries.

Many of the cases Frank is sent on from the Group differ stylistically from the cases he investigated in Season 1, when we believed the Group were a consulting firm. In "Monster," he is cryptically sent to a town where mass hysteria of possible child abuse is targeting a longstanding pillar of the community, with Peter instructing him to "find the evil"—a task Frank later discovers Lara also received as their initial antipathy turns to friendship. "Goodbye Charlie" again sees Frank and Lara paired together to investigate a series of deaths which are either a form of euthanasia, or the work of a manipulative serial killer, with the question from the Group: "Should we assist to arrest this person, or assist to protect?," which by the end Frank interprets as "Was he from Heaven or Hell?"[43] Repeatedly, as Season 2 progresses, Frank is on a journey filled with trials and tests being sent by the Millennium Group, though Lara herself interprets them as

2. The Monomytharc

"lessons"; the Old Man already represents the figure of a remote, God-like overseer of the flock, and the Group consistently seem to position themselves as all-knowledgeable bastions of a secret, arcane truth Frank is not allowed to understand until he is ready.

Season 2 was criticized in part for the fact Frank does not question the motives of the Group enough, his rationale being that deeper involvement with Millennium could help him understand a "facility" which he increasingly refers to as a "gift," and which over Season 2 develops into more of a psychic connection to objects and people. In Season 1, the initiation was that Frank used his ability to put himself in the minds of the killers he investigated, but in Season 2 he is far more often a receptor: the brilliant flash of Native American apocalyptic images in "A Single Blade of Grass," the rush of arrows in "The Hand of St Sebastian" which connects to the fate of a thousand-year-old corpse, the wave of Teutonic Nazi imagery in both "Owls" and "Roosters." The deeper he is radicalized by the Millennium Group, and the further he moves from Catherine and Jordan, the more his gift begins to evolve into something beyond psychological profiling.

This is where *Millennium* really displays how Season 2 is an enclosed Mytharc, which makes it quite a rarity in TV show terms. *The X-Files*, while it ebbed and flowed, had a consistent Mytharc for at least the first nine seasons of its run. (There is debate about how canonical Seasons 10 and 11 should be considered.[44]) *Millennium* did not start with any sense of a Mytharc, rather one or two character and story threads to be picked up on. Once Chip Johannesen took control of the show in Season 3, by which point Morgan and Wong had moved on, it only in places continued the Mytharc developed around the Millennium Group when it needs to. Indeed, it often works hard, as the Season 3 premiere "The Innocents" shows, to write itself out of the corner Season 2 backed the series into. Season 3 carries over thematic stylistic touches, and more of the fusion of Season 1's traditional horror and anxiety with the philosophical and metaphysical tales told in Season 2, but everything else is left very much behind.

In some respects, this includes Frank's Monomythical journey, which primarily takes place across the 22 episodes of Season 2. A key Campbellian event comes at the midway point, in "Midnight of the Century," as Frank faces the Atonement with the Father step on his journey.

The Mytharc of Season 2 of *Millennium* had several different layers to it, all of them moving in the same pre-millennial, fearful direction. There was the aforementioned aspect of Frank becoming more involved with

Myth-Building in Modern Media

the Millennium Group, and coming to learn of a philosophical schism in their belief system being exploited by old enemies,[45] a battle which sometimes puts him in conflict with the Group as he struggles with the more fanatical, cult elements of their organization. Beyond this, often on more of a symbolic level, are hints of a supernatural conflict between literalized Good and Evil. This is what Carter introduced late in Season 1 and it gets carried through into Season 2 as the Evil, manifested in a demon we later learn is known as Legion, who works to make Frank either sympathetic toward the Devil, or apathetic to the battle against Evil. He appears in numerous episodes in different guises and in different contexts.[46]

One of the most memorable is the Halloween episode "The Curse of Frank Black," a dark whimsical exploration of Frank's place in the world, detached from his family, on one dark and perpetually stormy night. He is visited by ostensibly the ghost of Crocell, a World War II veteran he briefly knew as a young boy and who killed himself as a presumed result of undiagnosed post-traumatic stress; a man who acts as a reflection of Frank's mental state and offers him a deal to "sit out" the battle to come, because "the time is near and He will win. There is no way He can lose."[47] Frank never knows for sure whether he imagined the entire experience—though the episode goes to spooky lengths to suggest he didn't—but this is as clear as the devious lawyer Al Pepper in "Powers, Principalities, Thrones and Dominions" offering Frank a job, or Odessa's hopes in "Owls" and "Roosters" that they may be able to court Frank into working for them through Catherine, or when in "Siren" the same force takes control of an illegal Chinese immigrant girl and throws Frank into a beguiling alternate reality where he never lost his family and never came into contact with the Millennium Group.

This is the mythic underlayer of Frank's quest, and the Mytharc surrounding the preparations to survive the coming millennium, which ripples across Season 2 but is unavoidable. It is present in "Midnight of the Century" which again, like "The Curse of Frank Black," explores Frank's psychological position over a holiday season (in this case Christmas) and gives him a level of closure through Atonement with the Father that allows him to further come to terms with aspects of his life, and his gift, which pushes him further on his journey back toward his family.

We learn in "Midnight of the Century" that Frank's mother died when he was a young boy, having taken her own life, and that for 50 years Frank believed his father Henry did not do enough to save her from what he considered to be depression and mental illness. In fact, Frank realizes that his mother had the same experience as Lara Means, seeing angels, and it

2. The Monomytharc

is heavily suggested that his daughter Jordan also is developing this ability as she grows older—given how she claims to have drawn an angel with her "grandma." Through Jordan's experience, and even a brief encounter in a graveyard with who likely could be the same "angel," Sammael, who fights off Legion in "Powers, Principalities, Thrones and Dominions," Frank comes to understand Henry's love and respect for his mother in the face of a gift she chose not to live with, even if it meant abandoning her children. In both a tragic and strangely uplifting irony, Frank letting go of this longstanding pain coincides with Henry's imminent death. While in the Campbellian lore, Atonement with the Father allows the hero to ascend to a higher plane of understanding; in this case, the father himself ascends by letting go of life.

It is a key episode to Frank's Monomythical journey because it draws him, if briefly, closer back into the orbit of a family, particularly Catherine, who has struggled to understand his choices over the season. This comes to a head soon after in "Luminary," arguably the single most important Monomythical story for Frank across the season, as it confronts the divide between his family and the Millennium Group. This is without doubt Frank's Apotheosis.

Taking a narrative cue from the book and film *Into the Wild*,[48] Frank undertakes a personal search for Alex Glaser, a young adventurer who went missing in the mountains after Catherine introduces him to the boy's parents. But the Millennium Group refuses to help him after an initiation meeting where Frank's loyalties are aggressively questioned by the assembled members. Frank walks out of the meeting. This puts him in conflict with Peter, who despite being revealed as a millennial zealot has across the season remained Frank's closest ally; Peter takes Frank's computer from his home and clashes with Catherine, upon describing Frank as AWOL. Frank's journey is in many senses one of self-discovery; like Catherine, who admits to Peter she has started looking to astrology books for meaning, Frank is lost in himself and his direction, aware he is torn in two directions—the Group in order to find the knowledge he seeks and defend against the coming darkness, and his family to heal. Frank finds the boy but, at first, he refuses to return to civilization after an arduous trek and exposure to the Aurora Borealis. He is at a crossroads in "Luminary" and he emerges from it with a renewed sense of purpose.

This becomes clear in "Owls" and "Roosters," which could be the two most important episodes in *Millennium*'s history, certainly when you consider the Mytharc in play. By default, given the myriad amount of narratives that have been building to this across the season (Frank and

Myth-Building in Modern Media

Catherine's marriage, Peter's obsessions, the Group's divisions, outside enemies, the Old Man, Lara's gift), Frank is more part of an ensemble across a two-part story which cuts to the heart of the Group and their belief system; some are Judeo-Christian end time believers who actively feel sacred objects like the Cross of the Crucifixion that serves as the MacGuffin of the episodes are crucial to battle an evil hundreds of days away, while the rest are secular, believing in unrevealed scientific proof that a cosmic tear in the space-time continuum will destroy the world halfway through the 21st century. In this sense, *Millennium*'s Mytharc feels like more of an apocalyptic battle of science vs. faith but akin to *The X-Files*' dread at a coming alien invasion inherent to its own Mytharc. In both senses, the present-day conflicts inherent in the drama are driven by anxieties of events to come in an unknown and unpredictable century.

Frank nonetheless emerges from the two-parter having overcome more examples of the Road of Trials, particularly the Brother Battle in Campbellian theory, whereby the hero must confront someone he trusts who can reflect some sense of their own persona or journey, and the long-brewing confrontation between Frank and Peter early in "Owls" exemplifies this step on his journey. It is a conflict which will deepen as we leave Season 2 and enter Season 3.

> The hero, whether god or goddess, man or woman, the figure in a myth or the dreamer of a dream, discovers and assimilates his opposite (his own unsuspected self) either by swallowing it or being swallowed. One by one the resistances are broken. He must put aside his pride, his virtue, beauty and life, and bow to submit to the absolutely intolerable. Then he finds that he and his opposite are not of differing species, but of one flesh.[49]

That step is taken across the two episodes at the end of Season 2 which conclude the Monomythical journey Frank takes across this season. "The Fourth Horseman" and "The Time Is Now" has Frank truly see the Millennium Group for what it is, and what he has always deep down suspected it to be: a cult. The Group's knowledge of the Marburg virus, a deadly modern plague capable of wiping out all human life, and their creation of a vaccine to protect their members, directly aligns them as analogous to the Syndicate of *The X-Files*; rather than collaborating with a hegemonic alien force intending to wipe out the human race with a viral apocalypse, the Group is accused of corrupting and brainwashing their members into believing the extreme systems of faith "Owls" and "Roosters" presented as a measure of control. Peter sees it but by the time he is prepared to help Frank, it is too late, and Lara loses the battle to retain her sanity as a result of Group initiation.

2. The Monomytharc

Frank undergoes the Rescue from Without on the Campbellian journey as Peter attempts to help him, after they again clash while Peter attempts to retain his faith in the Group's means and methods:

> The hero may have to be brought back from his supernatural adventure by assistance from without. That is to say, the world may have to come and get him. For the bliss of the deep abode is not lightly abandoned in favor of the self-scattering of the wakened state.[50]

In doing so, Frank manages to Cross the Return Threshold and reunite with Catherine and Jordan as a man resolved only to stay with the Group until he can extract people like Peter or Lara from its fanatical grip.[51]

Frank manages to get back to the Yellow House, the symbolic restoration of the family he drifted away from, but they all agree to move on from the shadow of darkness that cast over it while they lived there. This transformation becomes part of the Season 2 Mytharc in how they end up in, as Catherine describes pithily, "our new yellow house"[52]—an old, ramshackle cabin in the woods that Frank's recently deceased father Henry leaves him, and which the Black family escape to when the Marburg virus begins to infect the population. Frank manages to cross the Threshold, with the Ultimate Boon of his reunified family, but it is temporary given that Catherine tragically dies of the virus—one to which Frank and Jordan are immune. Season 3, in many ways, is Frank's consistent crossing of that Threshold as he works tirelessly, alongside the FBI, to bring down the Millennium Group, putting him in direct conflict with Peter who has, partly out of fear, been once again radicalized as a protector of the Group and their agenda.

Season 2 ends *Millennium* in a strange place, as Morgan and Wong complete their tenure as show runners and pass the baton to first Michael Duggan and later Chip Johannessen, which leads to a third and final season that tonally fuses the stylistics of both the first and third seasons to mixed effect. What Season 2 does, that no other *Millennium* season achieves, is to place Frank's journey in Monomythical terms as a cycle, much like the Ouroboros symbol of the Group—the snake eating its own tail. He journeys away from the Yellow House, and that place of safety and security away from the darkness, but successfully finds his way back, even if ultimately that journey leads to the sacrifice of part of Frank's salve against the darkness of the coming millennium.

At the end of "The Time Is Now," the now white-haired Frank is reborn to face a new cycle as Season 3 dawns. He is a character forever changed by the efforts to tell a Mytharc across *Millennium*'s second season and while it may not have been enough to make the show a popular piece of '90s culture, or indeed save it from eventual cancellation, it does make Frank an iconic hero on a unique, moving and powerful journey.

That is who he was.

This is who *we* are.

Master of the Two Worlds

If you wanted a perfect example of how Campbell's Monomyth runs alongside the modern interpretation of the Mytharc, it is hard to look beyond Jack Shephard, the nominal protagonist of one of the most ensemble-driven series ever made, *Lost*.

Jack's narrative arc neatly mirrors that of the show itself. *Lost* was never really a series about the survivors of a plane crash who must not just stay alive on a mysterious island in the middle of the ocean but also try and find a way to escape. That was the nominal premise but the Damon Lindelof and Carlton Cuse's series, co-created with J.J. Abrams and Jeffrey Lieber from an initial pitch by that would have been an altogether different series,[53] was really always all about a group of people who were lost in their lives and whose experience on the Island (with a capital I) gave them definition and meaning. Everything else was just one gigantic metaphor.

Principally, this was the character arc for Jack, and it underpins the entire Mytharc which *Lost* builds its foundations on in the most ambitious manner in TV history. *The X-Files* may have created modern TV mythology, with *Babylon 5* at the same time creating a novel for TV around it, but there has not been a show before or since with the scope and reach, from a narrative perspective, than *Lost*. In recent years, *Game of Thrones* surpassed it in terms of world-building and *Westworld* has online communities abuzz with theories and speculation akin to *Lost* in its prime, but the Mytharc of *Lost* is dense, fascinating, often absurd, often filled with one-way streets, but also boils down to a deceptively simple conflict: science vs. faith.

In that sense, *Lost* is no different from *The X-Files* or *Millennium* in the thematic battle at the heart of its concept. Fox Mulder believes in the existence of alien life against the scientific, rational skepticism of his partner. Frank Black is caught between a schism of secularism and Judeo-Christian belief within the Millennium Group of impending apocalypse. Jack Shephard, a medical doctor, refuses to believe the Island has a plan for him, refuses to believe in a destiny that may have been preordained from birth. It is only when Jack comes to believe, and has faith in the Island, does he find himself and find peace. His journey is classically the Hero's Journey of inner self-discovery which directly affects the outer world around him.

Lost dominated TV across the latter half of the 2000s. It debuted in 2004, two years after the rather quiet and ignominious end of *The X-Files*. While it never reached quite the pop cultural height of that show or came to acutely reflect and represent the decade it was made, *Lost* was a true phenomenon: high-concept, serialized, format-breaking TV, it served as one of the last significant "water cooler" network shows before the advent of cable and streaming services transformed television as we entered the 2010s. While *The X-Files* and *Babylon 5* both tapped into the early, formative years of online fandom via chat rooms and message boards,[54, 55] *Lost* took this to a whole other level; ARG experiences,[56] early podcasts,[57] viral marketing, even one of the first shows to have a Wiki-site created around it to keep track of the lore,[58] which is now commonplace for most ongoing TV shows.

Also, and this is quite important, *Lost* was strange. Really, really strange.

It began, admittedly, as a far easier concept for people to hook into, with the plane crash and disparate group of survivors from across the globe thrown together: faded British rock star Charlie, unhappy Korean couple Sun and Jin, intense former Iraqi soldier Sayid, pregnant young Australian Claire, etc., alongside the retinue of American characters, all with flashbacks every episode built in alongside the main Island narrative that explored who they were before the crash. In some cases, they peeled back mystery (as in why Kate was a prisoner) or simply revealed aspects of character (Charlie is a drug addict). Even as early as the pilot, however, *Lost* was telegraphing its innate weirdness; how else do you account for the roaring, stomping monster echoing through the trees which kills the pilot of Flight 815 halfway into the first episode?[59]

By the fourth episode of Season 1, "Walkabout," when we discover that the resourceful survivalist John Locke was in a wheelchair before crashing and the Island seemed to have allowed him to walk again, we understand as viewers that *Lost* is no ordinary survival adventure series. Each episode reveals aspects and fragments of the deeper Mytharc, much of which is telegraphed early on. *Lost* is frequently criticized as a show which "made it up as it went along"[60]—this claim has always been demonstrably false. In the pilot, Locke describes the fundamental dichotomy between good and evil, also depicted in the science vs. faith dilemma, to young Walt via the symbolism of a game of backgammon. In the sixth episode, "House of the Rising Sun," characters find the bodies of people who will be very important to the larger Mytharc of the series even six seasons hence. And very early on, Jack's Monomythical journey begins under strange circumstances.

Jack is the hardest-to-like protagonist of the three we have discussed when looking at the Monomyth. Mulder is obsessive but he's funny and charming. Frank, often dour and intense, is also dignified and warm. Jack is none of these things; the man we meet at the beginning of the series is self-righteous, uptight, emotionally closed off. Despite being resourceful and a natural leader, he's defiantly uncharismatic. Jack can lead a party inside the wreckage of a crashed plane to recover a satellite phone but in "Walkabout" he visibly recoils at Claire's request to lead a funeral service for those who didn't survive the crash. At the beginning of *Lost*, in terms of Campbell's Hero's Journey, Jack is firmly at the stage of the Refusal of the Call.

The Call to Adventure is different in this case to the other examples as the Call—the plane crashing on the Island—is not something Jack sought out. But the Refusal fits given Jack's initial struggle in being the person who the rest of the survivors rely on and look to for guidance. A major underpinning reason for this becomes clear in Jack's first "flashback episode," "White Rabbit." We know from the pilot that Jack was traveling to Australia to pick up the body of his deceased father, named (somewhat without irony) Christian Shephard, who died under mysterious circumstances. Jack, therefore, is swimming in the middle of a painful cycle of grief, particularly given the complicated relationship he had with Christian over the course of decades. He begins seeing visions of Christian on the Island in "Walkabout"; in the next episode, "White Rabbit," Jack races off into the jungles to try and find his father, and in doing so must confront his own inner realizations about his place on the Island. Jack consequently allows himself to be for the survivors what they need for him to be, after the visions of Christian lead him to a set of undiscovered caves where he finds his father's coffin ... but no body. Aside from the mystery of what that means, Jack resolutely returns to the flock and guides them, as a shepherd, to the caves, having embraced his role as leader.

Along the way, crucially, Jack is given Supernatural Aid from someone who will first be the ferryman on his journey and later grow into something else entirely: Locke. Locke encourages him to be the metaphorical Alice and tumble down the rabbit hole in search of his own truth, and to become that leader: "A leader can't lead until he knows where he's going."[61]

2. *The Monomytharc*

Locke already has his faith in the Island and while subsequent episodes will challenge his own security in what he considers his destiny, Jack is a world apart from any level of acceptance even at the end of "White Rabbit." He has nonetheless accepted the Call to Adventure. This plays into a defining aspect of his character, the hero complex fueled by his own historical anxieties about not being able to live up to his father's expectations. Jack is obsessed with "fixing" everything he can get his hands on in a literal context—problems that surmount amongst the survivors such as food rations, medical injuries and ultimately the hope that they may be rescued, even as it dwindles every passing day. The one area he cannot fix is the one area he consistently patches over: his own emotional acceptance at who he is, and the death of his father, over which he feels an incredible, personal sense of guilt.

Jack's flashback episodes over the course of the first three seasons primarily are designed to illustrate the relationship with Christian which drives Jack's psychology, and lines up with his central journey at the core of *Lost*'s Mytharc. "All the Best Cowboys Have Daddy Issues," "Man of Science, Man of Faith," "The Hunting Party," "A Tale of Two Cities," all of these episodes chart the breakdown of the professional and personal relationship between Jack and Christian as Jack is unable, morally and ethically, to conceal Christian's drink addiction from the medical association, leading him to lose his medical license. Jack also becomes paranoid and obsessed with the idea that Christian may be sleeping with his wife—a woman Jack helped "fix" when she was paralyzed in a car accident and who he subsequently drives away from their marriage with his levels of obsession.

Through all of these episodes, however, there is the distinct sense that Jack is both at points jealous of Christian and profoundly angry at him, secretly glad to have found a way to ruin his career. In fairness, Christian is by no means the best father figure; we later learn he also fathered fellow plane crash survivor Claire Middleton, and had traveled to Australia in a drunken fugue to try and see his estranged daughter. In "White Rabbit," after Jack is beaten up as a child by bullies in school, Christian chastises him rather than comforting and tells Jack, "You just don't have what it takes,"[62] words that haunt Jack into adulthood and inform his obsessive hero complex. Much like Locke's determined "Don't tell me what I can't do"[63] informs his psychology of overcoming a life of underachievement and victimhood, Jack's entire mindset is about proving his father wrong, even after he is dead.

Lost aligns both of these men on an axis of duality in the same way it later aligns Benjamin Linus and Charles Widmore,[64] the way it aligns

Myth-Building in Modern Media

Jacob and the Man in Black. Two players, two sides. Light and dark, science and faith. Jack and Locke's destinies are consistently intertwined, even if their approaches are fundamentally in opposition. *Lost* can almost be charted by many of the philosophical and ideological conversations between these two men, which serve as pivotal to the Mytharc. The aforementioned "White Rabbit" is the first, where Locke serves more as the ferryman aiding Jack toward his destination, but come Season 1's epic three-part conclusion "Exodus," their parallel position is defined and clear. Locke believes the Island is a special place which has a destiny for each and every one of them, while Jack believes Locke is an increasingly deluded, perhaps even dangerous fantasist. In many ways, both of them are ultimately proven right. A key step on the Campbellian journey comes after the Call is accepted and the first Threshold is crossed—the Entering of the Belly of the Whale.

> The idea that the passage of the magical threshold is a transit into a sphere of rebirth is symbolised in the worldwide womb image of the belly of the whale. The hero, instead of conquering or conciliating the power of the threshold, is swallowed into the unknown, and would appear to have died.[65]

Arguably, the first Threshold for Jack is the mysterious Hatch in the ground which Locke discovered (though this also can present as the whale), and which is blown open at the end of Season 1 as a means of hiding from the mysterious, unseen Others who live on the Island. The Whale for Jack in *Lost* is the domain of the Others, and in "The Hunting Party," in response to hot-headed survivor Michael entering Others territory in search of his abducted son Walt, Jack takes his first tentative steps at entering the zone of danger that will lead to his own Road of Trials in Season 3. The Whale is fully entered in the Season 2 finale "Live Together, Die Alone,"[66] as Jack leads a small party on a mission into the heart of the Others to find Walt, only to learn he has fallen victim to a trap laid by Michael, who made a bargain with the Others for his and Walt's freedom in exchange for Jack, Kate, Sawyer and Hurley's captivity.

If we consider the Whale to be a place of danger, then in *Lost*'s geography, the forested Dark Territory (or La Territoire Fonce, as coined by French scientist castaway Danielle Rousseau) serves as the entrance point to the metaphorical beast Jack enters—not just the domain of the Others but their entire world, system, society and ecology.

Season 3 was the point at which *Lost*, famously or indeed infamously, was accused of spinning its wheels.[67] Critics and commentators focused on the Jack-centric episode "Stranger in a Strange Land," principally geared

2. The Monomytharc

around how Jack gained tattoos that were only visible because actor Matthew Fox had tattoos of his own, as a sign that *Lost* needed significant forward momentum.[68] Around this time, Lindelof and Cuse decided on a plan for the show's endgame and chose, at the height of its popularity, to make a deal with ABC for a precise number of episodes and seasons *Lost* would run for before conclusively ending. Consequently, from the end of Season 3 onwards, *Lost* feels like a series that knows, with increasing certainly, of the direction it is heading and the Mytharc, through Jack's central journey, very clearly begins to reflect this.

Jack is changed across Season 3. In that year alone, he undergoes an arc from a prisoner inside the strange land alluded to above—determined to combat the psychological mind games of the Others' nominal leader, Benjamin Linus, and save the lives of the survivors he unwittingly led into captivity—through to a man who is almost corrupted by the lifestyle and safety afforded by the Others. They very quickly turn out to be far from the band of filthy island savages they try and make newcomers to the Island believe they are, and rather a longstanding, intellectually and technologically advanced mono-culture built around the cult of a demigod. Jack, through this prism and his righteous self-sacrifice to the Others in "I Do" to save passenger Kate Austen—a woman he has grown to love—makes the decision to stay with his captors, partly because of his experience of another Campbellian trope: the Meeting with the Goddess.

In the case of *Lost*, and Jack's Monomythical journey, the Goddess is Juliet Burke, one of the more immediately rational and more temperate Others. Apart from, as Ben Linus puts it, bearing "a striking resemblance to your ex-wife,"[69] Juliet at first represents the synergy of, in mythical lore, "sacred marriage" and a joining with the hero, operating as his female side, which in Campbellian terms is designed to make the hero stronger along his Road of Trials. Juliet is also a doctor, on a similar level of intelligence. At first she is as attracted to Jack as the reverse; *Lost* eventually segues into something of a "love quadrangle" with Jack, Juliet, Kate and Sawyer, all of whom at various points cross romantic paths in some manner.[70] Juliet also serves as the Woman as Temptress.

> The mystical marriage with the queen goddess of the world represents the hero's total mastery of life; for the woman is life, the hero its knower and master. And the testings of the hero, which were preliminary to his ultimate experience and deed, were symbolical of those crises of realisation by means of which his consciousness came to be amplified and made capable of enduring the full possession of the mother-destroyer, his inevitable bride. With that he knows that he and the father are one: he is in the father's place.[71]

Myth-Building in Modern Media

Designed to test the integrity of the hero, the Temptress is expressly there for the hero to reject, thereby displaying the pure virtue of the hero and allowing him to continue toward his ultimate goal without distraction. Juliet flits frequently between Goddess and Temptress in more of a direct way than Kate, who also can fulfill these roles in Jack's journey. She is the woman with whom he develops the strongest bond across the series, but her innate sense of duality between the good and evil in her nature frequently leads her to embroil Jack in situations which distract him from the primary goal on his journey. In Season 3, Juliet is first sent to become close to Jack as part of Ben's psychological manipulation to get Jack to perform spinal surgery on cancer that is killing him. But Juliet later seeks Jack's own support and heroic need to fix and rescue, given she secretly wants to escape the Others and Ben's own psychological manipulation of her.

Crucially, however, during the period when Jack is almost radicalized by the Others into joining their culture, he makes a choice to leave his journey behind and divert from the Road of Trials he is on. Before Locke destroys the Others' submarine, Jack had made a deal for he and Juliet to leave the Island on it in "The Man from Tallahassee"—he was ready to abandon Kate, Sawyer, Hurley, all of the crash survivors he had up until then protected, even despite reassurances he would try and get help for them when back in civilization. Juliet would have gone with him and, theoretically, the hero may at this point have given into his Temptress and allowed her to lead him astray from his quest. Locke, representing that duality with Jack across the series, is the one who ironically sets Jack back on the path toward the survivors he had previously protected as de facto leader.

At this point, *Lost*, and Jack's journey, shift quite dramatically. The end of Season 3 delivers a plot development audiences may well have reasonably expected to happen at the very end of *Lost*'s run: The survivors are rescued. In truth, this doesn't technically happen until the very end of the Season 4 finale "There's No Place Like Home," but Season 3's finale, "Through the Looking Glass," introduces a well-known twist which Lindelof and Cuse called "the snake in the mailbox"[72]: Viewers had made the assumption that the flashbacks across the finale featuring Jack were depicting the man at his alcohol-fueled, father-hating lowest, when in fact they were flash *forwards*. *Lost* moved seamlessly into a show which, from Season 4 onwards, told its story across both present, past *and* future, to when certain of the survivors were off the Island and attempting to reintegrate into their lives.

"Through the Looking Glass" famously saw Jack, at the end of the

2. The Monomytharc

flash-forwards, meet up with Kate and proclaim, "We have to go back," that they were never meant to leave the Island. Jack is haunted by the death of a mysterious figure of importance, Jeremy Bentham, and is in marked contrast to the man we see in the present; he had turned the survivors into a small army which has destroyed the Others' paradigm and are on the verge of being rescued by a boat off shore. He is a man convinced that getting off the Island, and getting everyone off the Island, is what he needs to do, despite what look like extreme, "gone native" proclamations by Locke ("You're not supposed to do this"). The question everyone was asking by the end of Season 3 was simple: How did Jack get from there to *here?* What could have turned the most ardent champion of rescue and "fixing" the survivors' lives into a broken man, on the verge of suicide, who just wanted to return to a place that he once wanted to leave?

The answer ripples out across Season 4, as *Lost* shows the build-up to the survivors leaving the Island—which doesn't see all of them make it and wracks up a lot of collateral damage along the way, as the rescuers are not all they appear to be—and Jack's steady transformation. At this point, *Lost* hints at Jack's necessary Atonement with the Father, as the seemingly dead character of Christian Shephard becomes more crucial to the mystical path of the Island. Jack glimpses him in "Somewhere Nice Back Home" in his surgery, while Locke finds the man acting as a guide and proxy in "Cabin Fever" for the enigmatic Jacob (who we will discuss in the next chapter). Though Jack's journey has almost strayed off its path, Season 4 reminds us of the importance of Christian to both Jack's arc and the larger Mytharc in play.

Before we can reach the Atonement, however, Jack must undergo Apotheosis and, without question, his moment of Apotheosis is in deciding that he needs to go back to the Island and to realize that he made a mistake in leaving. It takes certain profound realizations for Jack to get to this point. He helps Kate gain custody of Claire's newly born child in "Eggtown" and tries to fill the role of husband and father to them in "Something Nice Back Home," but his continued obsession with his father and fear of betrayal makes this unworkable. Locke, who is Jeremy Bentham, attempts in "The Life and Death of Jeremy Bentham" to convince him the Island needs him, that he has a destiny, but Jack refuses to listen to what turns out to be their final, tragic conversation—especially when Locke tells him that Christian, his father, was the one who sent him to bring back those who left. Jack's Atonement is calling out to him, pulling him toward a destiny he is running from, but he rejects it time and time again. It takes Locke's apparent suicide at having failed in his own quest—

and learning that Claire is in truth his half-sister—as the trigger for Jack, who has already spent years lying and pretending he can regain the life he had before, to gain the faith he needs in what Locke believed all along: that the Island has a plan for all of them.

Jack even believes he has gained the Campbellian Ultimate Boon, given what appears to be happiness with Kate and young Aaron. But this is a false reward. Jack may try and convince himself his journey is over but it's not, far from it. The goal of *Lost* becomes clear, as does the spread of the Mytharc and Jack's Monomytharc: This is about the process of escape, return and rebirth, even though in Jack's determination to make a life with Kate, he experiences the Refusal of the Return.

> When the hero quest has been accomplished, through penetration to the source, or through the grace of some male or female, human or animal personification, the adventurer still must return with his life-transmuting trophy. The full round, the norm of the Monomyth, requires that the hero shall now begin the labor of bringing the runes of wisdom, the Golden Fleece, or his sleeping princess back into the kingdom of humanity, where the boon may redound to the renewing of the community, the nation, the planet or the ten thousand worlds. But the responsibility has been frequently refused. Numerous indeed are the heroes fabled to have taken up residence forever in the blessed isle of the unaging Goddess of Immortal Being.[73]

Jack does exist within the monotonous daily life that he experienced before the Call, the crash of Flight 815. Only when he becomes involved in Ben's plan to unite the survivors who left the Island and embark on the Magic Flight, does Jack overcome the Refusal. "If the hero in his triumph wins the blessing of the goddess or the god and is then explicitly commissioned to return to the world with some elixir for the restoration of society, the final stage of his adventure is supported by all the powers of his supernatural patron."[74]

In Campbellian myth, the Magic Flight is about the return home with the Boon gained on the journey, but "home" in this context can be seen for Jack as the Island, a place his faith in a greater destiny he was running from will give him, the Boon being that awakening given to him by the Apotheosis—even if it is one born from guilt and tragedy. It becomes a race against time as Jack leads the survivors, who after all kinds of fate and happenstance manage to come together on another flight that has been precisely calibrated to deliver them back to the Island, and in this case the Magic Flight is quite literal. In "316," Jack and the survivors pass through a bright white light and are swept up, as if by magic, by the power of the Island, and thrown back to the year 1977 where their destiny continues.

2. *The Monomytharc*

This is by Season 5, a year in which *Lost* takes its most overt steps into full-fledged science fiction. Over the previous four seasons, *Lost* has certainly edged away from being a simple crash survivor character series what with hatches in the ground, scientific research initiatives, polar bears, black smoke monsters, etc. But in Season 5, immediately from the season premiere "Because You Left," *Lost* sees the Island and its main characters literally traveling through time after pulling a wheel hidden in an ice cave below the Island gets them unstuck, *Quantum Leap*–style,[75] flitting through periods as ancient as Egypt through to the Cold War 1950s, as Lindelof and Cuse build a complicated pre-destination paradox which had been layered in as early as "Orientation," the third episode of Season 2.

Jack in Season 5 has abandoned all pretext of being a leader. In the DHARMA Initiative structure of the Island in the late 1970s, he is a janitor, and subservient to Sawyer, who after unshackling his personal demons has grown into more of the leadership, heroic role Jack falsely inhabited across the first four seasons. Jack is now being guided purely by his faith in the power of the Island and whatever destiny he has been brought here to do, but this puts him in direct conflict with Sawyer when said destiny, Jack believes, is exploding an atomic bomb to change history itself. It becomes a question of faith as Jack fights in his belief that the Island brought him to 1977 in order to give them all a second chance and to correct a mistake—"The Incident"—that led, 30 years later, to their plane crashing on the Island in the first place.

All Jack ends up doing is ensuring that history happens as it originally happened. The bomb always exploded but the Island never blew up or sank to the bottom of the ocean. Jack and the survivors are flung back into the present day, which serves as Jack's Crossing of the Return Threshold and toward the final part of his journey.

> The hero adventures out of the land we know into darkness; there accomplishes his adventure, or again is simply lost to us, imprisoned or in danger; and his return is described as a coming back out of that yonder zone. Nevertheless—and here is a great key to the understanding of myth and symbol—the two kingdoms are actually one. The realm of the gods is a forgotten dimension of the world we know. And the exploration of that dimension, either willingly or unwillingly, is the whole sense of the deed of the hero.[76]

Having now returned to the Island, Jack has to face and understand his ultimate destiny in relation to the Island, and this speaks to the inherent duality at the heart of the entire Mytharc of *Lost*: light and dark, good and evil. For all his flaws as an emotional human being, all of his mistakes, Jack is still a healer. He may pathologically need to fix people, as a salve for his own inability to fix his own sense of ingrained inadequacy, but Jack has a goodness which drives him, in direct parallel to the evil encapsulated by the Man in Black, in the guise of the deceased Locke. We will discuss the Man in Black and this duality more in another chapter, but this Return Threshold is as key as the First Threshold on the trials Jack has faced to complete his journey. Now he must vanquish his opposite, and complete a symbolic rebirth toward the final step.

Jack's Monomytharc, much like aspects of Fox Mulder's, is Judeo-Christian in nature. His father's name is no coincidence, indeed names in general on *Lost* frequently have deeper levels of allegorical or symbolic meaning in its mystery play. In "The End," Jack dies to save the Island, on both a metaphorical and physical level. He defeats the Man in Black once he crosses the Return Threshold, after completing another key final step on the Campbellian journey: becoming Master of the Two Worlds.

> The individual, through prolonged psychological disciplines, gives up completely all attachment to his personal limitations, idiosyncrasies, hopes and fears, no longer resists the self-annihilation that is prerequisite to rebirth in the realisation of truth, and so becomes ripe, at last, for the great at-one-ment. His personal ambitions being totally dissolved, he no longer tries to live but willingly relaxes to whatever may come to pass within him; he becomes, that is to say, an anonymity.[77]

In this case, Jack is gifted the power of Jacob in order to access the magical "Heart" of the Island and, in the greatest act of CPR of his life, resuscitate the ailing Island which allows him to prevent the Man in Black's escape and confront him. Having overcome his fears about his destiny, Jack briefly becomes a master of the literal and spiritual worlds, and he can cross magical Thresholds. "Now you're like me," Jacob declares.[78] While Jack doesn't understand the mastery bestowed upon him in this case, he knows what to do with it. In the end, having suffered a fatal wound in his final battle, Jack gives his chief disciple, Hurley, the knowledge and mastery to guard the Island in the future, knowing Hurley to be the most virtuous of them all. This could be his most heroic act.

The final step of Campbell's Monomythical journey is taken, albeit in an unusual fashion: Freedom to Live.

> Man in the world of action loses his centering in the principal of eternity if he is anxious for the outcome of his deeds, but resting them and the fruits on the knees of the Living God he is released by them, as by a sacrifice, from the bondages of the sea of death. Powerful in this insight, calm and free in action, the hero is the conscious vehicle of the terrible, wonderful Law, whether his work be that of butcher, jockey or King.[79]

2. The Monomytharc

Jack's Freedom to Live ends up becoming his freedom to *die*, and to find peace. *Lost*'s Mytharc is cyclical. The first shot of the show, Jack's opening eye, becomes the last shot, as his eye closes. Jack's freedom may not involve life, going on to become a mentor or teacher or the ferryman giving Supernatural Aid to the next heroic journeyman, but it allows him to pass the greatest Threshold of all and achieve what his journey was all about—Atonement with the Father, or rather in this case an acceptance.

Lost tricked the audience in Season 6, its final year. Flashbacks or forwards became "flash sideways," showing what we spent the season believing to be an alternate reality in which Jack did change history with the Jughead bomb and our characters never crashed on the Island. Across the season, the characters—some of whom were long dead in the reality we had been following—seemed to remember what happened in this other life. But Jack, appropriately, remains the most resistant right up to the last scene of "The End," where in a church he finds Christian—his father. He learns, as we do, that this is no alternate reality but rather a "place" between life and death where Jack reunites with those on the Island he knew, all of whom are led by Christian into the literal afterlife together. It is, in theory, the ultimate happy ending.[80]

It also allows Jack to reach the end of his journey by finding, literally and figuratively, the father figure and acceptance he was always seeking. *Lost*'s Mytharc, for all of its complexities and concepts, always circled back around to people finding themselves and finding peace within themselves, and Jack's Monomytharc encapsulated that better than many others. His journey is heroic but unconventionally. Jack's quest is to save his soul as much as the rest of the world.

In the end, he lets go. He is lost no more.

3

The Divine Mytharc

We live in an age where the meaning of religion and faith have forever been altered. We never all believed in the same God, be it Jehovah or Allah. We never all believed there existed a pantheon of deities who needed worship in a variety of different ways, as the Greeks or Romans or Hindu faiths did in antiquity. Since the beginning of human history, since we were able to create parable from story, and imagination from reality, we have all *believed* in diffuse, often violently oppositional ways of existence.

What we all share, however, as a species beyond our different races or creeds or nations, is that we *do* believe. We all have faith in something.

For many, in the age of science and reason, faith does not derive from a God or a higher power. We have faith in scientific discovery or the power of technological advancement. Humanists have belief in pure human potential, in our own personal morality. More people are losing faith in organized religion, particularly in the traditionally devout United States, than ever before. Secularism and atheism are on the rise even in countries that have their bedrock in religious faith.

Narrative however, especially in television, remains fascinated by the concept of the Divine, and in faith as a broad idea.

A great deal of narrative mythology revolves around the search for something. We have seen with the Monomytharc, with how the hero's journey translates into the medium, how Mytharcs can be built around the quest of the journeyman to reach a goal, often an inner peace or equilibrium which affects external forces. Frequently, this journey can be driven by faith. Fox Mulder's faith in the existence of alien life, in contrast with Dana Scully's conventional faith in Christianity, underpins the belief systems of *The X-Files*. *Game of Thrones* is a TV series, and source material book series, littered with a monotheistic pantheon of deities and faiths across a multitude of lands, through which the tale of a prophesied savior will prevent the coming of darkness. *Westworld* has its own God figure controlling the balance between humanity and artificial intelligence. *Lost* has a deity pulling the strings of destiny. *Battlestar Galactica*, *Babylon 5*,

3. The Divine Mytharc

Millennium, some of which we discuss in detail, some not, but all at some point deal with this existential crisis of faith that TV's modern storytellers are dealing with. The list goes on.

In this chapter, we will look at the development of several Mytharcs driven by the search for a Divine truth. *Alias*' quest to understand the grand tapestry of 15th century prophet Milo Rambaldi, *Star Trek: Deep Space Nine*'s Judeo-Christian religious play at the heart of a secular space opera, *Lost*'s cyclical sense of fate driven by human deity Jacob, and how *The X-Files* underpins the search for alien life with the search for an all-consuming alien higher power. Each series places divinity and faith at the heart of their stories about heroes and villains, humans and monsters.

And all of them question whether, in the grand scheme, we are all searching for the same thing.

The Search for Rambaldi

Prophets and seers have existed in mythology since the dawn of time.[1] They exist within every major religious construct, from Christianity to Judaism to Islam. Often they play critical roles in the religious and social histories of these societies, with their power of divinity from God, conveying information or truth in the form of prophecy—the prediction of events to come. In the fictional Mytharc of ABC's science fiction–espionage series *Alias* (2001–06), a prophet played a singular role in the narrative structure of the show, and in many of its main characters' lives.

His name was Milo Giacomo Rambaldi.

In *Alias*' fictional lore, he lived in Italy during the Renaissance, a fertile period of scientific breakthrough, invention and discovery, often in direct opposition to the monolithic and corrupt Catholic Church. Rambaldi was designed as a cross between Leonardo da Vinci and Michele de Nostradame.[2] What's interesting about Rambaldi is that at no point does he serve as a character in the tapestry of *Alias*; the most we see of him is in montage flashbacks to the inventor as an old man, inside his classical study. Could these have been idealized visions of a man deemed to be a 15th century prophet? A man who claimed, through his work, that we would be able to "know God"?

J.J. Abrams and his creative team wanted Rambaldi to be a human MacGuffin,[3] a magical artifact of sorts to pivot the updated espionage concepts and nods to occult, arcane mythology they wanted to bring to bear, based on many of their inspirations—chiefly *The X-Files* which, much like

Myth-Building in Modern Media

Abrams' later series *Lost*, serves as a key touchstone for the adventures of the show's protagonist, super-spy Sydney Bristow.[4]

You could have made *Alias* without Rambaldi—in fact, there came a point later in the series' life when it flirted with doing just that. Following a complicated and rudderless Season 3, with viewers abandoning the series, the show attempted a soft reboot for Season 4, eschewing the Rambaldi mythology for well over half of those 22 episodes. By this point, however, the imprint of Rambaldi and the Mytharc surrounding him had become so dense and intertwined with the main cast's broader character arcs, the writers found it almost impossible to let go of the mythological monster they had created. Abrams seemed to be searching for the concept of a unifying narrative tether like Rambaldi, much like characters in the show who end up "searching for Rambaldi" himself.[5]

This becomes a recurring, interesting concept behind the Rambaldi Mytharc: the "search" for this historical figure.

Rambaldi is very much presented as a lost piece of history; a crucial, missing component to the Renaissance period where men such as da Vinci were innovating and laying the foundations for the age of scientific reason. The suggestion, across the show, is that Rambaldi's knowledge could may well dwarf the prescient prophecies of Nostradamus and the brilliance of da Vinci's inventions, and he very swiftly becomes equivalent to a Divine force himself. When characters such as villain Arvin Sloane "search" for Rambaldi, in truth they are searching for God, the Divine, for Creation itself. You can tell this comes straight from Abrams' own fascination with the "mystery box," which he's discussed at length[6]: his childhood obsession with imagining what lies inside a closed box, a core principle that, for much of his career, he's used to tell stories replete with a layer of enigma.

If Rambaldi, or essentially God, lies inside the box, then *Alias* never quite manages to figure out what God essentially means, or how he materializes. The show rarely overtly tips its hand to what ultimately Rambaldi's puzzle is supposed to mean. Immortality. The gift of eternal life. That to "know God" is to become Him, in a sense, and gain the kind of eternal longevity and dominion over the world a God would have. One has to factor in the real-life production factors of *Alias* when considering this. The writers consistently altered the game plan for the ongoing character arcs and mythology points,[7] and did not ever completely know what the end game of the Mytharc was.[8]

As the existential paranoia of *The X-Files* waned to the point it was cancelled, many shows of this period reflected the growing need to externalize an enemy beyond the borders of an America which had been

3. The Divine Mytharc

significantly wounded. *Alias* premiered just after the attack on the World Trade Center and by Season 2, Rambaldi's innovations had moved significantly away from clockwork devices and da Vinci's style manuscripts to essentially, weapons of mass destruction. "Salvation" re-conceptualizes the Red Ball as the carrier of an unknown virus. In "Passage," a nuclear warhead ends up being the carrier mechanism for a 500-year-old flower (more proof and hints of Rambaldi's Divine grand design). It is most overt in "Fire Bomb," where a Rambaldi device which can cause spontaneous human combustion through the release of a specific microwave electromagnetic pulse, is used to attack a Mexico City church—perhaps itself symbolically Rambaldi attacking the institution that tried to destroy his works and silence his "heresy." Never does *Alias* depict the horror of a terrorist attack on civilians more brutally, with shots of the charred corpses of worshippers underscoring that Rambaldi is more than just some Renaissance treasure hunt; that it's become an external force, delivered through occult, albeit *Indiana Jones*–style means, and threatens the heart of Western society.

From the outset of *Alias*, these existential fears about what Rambaldi may deliver upon the world exist in the form of prophecy. Invoking the Nostradamus aspect of the character, fused with da Vinci, Rambaldi hides inside a manuscript detailing many of his works, on the 47th page,[9] a prophecy or *the* prophecy as many refer to it. In the appropriately titled "The Prophecy," *Alias* takes its first overt steps toward the supernatural when the page reveals an exact drawing depiction of Sydney Bristow alongside this ominous passage: "This woman here depicted will possess unseen marks, Signs that she will be the one to bring forth my works; bind them with fury, A burning anger, unless prevented, She will bring the greatest power unto utter desolation."[10]

There are many ways to break down and read what would become Rambaldi's most signature piece of writing, but there is no getting away from the possibility the "greatest power" could well mean the United States, or Western civilization. That's certainly how the text is interpreted by the rather hawkish National Security Agency, or rather the mysterious, top-secret Department of Special Research,[11] who in "Q&A" use it as a pretext to imprison Sydney on the basis that she *could* be a threat to national security.[12] *Alias* is showing its hand here as a series worried about broad, unexpected threats to a country wounded and struggling to heal, and how both surveillance and human rights laws are beginning to erode under the fear and anxiety that anyone could be the enemy—even a woman as virtuous and honest as Sydney.[13] The show is already using

59

Myth-Building in Modern Media

Rambaldi as a prism through which, even in the popcorn, over-the-top, retro–60s stylistic approach it deploys, to explore a world post–9/11.

Arvin Sloane is one of the key reasons why *Alias* works so well as a reflection of the age it was made. Ostensibly he's a corrupted consigliere, the man in front of The Man,[14] but in reality Sloane is an example of the pernicious enemy within using the shield of protecting the people to forward his destructive aims. Crucially, by the end of the series, you can read Rambaldi's prophecy as Sloane being the "greatest power" for a range of different reasons; it explains Sydney's "burning anger" given Sloane kills her fiancé, kills her best friend, lies to her for years, keeps secret a sister from her, kills her sister, and ultimately causes her father's death. You can see why she would want to bring him "unto utter desolation." The show did not necessarily have this mixed interpretation in mind during "The Prophecy"; indeed, the show actively makes a plot point of negating Sydney being the woman in Rambaldi's prophecy with this quatrain: "This woman, without pretence, will have had her effect, never having seen the beauty of my sky behind Mt. Subasio. Perhaps a single glance would have quelled her fire."

She did see that sky, at the end of "Q&A," perhaps as the writers feared the connotation of their main character possibly being some kind of weapon of mass destruction. But the show ultimately refuses to let go of the idea Sydney could indeed be the woman central to Rambaldi's work or grand plan. They play with concepts of duality; partly between Syd's virtue on one side and Sloane's zealotry on the other, but also symbolized via the Rambaldi watermark symbol which appears on all of his writings and creations, a simple <O>, known as the Eye of Rambaldi. Considering the Rambaldi symbol, one cannot help but be reminded of the "Annuit Coeptis" on the Great Seal of the United States, visible on every U.S. dollar bill—a symbol many believe to be a key component of Freemasonry and Illuminati conspiracies in popular culture.[15] The U.S. State Department translates "Annuit Coeptis" literally as "He [meaning God] has favored our undertakings."[16] The Eye of Rambaldi isn't just a symbol, a watermark designed to protect real Rambaldi works from forgeries, but literally the eye of God, looking out into the future at those who would search for his secrets.

In Season 4, Syd is considered one-half of the eye, with either her rival Anna Espinosa or sister Nadia Santos the other, while the finale "Before the Flood" establishes Nadia as a virally infected, almost mind-controlled bringer of destruction. In conjunction with the Red Ball over the fictional Russian city Sovogda, Nadia is considered as the "greatest power" Syd

3. The Divine Mytharc

must bring down—which Irina claims forms part of another Rambaldi prophecy with the quatrain: "When blood red horses wander the streets and angels fall from the sky, the Chosen One and the Passenger will clash ... and only one will survive."[17]

The latter part of this quatrain appears far more on-the-nose than Rambaldi's earlier predictions, perhaps for expediency of the script, but the first part is realized by images and symbols seen by Sydney while in Sovogda. Yet in Season 5, the lines are again drawn between Syd and Sloane over a smaller Red Ball in the Tomb of Rambaldi. Quite how the prophecy can be interpreted and ultimately is actualized differs, perhaps thanks to the whims of the writers, and to some extent that could well be the point, fitting the nebulous interpretations of Nostradamus' predictions and some of the wilder theories proposed by da Vinci.

Take the late Season 2 episode "Countdown." As well as the Di Regno heart and ultimately the "fake out" of its significance as a weapon of mass destruction akin to what the CIA faced in "Fire Bomb," it pivots around the most overt Nostradamus comparison the show ever did with Rambaldi. The NSA has a manuscript listing times and dates, each marking an apocalyptic event. As Deputy Director Brandon states, "Napoleon's bloodiest battle with the Russians, 1813, the outbreak of World War I, 1914, dropping the bomb on Hiroshima, the list goes on."[18] Of crucial concern is a future date without any specific description, which instead of being an apocalyptic event of global magnitude has a far subtler and more ominous source: Sloane being given key, arcane knowledge of his own future, direct from Rambaldi through Conrad, one of his followers. It further plays on the suggestion that Rambaldi, in receipt of his Divine knowledge of the future, saw Sloane's role as the one who would "bring forth" his works, as he does with renewed purpose following receiving the letter[19] after experiencing a serious crisis of faith in his search. The question is, however: Did Rambaldi see Sloane's future or did he guide him toward it?

Sloane's own crisis of faith adds to the renewed idea of Rambaldi's positioning in *Alias* as a God-like being to be found and rediscovered. Sloane had spent years "believing" in Rambaldi after discovering a piece of his work by chance, and he admits in "Page 47" how it became "an obsession." We later learn in "In Dreams" that the closest Sloane probably comes to some level of redemption and acceptance from the people he wronged, that the stillbirth of his first child Jacqueline, pushed him further away from his beloved wife Emily and further toward pursuing Rambaldi to, as he describes, "fill the hole in my heart." This is quite clearly a religious conversion, much like people find God and Christianity after

Myth-Building in Modern Media

tragedy or trauma to help cope with their sense of loss. It takes Sloane losing Emily, who despite his obsession and terrible crimes to pursue it, loved her deeply, to suffer another crisis, one that threatens to push him away from the prophet. In "Countdown," we learn that Conrad, the Tibetan-based gatekeeper of Rambaldi truth, knew Emily would die and, though Sloane is angry he wasn't forewarned, the destiny he then discovers (or chooses) bestowed upon him by Rambaldi again fills that void. God, in this case, restores his faith by pointing him toward an appropriate revelation: a daughter he never knew existed, to replace the one taken from him.

Rambaldi acts, then, as God in controlling the destinies of people far into the future, seeing their paths and actively directing them through prophecy, written text and, in Sloane's case, direct contact. A scribed passing down of revelation. Nonetheless, it's a popular device for shows with a broad sense of their own mythology. Sloane here interprets his destiny as one of rebirth, attempting to cleanse the soul of past crimes through philanthropy while searching for Nadia. In circular fashion, Nadia's death is what pushes Sloane back to the obsessive, destructive search for Rambaldi's ultimate truth, and this is after he's given a choice: humanity or Godhood.

Nadia will forsake him unless he lets his obsession go but Sloane's own zealousness for understanding causes Nadia's death in "30 Seconds" and the circle (or the Eye) is complete. Rambaldi may have given him his daughter back but it could well have been one big test, pushing Sloane to choose between Man and the Divine. The choice ends up being Sloane's undoing, of course, but it feels almost inevitable in his role as the ultimate "Follower" of Rambaldi's truth. This cements him as analogous to *The X-Files'* own Machiavelli, the Cigarette-Smoking Man; both men give up their children and suffer the loss of wives and family in the pursuit of a greater truth, and in the end a greater sense of power.[20] Sloane's fate, gifted of eternal life but doomed to spend it trapped in Rambaldi's tomb as the memory of his daughter abandons him, is as ironically fitting as any character arc conclusion ever seen on television.

The "undeath" of Arvin Sloane could well parallel the same question whether Rambaldi ever truly died himself. There are consistent suggestions across *Alias* that Rambaldi didn't exactly die when he was burned alive for heresy in 1497; that he found numerous arcane, technologically advanced ways to experience a "Second Coming" 500 years in the future. In Season 3's "Full Disclosure," that term is even used by Assistant Director Kendall after Sydney discovers she was captured by the Covenant,[21] a

3. The Divine Mytharc

terrorist organization of extreme Rambaldi zealots who extracted her eggs in order to fertilize them with Rambaldi's DNA, long secreted inside an ancient vault deep in the Namibian desert. The Covenant's plan: To artificially bear a child of Rambaldi, with the woman he drew in his prophecy. Syd even wonders if this might be the meaning of that prophecy, that the "binding" of fury and "bringing forth" Rambaldi's works was more literal than anyone imagined. It's how the Covenant interpreted the words, and although their efforts are stymied and the DNA seemingly destroyed, the plan was clear: Rambaldi left all of the components in place for his own restoration and rebirth, centuries after his own death.

Quite what the Covenant planned to do beyond the birth of Rambaldi's child is uncertain, but it could connect to the ultimate revelations in Season 4. In "Before the Flood," we learn that the Covenant leader, Elena Derevko,[22] planned to bring forth one of Rambaldi's other prophetic manuscripts, *Il Diluvio* (*The Flood*). Rambaldi created the Red Ball virus, which essentially turns those infected into feral, zombie-esque automatons, as a doomsday device to "wipe clean" the world of those considered genetically and intellectually inferior. A true genocide. This is very interesting given the Third Reich's pursuit of Rambaldi's work, and Hitler's interest in the material lends a certain fascistic pallor over the Renaissance inventor's master plan.[23] Did Rambaldi intend to preside, as God, over the survivors of humanity following a flood, akin to the wrath imposed on Noah in the Biblical story, of his own making? Would the Second Coming of Rambaldi deliver the apocalypse and cleansing of mankind? If Elena planned to create a child, she could well have been planning to wait to unleash the virus longer than she did once the Covenant failed, combining it with another major and quite enigmatic Rambaldi creation: the Sphere of Life.

We first hear of the Sphere in the Season Three finale "Resurrection," after Sloane extracts its location from Nadia's genetic memory, and they both head off to discover it. That story is finally told in "The Descent," as we learn that the Sphere holds the consciousness of Rambaldi himself. Admittedly, even for *Alias*, this is the show pushing deep into science fiction territory, and it never knows quite what to do with the Sphere once its existence has been revealed, beyond acting as a character point for Sloane and Nadia.[24] This is, however, something the Covenant sought and Elena eventually retrieves, so in theory could the Rambaldi child have been meant to have this consciousness somehow "downloaded" into its brain? Could it have allowed Rambaldi's unique mind to be born into a new body?

It feels like the logical step for such a centuries-spanning master plan as this, even if *Alias* never wants to move too heavily into the overtly science fictional territory to show it on screen. The pieces of Rambaldi's truth, however, largely fit together. Until Season Five, that is, when new aspects complicate and potentially undo what could have been a level of Abrams' endgame.

In what became the final season of *Alias*, following the Red Ball incident and a potential Rambaldi doomsday scenario, some choice retconning goes on. A new organization, Prophet Five, emerges as the ultimate villainous group. They have been lying in wait for decades, with their tentacles in governments and crime syndicates, all of whom came together to pursue a key Rambaldi artifact—the Horizon.[25] Interestingly, the name "Rambaldi" isn't mentioned until well into the season, indeed roughly to the point *Alias* knew it wasn't long for this world. Following the narrative slump which many agreed Season Three took in its back half, with the wandering search for "The Passenger" (who turned out to be Nadia), Season 4 attempted a soft reboot with Abrams returning from focusing on *Lost* to oversee more of a streamlined, "spy-fi" concept where the trademark, heavily serialized storytelling was exchanged for a year filled with many more stand-alone stories, or stories which only etched at a deeper level of mythology.[26] An attempt to recoup viewers it may have been, but it was a creatively sharp move, even if it meant relegating Rambaldi until roughly the final quarter. Season Five attempts to do the same, but oddly seems to simply dress Rambaldi's works up in new clothes and alternative names.

Early on, we hear references to "La Profeta Cinque" ("The Fifth Prophet"), a Rambaldi manuscript which appears to detail how to clone a human being. But despite Prophet Five having taken their name from the search for this manuscript, this entire avenue is swiftly dropped so that everyone can go after the Horizon, and *Alias* very quickly edges back into serialized storytelling as it eats its own sense of history—replaying the early SD–6 storyline, essentially, through a new character, Rachel Gibson, created and designed to handle the series' spy derring-do aspects while star Jennifer Garner had a baby. *The X-Files* similarly had to creatively write around the real-life pregnancy of its female lead, but *Alias* chooses to incorporate the baby into Sydney's storyline.[27]

Despite the earlier flirtation with creating a Rambaldi child, it oddly doesn't try and fuse the unborn child with the Rambaldi Mytharc, instead drawing out the thematic ideas of motherhood between Syd and her mother Irina, which lead to a very misjudged climactic series beat: In the final reckoning, Irina, against a great deal of pre-existing reason,

3. The Divine Mytharc

is painted as one of the uber-villains with a plan straight out of a Bond movie.[28] Prophet Five and their plans end up being smoke and mirrors, purely to deliver the final revelation that Rambaldi's endgame involved immortality—which more than likely *wasn't* his endgame at all, and we almost certainly had telegraphed from early in Season 1.

The search for Rambaldi, therefore, ends up wholly being largely a game of misdirection and dead ends. There are bigger concepts which are established and then almost nothing is done with them. Much is made of Rambaldi having followers across the centuries, people who have at various points both sought to uncover and indeed have protected his works. Many of them have the Eye of Rambaldi marking their skin as a symbolic representation of their fealty and worship; these are disciples, protecting or looking for their one true God, but they never feel like the kind of collective organization or institution that would in other circumstances be representative of a church.

Late in Season 3, *Alias* also looks at the idea of genetic memory, suggesting strongly that the Derevko family members are descendants of Rambaldi himself; this is how Nadia manages to channel the location of the Sphere of Life through backwards, hieratic writing, having been drugged by an elixir, in "Legacy." Irina is considered to potentially be the woman in Rambaldi's prophecy, but in "The Telling" she explicitly tells Sydney it's *her* in the prophecy, suggesting that she knows of their family lineage and Sydney's role in events to come. But the idea is never expanded upon or given context.[29]

Perhaps the search for Rambaldi being so uncertain neatly parallels our own search for the Mytharc. From a creative standpoint, *Alias* is classically an example of a Mytharc which without question exists deep-rooted at the heart of a show concept but is never quite mapped out cohesively. There is no singular narrative serialized plan akin to J. Michael Stracyznski, nor beyond the first couple of season a particular strength of vision imbued in someone like Chris Carter, someone equally as fast and loose with cohesive narrative mythology. *Alias* is the first show in the post–1990s paradigm, on the cusp of a burgeoning new century and new age of television, to explicitly tether a Mytharc to a conceptual MacGuffin in the form of Rambaldi and, in particular, connect the grand design of that Mytharc to the exploration of faith beyond traditional organized religion.

Particularly interesting is how, toward the end of a run which overlaps with the beginning of *Alias*, *The X-Files* begins to explore the idea that its own formative Mytharc may also connect to a higher power.

Myth-Building in Modern Media

God Spelled Backward

Chris Carter spent a long time hinting in *The X-Files* that God was, in his overarching mythology, as alien as the strange creatures that Agents Mulder and Scully hunted for over two decades. It just took him a long time to voice it out loud.

In the second episode of Season 1, "Deep Throat," the eponymous, ill-fated informant tells Mulder, when he asks if "they" are here: "They have been here for a long, long time." The tenth episode of that season is named "Fallen Angel," specifically tying the idea of a crashed alien spacecraft with the iconography of a Biblical arrival from Heaven; the character of Max Fenig even disappears in a bright, magical beam of light. The finale of Season 3, "Talitha Cumi," is built around an alien shapeshifter in human form who heals people and saves them from death with the palm of his hand.[30] When Scully is diagnosed with terminal cancer across Season 4 and into Season 5, the alien microchip technology that serves as her cure is described as a miracle. Alien abductees in "Patient X" are called, Rapture-like, to the site of their abduction, looking en masse to the bright light of a UFO that beams down on them—the same site, Skyland Mountain, where Scully herself is taken early in Season 2. The name of the episode where that happens: "Ascension."

The examples go on but Carter, across the entire tapestry of *The X-Files*, conflates the existence of God with the all-powerful, destructive presence of a monolithic alien race controlling the destiny of our future. While there is a strong argument that the mythology of *The X-Files* was always about faith at the heart of Fox Mulder's quest to discover the truth about extraterrestrial life, Carter began to suggest faith, God and alien life were one and the same thing. Mulder's quest, the Monomyth central to *The X-Files*, may for him be a journey to find his sister, but in truth it is no less a journey to find God.

While *The X-Files* ostensibly is known as a series about aliens and monsters, either via the "alien mythology" or the so-called "Monster of the Week" episodes,[31] Carter's series from the very beginning was about faith. Mulder's faith was in the existence of extraterrestrial life but when you drill down into his psychology, his fervent belief in aliens—and in exposing their existence—stems more from the faith he has that his sister Samantha, abducted from the family home in front of him when he was just 12 by what appeared to be an extraterrestrial source, is still alive. Scully's faith in God, a present factor since childhood thanks to her role in a traditional American-Christian household, serves as a more traditional

3. The Divine Mytharc

belief system, one challenged frequently by her experiences investigating the paranormal.

For each of these characters, nonetheless, comes a journey of personal discovery. Mulder strives to recover Samantha while Scully seeks the affirmation of her faith in God. Early on, in "Beyond the Sea," following the death of her father, Scully shows a willingness to believe in the possibility of an afterlife thanks to Luther Lee Boggs, a Death Row murderer who claims he can pass a message on to William Scully through psychic means. This directly puts her in conflict with Mulder, whose only blind spot when it comes to belief lies in the idea of a monotheistic Christian God. We see this again in the third season's "Revelations," which pitches Scully as the believer and Mulder the skeptic, with Scully voicing this fear: "God is speaking, but no one's listening." This is a bigger existential fear which becomes more apparent when Carter begins tying both of these belief systems together.

Mulder refuses to believe in the faith-based Christian idea of the Holy Bible, of a God without some tangible basis in fact. The fascinating duality in Scully's character is precisely the fact that she *can* believe in God as an entity, as a spiritual force beyond human understanding, and it is the one aspect of the unknown she does not require the proof she demands of Mulder's X-Files in almost every other case. "Believing's the easy part, Mulder," Scully declares in "Nisei." "I just need more than you. I need proof." Mulder replies, "You think believing is easy?" Mulder is willing to have faith that science—which Scully otherwise places her faith in—simply cannot yet understand all of the supernatural or paranormal realities he is willing to believe in. He will take the same leap with a UFO or an E.B.E. that Scully will with God or a guardian angel.

As discussed in Chapter 2, Mulder is willing to take that leap with Jeremiah Smith in "Herrenvolk," the healer who is suggested to be a mere drone by the Cigarette-Smoking Man in a grandiose conversation that he and a captive Jeremiah had in the previous episode "Talitha Cumi." Darren Mooney suggests: "Smith is portrayed as a pacifist whose radical ideas threaten a corrupt status quo, the traditional narrative associated with Jesus Christ."[32] He works in precise opposition to the Smoking Man's protection of a conspiracy central to the Mytharc of *The X-Files*, and it is in "Talitha Cumi" that Carter stitches together the principle of a higher power with the meat and potatoes, science fiction reality of extraterrestrial interlopers for the first time. "The people believe in authority," the Smoking Man tells Smith. "They've grown tired of waiting for miracle or mystery. Science is their religion, no greater explanation exists for them. They must never believe any differently if the project is to go forward."

In this, *The X-Files*' own Machiavelli confirms that the alien force with which his Syndicate is collaborating are more than mere beings from another world; they are deeply connected to the ongoing battle between scientific rationality and religious faith of the modern age. Carter has flirted with this before in the show. In "Genderbender," the strange Kindred cult who live very much like an Amish community, and whose members appear to be able to shapeshift between sexes, are suggested in the final frame to have left Earth via spacecraft. Another example of Carter conflating God's influence with alien influence is found in "Fearful Symmetry": the abduction and return of numerous animals by extraterrestrial forces who remove their ovum with the intention, as Mulder believes, to create a genetic Noah's Ark in the event humanity destroys itself through its proliferation of weapons of mass destruction.[33]

Mulder struggles with Scully's definition of faith, the Christian Biblical paradigm, but framed in the context of the great revelation of alien life, he is willing to let his belief system drive him. Jeremiah, the prophet from above, promises, "I can explain everything to you," but despite numerous opportunities, he seems unable or unwilling to follow through on that before he is removed from Mulder's orbit. Jeremiah has the pacifistic calmness of a God figure, but he is unable to provide Revelation. The Truth, for Mulder, and for the audience, remains elusive.[34] The Mytharc, however, has forever fused miracle, mystery and science together and in the next major narrative step for the mythology, in the Season 4–5 bridging episodes "Gethsemane" and both parts of "Redux," they are explicitly brought together. Mulder and Scully's respective faiths are both shaken.

The Season 4 finale is called "Gethsemane," which refers to a garden at the foot of the Mount of Olives in Jerusalem, famous for being the place Jesus Christ prayed and his disciples slept the night before he was crucified by the Romans. Carter has stated that the episode title referenced how the tale debates "the existence of God,"[35] a story in which Mulder is led to the hard proof about alien life he has sought all his life, in the form of a buried Extra-Terrestrial Biological Entity on the slopes of the Yukon Mountains in Canada, only to discover that the E.B.E. was faked to make him believe and go public with the information, as the ultimate means to discredit him. Mulder is told by DOD official Michael Kritschgau (among the least suspicious and most rational government employees he encounters) that the entire conspiracy he has investigated for years is a lie perpetrated by the military-industrial complex[36] to cover up experiments on

3. The Divine Mytharc

human citizens. As a result, he fakes his own suicide in order to infiltrate the DOD to prove, or disprove, what he has learned.

There are clear Biblical parallels in this crisis of faith, beyond just the title. Carter intentionally uses this idea to question the entire Mytharc we have followed for almost five years, detailing in "Redux" a different, far more mundane Revelation of Truth for Mulder than the alien genesis he has come to believe. If the garden of Gethsemane is the veritable olive mountain in Canada which Mulder climbs, then his apparent suicide is his own crucifixion, martyred as a Christ figure for his beliefs.[37] "Redux" is almost his resurrection, emerging from his tomb into a new realm of enlightenment, even if that Revelation ultimately turns out to be false.

Conversely, at the same time, Scully is on the verge of death from a cancer which has metastasized ever since she removed from her neck an implanted chip, placed inside her during her abduction by either aliens or Syndicate members in Season 2. It triggers her own significant crisis of faith in the God she has believed in since she was a child. "Why do I wear this?" she asks her mother,[38] referring to the cross around her neck, as she traumatizes herself over undertaking what she deems "crazy treatments"[39] in order to preserve her life. In truth, Scully's crisis is about how she feels she has *lost* her faith, which you sense has been building across the run of the series so far.[40] The closer she works with Mulder, the deeper she goes into his world of events and circumstances that contrast with her scientific rationality, the less her own belief in God makes sense. How can she be skeptical at Mulder's faith in the idea of extraterrestrial life when she too believes in a supernatural force she cannot prove or disprove with science?

Yet in her time of need, she turns back to her faith, to God, and is rewarded with a miracle in a swift and unexpected recovery, once the chip she previously removed is re-implanted.[41] While Scully is reminded of how important her faith is to her, almost as a trade-off, Mulder briefly loses his. The Mytharc here places not just the characters front and center but the centricity of God and faith, belief in the Divine, with the conspiracy narrative. The Gethsemane trilogy, in the grand scheme of the bigger story, could almost be considered incidental; Mulder after all learns by "The Red and the Black" later in Season 5 that he was deceived in being led to believe the conspiracy had been a deception. Yet, in fact, these three episodes are crucial in marrying together the Mytharc's developing obsession with divinity.

The three-part story "Biogenesis," "The Sixth Extinction" and "The Sixth Extinction II: Amor Fati," bridging Seasons 6 and 7, stitch together these conceptual dualities and place Mulder *and* Scully on the same mythological journey of discovery. Scully ends up being the one to find, crashed on the beach shores of Africa's Ivory Coast, an alien spacecraft. On the outside of the craft, there exists, etched in the form of hieroglyphic markings, a complete example of the human genome, and passages from half a dozen religions—the Bible, the Qur'an, Pagan religions, from ancient Sumeria, "science and mysticism conjoined" as Scully remarks at one stage,[42] while documenting a discovery which, even for Scully, is staggering in how it bridges her firm belief in the scientific constructs of humanity with the existence of God. God, in this case, is simply an alien intelligence.

This is confirmed by the dying Cigarette-Smoking Man in the Season 7 finale "Requiem" when he states, "There is no God. What we call God is only alien. An intelligence much greater than us." What is interesting is how, by this stage in the Mytharc, what started as a myriad collection of alien species from invisible monsters,[43] to alien Grey abductors,[44] to even the aforementioned creepy Amish cult, had manifested as a race known as Purity. According to abductee Cassandra Spender in the sixth season's "One Son," they are "taking over the universe" and "infecting all other life forms" with their own life force—the same black substance we have seen, on several occasions, can jump from body to body and infect human beings. The mythology had well established the devastating, apocalyptic end game for these aliens, in colonizing and destroying all human life on the planet.[45] The "Biogenesis" trilogy goes further in directly suggesting that not only are these aliens returning after millions of years to destroy us, but that they originally created us.

This is not a new idea that can be credited solely to Carter and Spotnitz. The Biogenesis trilogy plays heavily off the work of pseudo-scientists such as Erich Von Daniken, who came to international prominence in the 1960s with books such as *Chariots of the Gods?*, which posited the phrase "ancient aliens" in suggesting that alien visitors in antiquity influenced the earliest civilizations in human history. These claims are repeatedly refuted by mainstream scientific authorities as science fiction rather than science fact, but there is no doubt these ideas struck a chord in popular culture.[46] In the Biogenesis trilogy, there is even a doctor, Barnes, who travels the world debunking theories like Von Daniken's, until evidence of the crashed alien spacecraft compel him to murder in order to cover up a discovery he can't disprove. *The X-Files* includes the term "alien astronauts" in "The End," where Mulder posits that a gifted child with possible alien genetics is the "missing link" between human and alien genetics.[47] "The Beginning" goes further, with Scully discovering evidence that all humans have DNA that is switched off, a so-called "genetic remnant,"

3. The Divine Mytharc

which further edges closer to the mystical revelations of "Biogenesis" that human and alien life are one and the same.[48]

Over a decade after *The X-Files*, these ideas would be repurposed by film director Ridley Scott in *Prometheus*, his prequel revival of the *Alien* franchise. It suggests that human life was seeded billions of years ago by the Engineers, alien visitors theoretically not too dissimilar to *The X-Files'* advanced Purity species, who by all accounts left behind the building blocks of human existence.[49] The ideas that Carter draws together in the Mytharc of *The X-Files* that bring God and alien life into the same sphere never seem to quite disappear; rather, they permeate.

What is equally interesting about the Biogenesis trilogy is how it serves to mythologize Mulder by presenting him, and the Cigarette-Smoking Man, as self-sacrificing Christ figures in a Biblical narrative. Mulder never sees the alien spacecraft, which disappears from Scully's reach as soon as she begins to unpack its secrets, but he is riven with the literal effects of its power, thanks to a rubbing from an artifact found near the craft. It has a psychological effect on his brain and begins unlocking certain latent genetic gifts which the remnants of the bigger American conspiracy attempt to exploit to their own ends.[50] "Amor Fati," concluding the trilogy, presents Mulder with a key step on his Campbellian heroes journey: Tempted by the Smoking Man—aka the Devil—with the promise of happiness, Mulder must reject inner peace in order to conquer his own demon within and come back to reality.

The X-Files could have easily given Mulder the opportunity to confront this combined reality of God and extraterrestrial life and explored the consequences on his own journey of discovery, but the journey is more interesting through the prism of Scully. She is fundamentally faced with what appears to be hard, scientific evidence that technology not of this world, only from an alien source, has knowledge of the building blocks of human life and of the arcane, prophetic warnings of our own destruction across dozens of texts from monotheistic and polytheistic religions which have existed since the first human civilizations.[51] The "Biogenesis" trilogy presents this alien spacecraft as the Tree of Knowledge,[52] with Scully as Eve picking the fruit, only for higher spiritual forces blocking her path to true understanding and enlightenment. While Mulder undergoes his own mythic Christ parable, Scully faces the reality that her own faith and Mulder's faith may essentially be the same quest.

This experience changes Scully's belief system when it comes to alien life for the remainder of the original run of the series, even though the idea of "God as Alien" is only revisited to a lesser degree directly in the ninth season episodes "Providence" and "Provenance."[53] She ends up bearing a son, William, who could well be an Immaculate Conception given how Scully believed she was barren thanks to invasive government experimentation. The eighth season's "Essence" and "Existence" play with the idea that William is a Christ child, born under the weight of religious symbology, but coveted as much by an alien power as a fundamentalist human religion.[54] These direct allegories lessen in the story of William through to the modern revival seasons, but Scully remains far more open to the possibility that alien life exists before her discovery of evidence directly tying their existence into the higher spiritual power she spent a lifetime believing in.

But *The X-Files* does not believe that God or Christ is here to save us. Much like in Ridley Scott's *Alien* saga, Carter's alien gods seek to destroy their creations. We exist, in the *X-Files* mythology, only to die in service of breeding more alien life forms, completing a long-gestated circle of conception from the primordial soup to modern humanity capable of questioning its own existence. It could even be a scarier idea that, in Season 11 most recently, the aliens are said to have sundered us completely, believing our destruction of the natural world (which they would have inherited after colonization) has rendered us unworthy even of our own apocalypse.[55] Carter's modern message is simple: God doesn't need to destroy us given we are almost certainly likely to destroy ourselves, and sooner rather than later.

If there is a truth that both Mulder *and* Scully, from both of their diametric ends of the belief spectrum, can both come to believe in, perhaps that is it.

It Only Ends Once

If the 1990s was dominated in television terms by the legacy of *The X-Files*, there is a strong argument that *Lost* metamorphosed into the TV phenomenon of the 2000s. While *Alias* and its Rambaldi mythology was still on the air, J.J. Abrams diversified and co-created a show he will never quite escape. Though Abrams soon moved into producing and directing motion pictures with *Mission: Impossible III*, leaving *Lost*'s production largely to co-creators and joint show runners Damon Lindelof and Carlton Cuse,[56] the foundations were very much laid for the series which would boast the next significant Mytharc in network television.

Though *Alias* suffered from the lack of a truly cohesive, singular voice

3. The Divine Mytharc

which carried across the mythology and series development, *Lost* very swiftly gained those voices in Lindelof and Cuse, who much like Chris Carter a decade earlier packed their show with deep philosophical, mythical, post-modern conspiratorial concepts, characters and storylines you would need an entire book to analyze and decrypt.[57] They created what remains, outside of perhaps *Game of Thrones*, the densest patchwork and tapestry of in-world narrative mythology that TV has ever offered.[58]

And like *Alias*, ultimately, the Mytharc of *Lost* revolves around the search for a Creator, making it almost a natural evolution of the search for Rambaldi. Even more so than *Alias*, *Lost* pitches this mythological search ostensibly in secular, non-denominational terms, before revealing itself to be a grand Judeo-Christian saga.

The search for Jacob is primal, lyrical and mythical.

Lost is a fascinating TV series and may go down in history as a watershed conflagration of mythological storytelling in tandem with the rise of obsessive online fandom.[59] Though it now remains divisive amongst audiences, given its propensity to pose more questions than answers in the saga of a commercial airline flight filled with survivors who crash on a deserted island in the South Pacific, only to find themselves trapped on a mystical island with a mysterious history and a centuries-old conspiracy that has global ramifications. Perhaps its most intriguing creation, however, is Jacob, the God of the Island.

Jacob only becomes a presence in *Lost* toward the end of a story which serves as the next stage, in evolutionary TV terms, from *The X-Files* (by way of *Alias*) in the ongoing battle between science and faith as rational vs. mystical constructs.[60] *Lost*'s two principal characters are Jack Shephard, a rationalist, troubled medical doctor, and John Locke, a disabled failure in life who the Island "heals" and who becomes a shamanistic seeker of truth. The bigger concepts circle around the theological battle between Jack's science and Locke's faith, with the show's ultimate message being that Jack needs more faith, and Locke perhaps would have benefited from not following blindly.[61] All roads in this battle ultimately lead to Jacob.

To explain the nature of Jacob is as impossible as attempting to explain who created Q in *Star Trek: The Next Generation*,[62] where the God-like Purity aliens in *The X-Files* come from, or how Rambaldi in *Alias* could foresee events five centuries in the future. Jacob represents the power of the Island, which is both frequently anthropomorphized in *Lost* as a character as vivid as those who land on it, and equally as a representation of a higher power. The Island can exist in different points in time. The Island cannot be found on a map. The Island can heal the sick and raise the dead.

Myth-Building in Modern Media

The Island itself is equivalent to God. It is as unknowable and as alien as Q, Rambaldi or Purity. It simply *is*. The mythology of *Lost* sprinkles enigmas within enigmas going back as far as ancient Egyptians,[63] but the Island has always been there, and likely always will.

Jacob is different because Jacob was not always God. Jacob was a human man who became the divine representation of the Island and its Godhood. Toward the end of *Lost*, a much-pilloried episode called "Across the Sea" provides the backstory of Jacob and his twin brother, known only as the Man in Black,[64] given he was never named by their birth mother, a shipwrecked young woman in antiquity. She is swiftly murdered by a woman already on the Island, who raises the children as her own. She named Jacob as he came out first. We never know where "Mother" comes from or who she is, and when her sons begin asking, she simply responds: "Every answer will simply lead to another question."[65] This reply precisely fits the philosophical thinking behind Creation. If God created the Universe, then who created God? And who created whoever created God? The answer is maddeningly Lovecraftian in its unknowability.

We learn that Jacob represents a mythic duality visible in dozens of examples of genre fiction: light and dark, good and evil. Jacob is purity and innocence, while his brother challenges orthodoxy. Neither knows of any world which exists beyond the Island, not being aware of their real mother,[66] until the Man in Black sees his birth mother, who tells him the truth. Jacob just wants to stay with Mother and clashes with his brother, who wishes to leave the Island and seek out the world that exists beyond, a world Mother claims is full of people she is protecting them from. It is a Biblical narrative without any sense of denominational religion at this point. They are not Christians or Pagans or Egyptian descendants. They exist outside of time and history but are playing out a religious parable, and a Biblical one at that.

What Jacob learns is that Mother protects the Heart of the Island, a light inside a cave which can never be allowed to go out, because "if the light goes out here, it goes out everywhere."[67] The implication is that the Island could well be representative of the heart of the Earth itself. The Island is therefore perhaps more representative of the Gaia, the Earth Mother, than the orthodox God of judgment and Creation.[68] It is the Man in Black's determination to leave the Island, and Mother's genocidal attempts to prevent this result in fratricide—Mother dies at her son's hand. In his fury, Jacob kills his brother by throwing him into the Heart but, as a result, seems to create a darkness which keeps the Man in Black alive in the form of a "smoke monster" which stalks the Island for millennia, at-

3. The Divine Mytharc

tempting to exploit the minds and hearts of those who come to the Island as part of his mission to leave.

If it sounds nebulous and complicated, that's because it is. Jacob takes over his Mother's role as the protector of the Island, of the Heart, but he spends the next 2000 years "bringing" people to the Island by influencing their lives. He is able to leave the Island and enter the real world in a way the Man in Black cannot, perhaps thanks to his corruption of the Heart.[69] A glamor, in magical terms, is placed around the Island keeping the Man in Black in, while Jacob constantly seeks to find a worthy successor to his role as the protector of the Island. He is immortal, never aging, and evolves to a beatific level of calm and assuredness in his place on the Island, but he is filled with sadness at the fact that his entire life, from birth to death, was in service of protecting a Truth he cannot ever truly know.

The morality play that is *Lost*, and ultimately the very core of the Mytharc, is about how the characters who crash on the Island do not just become literally lost on a desert island, but are metaphorically lost in their lives. Jack, as we have previously discussed,[70] is crippled by his own neuroses and a significant hero complex thanks to years of psychological abuse from his troubled, alcoholic father. Kate was the victim of an abusive stepfather and this triggered violent impulses, not to mention a highly dysfunctional relationship complex with damaged men. Sawyer saw his father kill his mother over sexual infidelity and became so twisted by it that he actively *became* the con artist who seduced and tricked his mother, even down to taking the man's name. And Locke, who completes the quadrangle of *Lost*'s cluster of protagonists, grew into a vulnerable underachiever due to being rejected by a weak mother and an amoral father who, as it turns out in perhaps *Lost*'s most staggering connection, to be the same con artist who destroyed Sawyer's life.[71]

What do all of these characters, and Jacob, have in common? Mommy or daddy issues, as Sawyer memorably remarks.

If you look across the swath of mythological fiction that has emerged in cinema and TV over the past 50 years, so much of it connects back to issues between parents and children—whether it's the high space fantasy of *Star Wars* through to the existential paranoia of *The X-Files*.[72] *Lost*'s morality play, and indeed the crux of its entire Mytharc, is not just about finding and discovering the Creator in a religious or divine sense, but in children looking for a way to let go of the issues they have with their literal Creators—their own parents. Jacob was able to do this, laying to rest his mother and spending his immortal existence protecting the Island, all the while looking for a way to "pass on" and, essentially, ascend to another plane of existence.

The way in which Jacob brings people to the Island is never quite explained, as tied up as it is with the "magic" of how the Island works, but "Lighthouse" suggests that Jacob has some preternatural ability to look into the pasts of people who have suffered trauma and, consequently, have found themselves "lost" in their own lives. People searching for a purpose or trying to figure out how to exorcise their demons. The suggestion is that Jacob spends centuries bringing people to the Island by influencing their lives in small but crucial ways, as "The Incident" shows us—whether it's a brief metaphor whispered to Jack in a hospital or reassuring child Sawyer, at his parents' funeral, that he will be okay. He can transcend time as well as space, even though he remains physically tethered to our world. It just takes him hundreds of generations to find the right confluence of people to help him ascend to true godhood.

The Man in Black, early in "The Incident," during a philosophical debate with Jacob which cuts to the core of their relationship, suggests that their seemingly eternal conflict "only ends once. The rest is just progress." This taps into the deeper, symbolic, cyclical nature of *Lost*'s storytelling: the suggestion that Jacob's efforts have some level of futility to them until Fate, or the larger spiritual forces underpinning the Island which transcend even the powers of Jacob and the Man in Black, decide that the time has come to hand over the charge.[73] *Lost* suggests that it takes the survivors of Flight 815 and their desperation to return to the lives in which they were unhappy and unfulfilled, to reach a point of understanding that the Island, and their "destiny" in being brought to it since they were born, is how the back and forth between Jacob and the Man in Black ends. In some sense, the crash survivors have to become "woke"[74] in their own existences to take their place in the path the Island has chosen for them.

It becomes clear that while Jacob and the Man in Black may be playing out an archetypal God-Devil narrative function, neither is precisely one or the other. Jacob has Divine powers but he is not strictly Divine, and seeks the solace of the afterlife as keenly as worshippers of God themselves do.[75] The Man in Black is malevolent and warped by his own feelings of being trapped in the confines of a world he feels too big for, but he was not born "evil." (Nor was Lucifer.) If there is a true, unknowable God parallel in *Lost*, it is most definitely the Island itself; it can preserve the souls of the dead, it can bend time, and it has existed since time immemorial. Sagas were played out before the story of Jacob and the Man in Black, and *Lost* ends

3. The Divine Mytharc

suggesting that sagas could theoretically play out again unless the Island is watched over by a protector.

In the end, Jacob passes on his gift beyond the point his physical form has been destroyed. He is, in all essences, a ghost when he tells Jack "Now you're like me" in the series' penultimate episode, "What They Died For." His powers are transferred through the consumption of a holy water equivalent, running from the stream which leads to the Heart of the Island, and a mumbled few words of Latin. Given Mother didn't pass this knowledge on to her son, or so it appears, it's unclear why Jacob needs to speak what would, theoretically, have been his native tongue in antiquity. When a dying Jack passes the gift on to Hurley, he only uses the water to grant the presumed "immortality" and knowledge. "What the hell am I supposed to do?" is Hurley's pained response.[76] Jack has no idea. You feel that it probably took Jacob quite a few centuries to figure that out too.[77]

In this sense, *Lost* is decidedly spiritual in purely a mythic sensibility. It is a show about archetypal belief systems rather than a core, ingrained spirituality. Jacob is rarely referred to as "God" by anyone on the Island.[78] He is considered by many as almost mythical himself, given how the only character to ever have *seen* the man the Others society worships and venerates, is Richard Alpert—who as we see in the final season's "Ab Aeterno," is gifted some level of Jacob's magical immortality to act as his Island steward over at least a period of 150 years. Jacob fits the mould of God in that he doesn't get involved in the actions and conflicts on the Island played out over the first five seasons, whereas the Man in Black spends much of that time plotting to bend the survivors to his master plan. The first voiced mention of Jacob isn't even particularly grand and meaningful, merely as a throwaway line from a minor Others functionary in "I Do" in Season 3. Lindelof and Cuse intentionally creep Jacob into the storytelling as opposed to the Man in Black who, even if we didn't know it, has been in our faces since the pilot episode.

Lost thereby does subscribe, certainly in a broader theological sense, to the Christian deity. God is everywhere but leaves His children to direct their own existence. God "works in mysterious ways," which means that His followers have no real conception of what He wants or believes, or if He even exists. Jacob is very similar. He only becomes involved in the saga when the Man in Black–the Devil brings the conflict to his door, and he very passively allows himself to be destroyed. He could almost be Obi-Wan Kenobi, taunting Darth Vader to strike him down, so that he will "become more powerful than you could possibly imagine."[79] Jacob's power, existing in an Island limbo between life and death, comes through the survivors who believe in him, and believe in the Island. This is Jack's arc, completely, in a nutshell—and like Christ, he dies to save the Island and save the world as a result.

Where *Lost* concludes its quasi-religious metaphor is in how it approaches the afterlife. Since the show began, it fielded fan theories about how the Island was, in fact, purgatory. So much so, that by the end of Season 3—when the series had cemented itself as a phenomenon in popular culture—the episode "S.O.S." even deigned to suggest maybe this theory was true and that the crash survivors were all dead.[80] Ultimately, the final season plays a big long con on the audience, in how it presents what appears to be a season-long alternate reality in which the plane never crashed on the Island, which turns out to be a "place" created by the souls of the crash survivors after death so they could be together, and "move on" to the real afterlife.[81]

But there is no place for Jacob in this afterlife. If there does exist a way to reconnect with the souls of those you loved, those who as Christian puts it "the most important part of your life was the time that you spent with these people,"[82] then Jacob (one would assume) found his own space with Mother, or even his *real* mother. And perhaps the Man in Black—though like the character of Ben Linus, a sinner in the eyes of the church—must spend longer atoning for his actions outside of the place beyond. *Lost* doesn't show us any of this but it can be assumed, given Jacob touches divinity but never directly becomes a God for mortals to discover. He presents the very humanist aspect of *Lost*'s message: that only together can we become more than we are.[83]

What the characters of *Lost* learn through the shows Mytharc, and that includes Jacob, is what it means, ultimately, to be found.

We have already discussed how *Lost* is the depiction of a mystical, quasi-religious Christian mystery play which distills the Divine concepts of gods, devils and mortals into a swirling concoction, but this would be impossible to construct without the level of cyclical storytelling inherent in the very DNA of Carlton Cuse and Damon Lindelof's series.

This really becomes apparent in the second season of the show when the Flight 815 crash survivors discover the Hatch. After a season of surviving the hardships of a South Pacific desert island, the discovery of a strange metallic Hatch in the ground is seen as a refuge for the characters now under threat from the mysterious Others, apparently the original inhabitants of the Island. They discover that the Hatch is part of a much bigger connected web of installations belonging to the DHARMA Initiative, a social science research organization that came to the Island in the 1970s

3. The Divine Mytharc

to study its unique properties. The Hatch, in fact, is known as the Swan Station.[84]

Early on, watching an "orientation" video made by one of the DHARMA scientists, characters (including central figures Jack and Locke) hear about an incident which led to a bizarre ritual in which a series of numbers had to be entered into an antiquated computer system in order to stave off some unknown catastrophe. Successive DHARMA employees over the last three decades have entered the numbers and "pressed the button" and, conversely, disaster has been averted. Season 2 plays with the philosophy of this idea, using it as a tool of science vs. faith; Jack believes it's a fallacy, that nothing will happen if they don't push the button, whereas Locke believes if they don't enter the numbers, something terrible will happen.

As becomes the standard with *Lost*, belief and faith tend to win the day, and this turns out to be the case with the Hatch. When Locke finally loses faith and resolves to make sure the button is not pushed, it triggers a singular electromagnetic implosion which leads directly to a chain of events in which both some of the Island inhabitants are rescued, and the Island is placed in terrible danger. It also leads to the conditions in which the "incident" happens in the first place, thereby ensuring the fate of certain Flight 815 survivors, and the Island, is caught inside a cyclical pre-destination paradox: The incident is caused by the same people who end up discovering the Hatch three decades later.[85]

To try and explain the whys and wherefores in how *Lost*'s science works would be a foolhardy endeavor. The Island simply just *exists*, as does one of the strangest narrative devices the series introduces, at least on the face of it: the Frozen Donkey Wheel.[86] At the end of the Season 4 finale, the deposed leader of the Others, devious Ben Linus, digs beneath the DHARMA Orchid Station into a frozen, icy, subzero subterranean layer containing a ancient wheel device built into the rock. On turning it, DHARMA "negatively charged exotic matter"[87] transports Ben magically through time and space (he arrives in the Tunisian desert) but moves the Island itself through time.

Again, trying to explain exactly how this is possible is not the point of this exercise, but it rather further demonstrates the idea that *Lost*'s entire storytelling structure operates in a cyclical manner—an ever-spinning sphere of time and space. The Frozen Donkey Wheel, we eventually learn, was created by the Man in Black as part of a mechanism to tap into the spiritual, unknowable power of the Island and, in his belief, provides him the means to "escape" the Island. By the point of the Season 6 episode which reveals this, "Across the Sea," we have already seen both Ben and Locke turn the wheel and travel in this manner, "moving" the Island as a result.

Consider the wheel itself and how it appears in numerous ways across *Lost*. The word DHARMA, an acronym for Department of Heuristics and Research on Material Applications, is a Sanskrit term used in a range of Eastern philosophies, particularly Buddhism. While the story of Jacob and the Man in Black might be a Christian religious play, the concept of "Dharma" directly relates to teachings of "law and order" in a cosmic sense, a prescribed way of living.[88] The logo of the DHARMA Initiative even displays a circle with the word "dharma" inside, inscribed within a "bagua"—the eight symbols used in Taoist Chinese cosmology to represent the eight fundamental principles of reality, representing yin and yang. It is not difficult to connect the fact DHARMA has eight research stations on the Island, all investigating properties linked to the "light" and "dark" of the Island, all positioned in a circular fashion around a ninth at the center.

The wheel recurs repeatedly in terms of *Lost*'s narrative: the aforementioned DHARMA stations in a circular pattern; the Donkey Wheel which turns, in a similar fashion to the "dharmacakra," otherwise known as the "Wheel of Dharma" (an eight-spoke wheel which to turn it means to reveal the truths of the universe central to the path of enlightenment, according to Buddhist tradition[89]); how the Island is described in "316" as akin to a wheel spinning through time itself. Everything comes back to the almost cosmological, philosophical spin of time and space, of the forces of nature spiraling around in a recurring pattern. This is both metaphorical and literal in how *Lost* conveys its historical narrative.

There is plenty of evidence to suggest that the series' "origin" story, the tragic Cain and Abel adaptation that is Jacob and the Man in Black, is by no means the first example of this balance between good and evil taking place. The "light" and "dark" at the heart of the series, which the survivors of the crash must battle, which exemplifies the battle between the survivors and the Others and ultimately Jacob and his brother, is described ultimately as a level of balance. Jacob in "Ab Aeterno" suggests the Island is essentially a cork in the bottle of an immense darkness which can swallow the entire Earth. This ends up being more than just metaphor, as we see an electromagnetic black hole threaten the Island in "The Incident" before a literal cork at the heart of the Island does even more in the series finale "The End," when the cork is removed from the bottle.

Season 5 presents a mystery which *Lost* never entirely answers. From

3. *The Divine Mytharc*

Season 2, when the numbers on the Hatch once counted down reveal Egyptian hieroglyphs,[90] there was a strong suggestion forces more ancient than even Jacob and the Man in Black may have existed on the Island. In the Season 2 finale "Live Together, Die Alone," crash survivors discover the mostly destroyed, four-toed statue of someone we find out come Season 5—when the Island begins moving through time, allowing the series to explore its own mythological past—represents the Egyptian goddess figure of Tawaret, who is described as the deity of childbirth and fertility.[91] This is intentional and central to the idea in *Lost* that the Island is a place of rebirth and of the importance of new life to continue the cycle of life and death.

Tawaret's presence is expanded on in Seasons 5 and 6 when we learn that the Others have for a long time been using an ancient Egyptian temple as a base of operations, a temple which again predates Jacob and the Man in Black and presumably was built by the same Egyptian settlers who constructed the Tawaret statue on the coastline, looking out to the world beyond. This suggests that Egyptian colonists may have existed on the Island for many years, long enough to construct a large temple structure which includes underground caverns containing a mural which we see in the episode "Dead Is Dead," an Egyptian hieroglyphical depiction of what is quite clearly the infamous "Smoke Monster."

Lost does not even hint at the reason for this but mythologically it has significant implications on the history of the series and the cyclical nature of the religious play unfolding. We see in "Across the Sea" that the Smoke Monster, which stalks the Island's jungles with an intelligence capable of "scanning" the souls of those it encounters and inhuman strength with the power to kill, is created after Jacob throws his brother the Man in Black—after the murder of their mother—into the cavernous heart of the Island. The suggestion is that his dark soul ends up turning man into mythical creature, given the Man in Black's body washes up later in a river. Even though Jacob buries him, his brother spends the next 2000 years appearing in spectral, undead form when not the Smoke Monster.

If the Egyptian murals that predate the events of "Across the Sea" are to be taken at face value, however, then this strongly suggests that the events that caused the Man in Black to become the Smoke Monster were not the first time the Island has played host to such a malevolent creature. There are hints in "Across the Sea" that Mother could have been another incarnation of the Smoke Monster; it is heavily suggested that she murders a native group of possibly Greeks (or Egyptians) Island settlers with such power and brutality it would be almost impossible for one single person to achieve alone.[92] Again, *Lost* does not qualify this with a definitive answer.

Lost, of course, tells the story of how, presumably, the wheel finally stops turning. The suggestion is made that the conflict between Jack and Locke (which distills so completely into its purest form when Jack "becomes" Jacob and Locke dies, allowing the Man in Black to take his form) is the conflict designed to decide the fate of the Island in perpetuity. Is the cycle broken when the Island is almost destroyed in finally ending the life of the Man in Black? While *Lost* may suggest this to be the final conflict, on the other hand it stresses the continued importance of a "guardian" who, like Jacob, must protect the Island from those who would corrupt the power within. That person turns out to be the cheery, likable, troubled Hurley, supported by the reformed Ben and, as we later see in the epilogue "The New Man in Charge," a grown-up Walt. If the Island is safe, why would they need to remain?

In many ways, the fact that the final episode of *Lost* is called "The End" is the biggest mistruth of the entire series, and its own Mytharc. There is no true sense of an ending to the broader concepts that underpin the storytelling of *Lost*. The characters involved receive some level of closure, whether in death, escape from the Island, or in whatever lies beyond existence, but mythologically the precepts of the Island remain. It will always need to retain that balance. There will always need to be a Jacob because there will always remain the potential for a Smoke Monster. *Lost*'s cyclical mythology reflects the eternal, very human and very delicate conflict between good and evil, and our search for the Divine.

Everything is just progress.

Far Beyond the Stars

When you consider TV shows with built-in mythology, the *Star Trek* franchise is not necessarily an example which comes to mind.

Star Trek has a powerful cultural resonance when it comes to developing a mythology in TV, as we will discuss in the next chapter, but the *Original Series* through the 1960s, and sequel shows including *The Next Generation* and *Voyager* into the 1990s, simply did not have an ongoing, over-arching mythology to their storytelling. There was backstory aplenty, and '90s *Star Trek* became a master of the two-part "event" episode.[93] But *Star Trek* series simply did not tell broad, mythic, long-form narratives.

Until the third spin-off series, created in 1992: *Deep Space Nine*.

3. The Divine Mytharc

This was just one year before *Babylon 5*, one of the key touchstones of TV mythology, was released, and the two series would often be compared and contrasted over their respective runs—given they started and ended within a year of each other. While *Deep Space Nine* would be accused of copying *Babylon 5*'s space station formula (only with a much higher budget),[94] it would also have the charge leveled at it that, once it embraced serialized storytelling, it was trying to take a cue from the heavily serialized "novel for television" being created by J. Michael Straczynski.

Neither were particularly true given how, texturally, both of these series were telling different stories. *Babylon 5*, much like *Deep Space Nine*, builds to a galactic war in which human and alien races must unite to defeat a powerful enemy. But it tells a tale of resistance against Totalitarian rule, underpinned with a quasi-Buddhist religious philosophy of cyclical death and rebirth. *Deep Space Nine*, though it does not truly becomes clear until the fifth season, is a Judeo-Christian tale about a messiah learning of his place in the world, and how he must save it.

As a result, *Deep Space Nine*—a show born into the era of Bill Clinton's presidency,[95] rising governmental scandal[96] and the broad, post–Cold War American question of who we are and where we are going[97]—nonetheless becomes a radical prospect in how it fuses the scientific, near-atheist worldview of *Star Trek* creator Gene Roddenberry with a grand, mythical religious apocalyptic battle between good and evil.

Roddenberry was famously an atheist. The world he created, "Wagon Train to the Stars,"[98] a futuristic take on the Western genre originally, was meant to exist as a Utopian vision of human society who had put aside their petty Earth-based differences and left behind the idea of monotheistic or polytheistic worship, i.e., the worship of one singular all-encompassing deity (as in Christianity, Islam and Judaism) or the belief in a multiple array of gods all depicting and representing different cosmological elements (Hinduism, Shinto, Santeria, etc.).[99] By the 23rd century and beyond, gods would mean nothing in Roddenberry's world.

Roddenberry wasn't just a futurist, he was a self-confessed humanist. Having suffered psychologically through the Second World War as a pilot,[100] he came out of that conflict with a determination to imagine a future where humanity had evolved past the need for war, and perhaps recognized the importance of religious belief in many of the major conflicts which have occurred across human history. His crew of the starship *Enterprise*, exploring the final frontier, were made up of nations, colors and creeds with now one goal: to portray the future of humanity as a collective, united species.

What's fascinating to see, when you look back on the *Original Series*, is how prevalent religion is in many of the episodic storylines and galactic adventures faced by Captain Kirk, Commander Spock and the *Enterprise* crew. For a man who didn't believe in the monotheistic Christian god he had grown up surrounded by in 20th century America, Roddenberry was fascinated and obsessed by applying concepts of faith and worship to the vision of the future he had created.

In the first season *Original Series* episode "Where No Man Has Gone Before," Roddenberry pitches former Starfleet officer and friend of Kirk, Gary Mitchell, as a man who develops godlike powers which threaten to destroy the ship. "The Squire of Gothos" introduces Trelane, a forerunner in many respects to Q in *The Next Generation* some two decades later, mischievously playing with matter and existence for his own ends.[101] Many episodes feature races being led and controlled by false gods, such as Landru in "The Return of the Archons." In "Space Seed," perhaps Trek's most celebrated antagonist, Khan Noonien Singh, exhibits evidence of God-like grandeur, the result of late–20th century genetic engineering which would ultimately send him spiraling into madness when he returns to seek vengeance on Kirk in *Star Trek II: The Wrath of Khan*.[102] The examples go on and many suggest the same conclusion: Roddenberry was fascinated by the idea of faith but couldn't bring himself to believe in the Christian God especially, and wanted to use *Star Trek* to denounce religion as a false and dangerous human concept.

Whenever Roddenberry introduces a being of supreme power into the *Original Series* or *The Next Generation*, they are almost always false deities seeking to bring harm to the intrepid humans seeking answers about the universe, or aren't nearly as powerful or beatific as they claim to their brainwashed followers. We see this trope repeated time and time again, even in *Star Trek V: The Final Frontier*, which involves the literal search for God and the memorable discovery, beyond the Great Barrier, that the traditional representation of the Christian God, an old man with a white beard, is just another alien tricking humanity.[103]

What, indeed, *does* God need with a starship? William Shatner's fifth Trek film may ask this question in a rather pulp 1960s context, but again it's a symbol of *Trek*'s unsophisticated approach to religion in the future until we reach *Star Trek* in the 1990s. It was only then, oddly enough, that *Trek* stopped using the word "God" in the same context as was used in *The Final Frontier* and the 1960s series before it. Intentionally or not, religious ideas and faith were explored and couched in different terms in subsequent series and movies, further moving the franchise away from depicting, and criticizing, monotheistic Christianity.

3. *The Divine Mytharc*

Until we get to *Deep Space Nine*, when the Christian myth story plays out very keenly with the character arc of Benjamin Sisko, only couched in non–Christian terms. The Prophets of Bajor, the Emissary of the Prophets, the Pah'Wraith fire demons trapped for centuries, the idea of an apocalyptic holy war, between beings who exist out of linear time and space, to end all of existence, with prophecies of sacrifice and a "golden age" for the Bajoran people once the battle is fought. Sisko as Christ and Gul Dukat as Satan equals Christian Armageddon, with Bajor's future the Promised Land or Garden of Eden.

For a show ostensibly about frontier politics, Holocaust allusions and ultimately the devastation and cost of war,[104] *Deep Space Nine* is ultimately *the* most overtly religious, and overtly Christian, *Star Trek* series. In some ways it's a good thing Roddenberry was dead before it aired as the very idea of the show would probably have him spinning in his grave. His vision of *Star Trek* is fine with the idea of gods existing in space, existing in the mythologies and psychological constructs of less advanced alien worlds, but for humans? Sisko, a human, becoming a literal Christ would almost certainly have offended all of his atheist, humanist sensibilities.

When *Deep Space Nine* began, it showed no particular inclination that then–Commander Sisko was going to have anything other than the narrative arc the two previous *Star Trek* leading men would have. William Shatner's James T. Kirk went from roguish man of action to middle-aged, disconsolate admiral, back through to a captain pining for his youth.[105] Patrick Stewart's Jean-Luc Picard was the steadfast, educated, seasoned captain who developed from brittle taskmaster through to a benevolent father to not just a crew, but a family.[106] Avery Brooks' Sisko was not just different as a man of color, but also for the fact he was "grounded"; unlike Picard or Kirk, racing around the galaxy on their *Enterprise*s, the action had to come to Sisko as the peacekeeper of a rickety political situation in formerly occupied territory on a space station filled with as many crooks and ne'er-do-wells as Starfleet officers.

Nonetheless, in the first couple of *Deep Space Nine* seasons, Sisko operated in the vein of a traditional *Star Trek* show leading man, apart from one key difference: his role as the emissary to the Prophets of Bajor, gods to the superstitious, highly religious world recently freed from decades of fascist oppression. In an uncertain world filled with the need to rebuild after their sociological trauma, the Bajorans looked for a symbol to fulfill ancient prophecies of restoration. Sisko, as the man arrived to facilitate Bajor's aid from Starfleet and begin their process to becoming a Federation member, fitted that bill nicely. "You are of Bajor," he is told by the

Myth-Building in Modern Media

mystical Opaka, Kai (read: pope) of Bajor.[107] The pilot episode "Emissary" establishes this as a key aspect to Sisko's place on *Deep Space Nine*, lending him a tether and connection to the incorporeal beings who his crew call "Wormhole aliens," by virtue of the fact they live in a "Wormhole" which gives Starfleet access to the distant Gamma Quadrant—thereby fulfilling *Star Trek*'s mantra of exploring new life and civilizations.[108]

Despite this connection, Sisko never really believes he has anything close to a mystical purpose or spiritual destiny. He respects the Bajoran belief system but in the first few seasons he indulges it more than he takes it seriously, often for the purposes of political relations. He is treated differently by key Bajoran religious figures, such as the ill-fated Kai Opaka and the cunning Vedek Winn,[109] but Sisko never uses their belief system against them. In the "Homecoming" trilogy, he actively pushes rescued Bajoran resistance fighter Li Nalas into becoming more of the post-occupation symbol of hope for his people than the emissary. "Dying gets you off the hook. Question is, are you willing to live for your people? Live the role they want you to play? That's what they need from you right now."[110] Though perhaps more romantic (in the classic sense) than Kirk or more emotional than Picard, Sisko is first and foremost a man of science. Yet what happens over the course of *Deep Space Nine*, particularly when Ira Steven Behr takes control of the series,[111] is that Sisko becomes a man of faith—undergoing a classic Monomythical heroes journey to enlightenment, and in the process building the first, and to date last, Mytharc within a *Star Trek* series.

The change begins to happen across Seasons 3 and 4, as Sisko becomes a captain and the threat of the Dominion begins to rear its head. In "Destiny," Sisko comes to believe the prophesied warnings of a Bajoran Vedek about a pair of Cardassian scientists who may destroy the Celestial Temple (aka the Wormhole). "Do you really believe I'm the emissary?" Sisko asks his trusted first officer, Bajoran Major Kira. "I guess I always have. But I've never wanted to admit it to myself. It's hard to work for someone who's a religious icon."

In "Accession," poet Akorem Laan reappears after centuries and proclaims himself the Emissary. Sisko is at first relieved that he no longer bears the responsibility: "No more ceremonies to attend, no more blessings to give. No more prophecies to fulfill. I'm just a Starfleet officer again; all I have to worry about are the Klingons, the Dominion and the Maquis. I feel like I'm on vacation." Yet Akorem's entire reappearance is designed as a reminder to Sisko from the Prophets, a wake-up call about the importance of his role as the emissary.

3. The Divine Mytharc

The crux point comes in the fifth season episode "Rapture," in which Sisko becomes obsessed with the ancient Bajoran lost city of B'Hala and undertakes a vision quest to find it, spurred on by visions from the Prophets, even to the point he starts reciting prophecy, foreshadowing events that would take place later in the series:

> But then a shadow blocked out the sun. We looked up and saw a cloud filling the sky. It was a swarm of locusts. Billions of them. They hovered over the city, the noise was deafening … but just as quickly as they came, they moved on. Now I know where they were going. Cardassia.

From then on, upon discovering B'Hala and subsequently heeding ancient prophetic warnings to prevent Bajor's admittance to the Federation which was about to take place, Sisko crosses over into something else. He becomes both captain of *Deep Space Nine and* the emissary, for all those roles entail.

This journey goes beyond that of a mere story arc, the kind *Star Trek* had been used to telling up to this point. *The Original Series* existed in an age of television where stories remained largely self-contained, but even *The Next Generation* only engaged in arc-based stories: Worf's ongoing journey to retain his honor amidst a Klingon Empire overcome by civil war and insidious Romulan forces[112]; Picard's assimilation by the terrifying Borg Collective and how it informs subsequent encounters with them[113]; Data's ongoing quest to become more human,[114] etc. Even *Voyager*, which came after *Deep Space Nine*, merely dealt in continuing story arcs, some of which would reappear across different seasons, much like *The Next Generation*.[115]

Deep Space Nine was different. In its corner of the *Star Trek* universe, *Deep Space Nine* crafted a mythology around Bajor, the Prophets and the Cardassians which eventually became seamlessly intertwined with the bigger, ongoing story arc that saw the Federation go to war with the Dominion, encompassing a whole host of main and supporting characters. Sisko's ultimate journey inwards, to that discovery of truth, leads him back to his own past in "Image in the Sand," discovering that his mother was a Prophet and, essentially, his entire life was designed by the mysterious aliens in order for him to fight what is quite clearly a Judeo-Christian myth by the time we reach the final seventh season, and particularly the series finale "What You Leave Behind." "The Sisko is necessary," he is told by the Prophet who appears in the form of Sisko's late mother Sarah.[116] Sisko was the Christ amidst an apocalypse driven by destiny to destroy his opposite—the emissary versus the Kosst Amojan, a Devil figure from

Myth-Building in Modern Media

Bajoran antiquity who takes control of Sisko's long-term antagonist, his wily Cardassian predecessor on the station, Gul Dukat. "I should have known the demon would be you,"[117] Sisko barks as their final confrontation in the Biblical setting of the ominously named Fire Caves takes place, as if the apocalyptic point needed further underscoring.

When you look at the tapestry of *Deep Space Nine*, the presence of a Mytharc is not immediately obvious in the same manner as it is with its non–Trek opposite, *Babylon 5*. *Deep Space Nine* organically finds its way to the mythic story of Sisko's destiny and how, ultimately, it factors into how he protects Bajor from the Dominion and ultimately defeats Dukat in their final reckoning. *Babylon 5*, from the outset, had the aforementioned "five-year plan" that J. Michael Stracyznski wanted to achieve, which he managed to do despite challenges along the way.[118] While both shows undeniably share DNA in terms of their long-form arcs, principally how they both go from initially telling relatively stand-alone stories on a space station designed as a beacon of peace, through to depicting a devastating galactic war in which *Babylon 5* and *Deep Space Nine* are both critical in how they defeat the threats to their way of life, *Babylon 5*'s mythology was far broader in more of a polytheistic approach to godhood and the afterlife, whereas *Deep Space Nine*'s journey for Sisko is quite explicitly a Christian apocalyptic denouement in the fires of Hell. But *Deep Space Nine*, from a storytelling perspective, never prepared the ground for this conclusion in the manner that would suggest a broad, cohesive Mytharc in play.

The turning point arguably comes around Seasons 3 and 4, when Ira Steven Behr places his stamp on the material and begins to more expressly engage in longer-form storytelling, before fully experimenting with serialization in the first six or seven episodes of Season 6 and the last half of Season 7.[119] Building up to that, you can point to the Mirror Universe episodes,[120] or the Ferengi comedy pieces[121] and the Klingon politics stories,[122] or perhaps the Sisko–Michael Eddington confrontations,[123] as examples of long-form story arcs in play, but these do not encompass what we consider a mythology. The Mytharc of *Deep Space Nine* is synonymous with the internal show mythology of Bajor, its religion, its prophets and the role of its emissary. Once the show realizes, during Season 5, that Bajor's destiny is uniquely entwined with the brewing Dominion conflict, the final two seasons play much more into the pattern of Mytharc-based storytelling. Episodes such as "Waltz," establishing Dukat's mania, followed up by "Covenant" and beyond, or "The Reckoning" with its epic non-corporeal battle between veritable angels and demons on the *Deep*

3. The Divine Mytharc

Space Nine Promenade, leading directly into a fusion of Bajoran mythology and Dominion conflict in the Season 6 finale "Tears of the Prophets." These are pieces of a whole, as opposed to connected but at the same time disparate arcs inside the framework of *Deep Space Nine*'s tapestry of characters, worlds and stories. They move the series away from the same story or character arc two-part tales in other *Trek* series up to this point, which acted more like cinematic sequels in television terms than a mythology.[124]

Perhaps the most fascinating idea running through *Deep Space Nine* is that the whole show, and by extension potentially the entirety of the *Star Trek* franchise, exists solely in the head of Benny Russell, a 1950s pulp science fiction writer played by Avery Brooks, a.k.a. Sisko, in the Season 6 episode "Far Beyond the Stars" as part of a searing commentary on institutionalized racism, and who then reappears early in Season 7 as part of the mythology when Sisko learns of his own personal biological history with the Prophets. Though all of the main cast appeared in alternate roles within what appears to be a fictionalized world Sisko imagines, as opposed to the other way around, show runner Ira Steven Behr had a striking conceptual idea of how this could have been weaved into the *Star Trek* universe:

> I did pitch to Rick Berman that the final episode would end up with Benny Russell on Stage 17 at Paramount, wandering around the soundstages, realizing that this whole construct, this whole series, that we had done for seven years, was just in Benny's head. That is how I wanted to end the series. And Rick said, "Does this mean *The Original Series* was in Benny's head? Does this mean *Voyager* was in Benny's head?" I said, "Hey man, I don't care who is dreaming those shows, I only care about *Deep Space Nine* and yes, Benny Russell is dreaming *Deep Space Nine*." He didn't go for it.[125]

If Berman *had* gone for it (and some would say it could have been a better "ending" to the glory years of televised *Star Trek* than *Enterprise*'s "These Are the Voyages…"),[126] this *St. Elsewhere* conceptual rendering[127] could not only have had profound consequences on *Star Trek*, but on television as a whole. It would have rendered *Deep Space Nine*'s Mytharc open to question and left *Star Trek*'s most daring series with an open, philosophical ending we would still be debating some two decades later.

4

The Cultural Mytharc

Take any piece of fiction on TV today and analyze it critically and you will find, baked into the structure, some kind of reflective element to where we are as a culture.

This is nothing new. As we will discuss, *Star Trek* led the way for popular culture in the 1960s by tackling a smorgasbord of social, political, religious and philosophical issues under the veil of harmless science fiction escapism. We discussed in Chapter 2 how many of the precursors to the modern age of television mythology tackled issues directly relating to our culture, many of them under the "genre" umbrella where they could hide their coded messages, critiques or rebukes against the establishment, corporations, government and individuals under the guise of simply telling a story.

Those subtexts, however, are very clearly present, and many of them shape and underpin the most successful television, and the most powerful TV mythologies, of the age in which they air.

The X-Files tapped into and defined a latent American guilt about historical misdemeanors and a latent fear amongst their society about the "other," be it aliens or monsters of the week. *Millennium* accentuated that by examining the very primal fear of the human monster and pre-millennial anxiety about our future as a species. *Fringe* picked up the baton *The X-Files* left behind but focused the same anxiety about conspiracy and maltreatment of society less through the prism of big government than the emergence of unchecked corporations with power and resources; theirs was a world in which the monsters were us, transformed and mutated into aberrations by old white men intent on playing God.

Mythologies continue to reflect our emergent concerns and cultural touchstones through which we define our place in the world. *Game of Thrones*, while set in a medieval-styled fantasy realm, is as much about post-truth and the manipulation of populations by an elite determined to retain their power in the face of sweeping social, economic and political change. *Westworld* worries about our growing interface with technology

4. The Cultural Mytharc

and artificial intelligence, and where our dehumanizing thirst for entertainment and spectacle will take us should we create machines that exceed our own capability.

Many of these Mytharcs intertwine with the central Monomyth and the hero's journey, frequently aligning with religious meaning as characters within these narratives strive to find their place in the universe. Our meaning we find by digesting and becoming invested in these stories, which repeatedly reflect the culture in which we live, where we are heading, and how, in many cases, we should prevent making the same mistakes as the characters we follow, revere and adore.

This is not just their story. It's ours.

The Road of Discovery

Though the Mytharc may have been propagated by the aforementioned series which launched in 1993, another major TV series of the early 1990s which came to pass only slightly before *The X-Files* and *Babylon 5* would without doubt take a cue from those shows in not just adopting Monomythical, arc-based storytelling, but bringing such stylistics to the most well-established franchise in entertainment history.

Star Trek.

If *The X-Files* established the idea that the underlying Mytharc would concern deep-rooted explorations of American cultural history, discussing them within the prism of narrative and storytelling, then back in 1966, *Star Trek* was the touchstone of that foundation.

Star Trek was the first television series to truly bring to the mainstream the idea that ongoing science fiction or so-called "genre" fiction is far more about *our* world than the fantastical one presented on screen.[1] It is fair to suggest that creator Gene Roddenberry builds off Rod Serling's seminal *Twilight Zone* (1959-64), one of the first TV series to tell fantastical stories through a prism which reflected modern society. But the anthological aspect of that show was in some respects a restriction. *Star Trek*, like *The X-Files*, introduced characters and a "universe" which have eternally become part of popular culture and have resonated across half a century.

Star Trek began as a kitsch, rather throwaway series which lasted three seasons before being ignominiously cancelled. Given how Roddenberry's little show that could survive a decade of repeats, letter campaigns championed by authors such as Harlan Ellison[2] and super fans such as Bjo and John Trimble[3] and convention circuits before a big-screen revival in 1979,[4] it was perhaps inevitable that a golden age of *Trek* would be kickstarted. This came to be across the 1980s and 1990s, spawning as of today five successful spin-off series and 13 motion pictures (with more on the way).[5] It was a series which became a franchise. A significant reason for *Trek*'s enduring appeal and success comes down to its internal mythology, a mythology which cannot quite be defined in the same terms as *The X-Files* or *Babylon 5*.

Star Trek, across all of its incarnations, has never held true to what would be considered a Mytharc, or even historically a Mythos. There is no broad narrative and thematic sweep which covers all of the different shows, from the *Original Series* through most recently to *Discovery*. *Star Trek* does employ serialized storytelling in some of its series, but these cannot be considered a connected mythology in our defined sense of that word. *Deep Space Nine* created what could be considered the first long-form serialized narrative in *Star Trek* with the Dominion War and the mystery about Captain Sisko's role as the emissary of the Prophets, particularly in its seventh and final season[6]; *Voyager* during its second season attempted with ongoing villains the Kazon to drip-feed a recurring narrative, even if it took place across the season between stand-alone stories. *Enterprise* with its third season adopted a season-arc concerning a dangerous mission in a region of space called the Delphic Expanse to stop the Xindi, a species building a super-weapon to attack Earth, but built stand-alone stories inside the overarching narrative the crew were undertaking.

The newest series, *Discovery*, has fully embraced serialization unlike any previous *Star Trek* show. Arriving in the age of what is described as "peak TV,"[7] launching on a streaming service in CBS All Access which is directly competing with streaming giant rivals who are making gigantic hit series which live and breathe on a serialized narrative,[8] *Discovery* hit the ground running with the ongoing story of Lieutenant Commander Michael Burnham's fall from grace, helping to trigger a Federation-Klingon war, and later joining the crew of the *Discovery* in an extended sojourn to the sinister Mirror Universe. There are no direct stand-alone episodes in the manner of previous *Star Trek* series, which acted more as parables or television plays working with allegory or making a social commentary. Rather, *Discovery*'s 15 Season 1 episodes form a connected, ongoing, developing narrative structure under the umbrella of the *Star Trek* world we are already familiar with, and this same structure continued with Season Two and likely will do so beyond.[9]

Unlike *The X-Files*' dark reflection of modern American history, Rod-

4. The Cultural Mytharc

denberry's series is the very definition of futurist optimism. Humanity, come the 23rd century, have united the planet Earth and created a vast United Federation of Planets, a banner under which they explore the galaxy to "seek out new life forms and new civilizations," and "to boldly go where no man has gone before."[10] One of many starships on such a quest, the *Original Series'* USS *Enterprise* is on a five-year mission[11] to achieve this purpose, filled with a crew Roddenberry intentionally developed as a mishmash of human countries and races brought together in common purpose: the Chinese navigator, the Russian security chief, the Scottish engineer and the African-American communications officer. Naturally, of course, the captain is white American, but his second-in-command represents the "other": He's an extraterrestrial from the planet Vulcan, a world built around philosophical and religious precepts which reject emotion.[12]

These decisions were as intentional as they naturally seem. Roddenberry's vision as a futurist relied on the idea of races who in the 1960s, at the height of the Cold War, distrusted each other across border lines intensely, but by the year 2265—when his show was set—would have put aside their enmities. "Intolerance in the 23rd century? Improbable!" Roddenberry stated at the time. "If man survives that long, he will have learned to take a delight in the essential differences between men and between cultures."[13] To portray a unified crew of former enemies of the American people through two difficult world wars was a bold step, helping to cement the central concept of *Star Trek*, and it arguably served to enhance its durability. These decisions helped render the underlying idea of the Federation as a broader ideal which Roddenberry, and the creatives who steered *Star Trek* after his death in 1991, would develop, expand upon and deepen over the decades of television stories and movies the franchise would produce.

In the 1960s, the Federation was far less a concrete idea with detailed rules and specifications. Later movies and particularly TV shows would set the core tenets of the organization, chiefly the Prime Directive of non-interference in civilizations which had yet to achieve space travel.[14] Here, the Federation is a loose backbone on which Roddenberry pinned his morality plays and escapist science fiction tales. Mythologies within fictional worlds and franchises often rely on rules or precepts which, at this stage, *Star Trek* didn't have.

Much like Martin Luther King Jr. had a dream,[15] around the time *Trek*'s third season was being broadcast, *Star Trek* had an idea.

Gene Roddenberry died in 1991, just after watching a cut of the final *Original Series* movie, *The Undiscovered Country*, in some level of circular kismet.[16] He fashioned the beginning, and bore witness to part of its end. Roddenberry's death massively loosened the dramatic box he believed was crucial to *Star Trek*'s evolution, but seemed out of place in a more cynical world than the 1960s; a world in which the American people no longer believed everything would necessarily be all right in the end.[17] The '80s may have been colorful and festooned with popular culture in entertainment, but it was also a decade of rampant capitalist expansion and growing inequality; it gave birth to a paranoid, cynical, distrustful '90s in which the American people started believing again in conspiracy theory. TV series such as *The X-Files* now had the cultural space to become a phenomenon. Idealism was not enough.[18]

The Undiscovered Country is haunted by the shadow of the end of the Cold War. Arriving just two years after the Berlin Wall fell, and the same year the Soviet Union ceased to be and ended almost 50 years of post-World War II hostility, Nicholas Meyer's final voyage for Captain Kirk and his crew openly questioned the morality and political honesty of the United Federation of Planets in a way no *Star Trek* story had ever done. "It's about the collapse of the Soviet Union, and it's about change and fear of change and 'Have we reached the end of history?' as Francis Fukuyama wrote when the wall came down," Meyer said.[19] Kirk, who sports an ugly vein of resentful, open racism against the Klingons following the murder of his son by one of their kind in the third movie *The Search for Spock*, ends up with his crew exposing a conspiracy within some of the highest ranks of the Federation to assassinate the Klingon chancellor and destabilize their ailing empire.

These events open up some significant questions about the Federation as an organization, as the underpinning world-building of the *Star Trek* universe revolves heavily around this institution. The Federation has little sense of definition in the *Original Series*. The prequel series *Enterprise*, produced over 30 years after the *Original Series*, works hard to fill in many of the blanks, primarily because Roddenberry was more concerned in 1966 with creating an allegorical series of science fiction morality plays than building a world riven with continuity and defined rules.[20] In early episodes, Captain Kirk often doesn't even use terms familiar in later shows such as "this is the Federation starship *Enterprise* or *Voyager*." Often his terms are fluid, such as "the Starfleet ship" or the "spaceship *Enterprise*." Roddenberry is not fixed on detail, beyond one or two particulars. The Federation is a concept, not an entity to be detailed and examined in its own right.

While *The Next Generation*, *Deep Space Nine* and *Voyager* all shade

4. The Cultural Mytharc

in significant detail—after some legwork delivered by the *Original Series* movies in the 1980s—*Enterprise* sketches in the formative particulars about the Federation. Crucially, the Federation is formed primarily out of crisis.[21] The prequel series, set in 2151 and featuring the first starship *Enterprise* to explore beyond Earth's solar system, establishes Starfleet as an entity of a unified Earth government which itself is fairly indistinct— yet it, too, was forged out of the recognized World War III which takes place in fictional *Star Trek* "future history," best characterized by *The Next Generation*'s "Encounter at Farpoint" and the movie *First Contact*.[22] That mid–21st century conflict which killed billions of humans led to first alien contact with the Vulcans, which begins the "long road getting from there to here" that leads to *Enterprise*.[23]

In the mythological backstory of *Star Trek*, World War III, and the so-called "post-atomic horror" which is described in "Encounter at Farpoint," are much more akin to a dystopian worldview in science fiction born out of modern-day conditions than born out of the traditionally utopian outlook of *Star Trek*'s future. These aspects were developed in the '80s and '90s across the sequel series, but there is a strong sense that writers such as Michael Piller and Ira Steven Behr never truly believed humanity would be so self-destructive as to actually succeed in allowing their civilization to be eroded and destroyed. We reached an idealized worldview in this universe precisely because we had the intelligence, foresight and resilience to overcome our mid–21st century mistakes and, with the help of the Vulcans, rebuild our society.

The years between the post-atomic horror and the formation of Starfleet, and then the beginning of the series that would become *Enterprise*, have been vaguely referred to or dealt with. It appears that many writers have considered them relatively unimportant to the tapestry of *Star Trek*'s internal world-building and mythology. But if anything, they could well be the *most* important; these were the decades in which Zefram Cochrane's warp-drive[24] were developed and built upon; the decades in which humanity overcame centuries of nationalistic divide, cultural animosity and protective borders to become one Earth government; and, in a huge move, the decades in which they chose to abolish an economic structure to human society. The absence of money is one of the more hard-to-imagine utopian concepts in the *Star Trek* universe.[25]

Therefore, while *Enterprise* may be important for representing the first steps of exploration into the so-called "final frontier," the ideals that Roddenberry developed in his original show, which canonically takes place a century *after Enterprise*, were already laid down by the time we

Myth-Building in Modern Media

began exploring the galaxy with Captain Jonathan Archer and his crew. *Enterprise* worked hard to make its cast and crew more like futuristic astronauts than deep-space humanoids; often they spoke more like 21st century people than mid–22nd century ones likely will, but it grounded them in a humanity Roddenberry seemed to think we would have ended up losing the closer we got to his utopian future. *Enterprise* itself became a show compromised by changing TV trends, and the impact of 9/11 on entertainment, but it remained a formative, pre–Federation step toward that original idealism.[26]

Humanity is known by many *Star Trek* alien species as Terran, a play on the Latin *terra firma* meaning "earth" in a literal sense. But outside of the aforementioned Mirror Universe, the Federation never refer to humanity as "Terran," rather just "the human race." Such terminology is decried as racist by Azetbur, daughter of the Klingon chancellor, in a discussion about human rights: "If you could only hear yourselves. 'Human rights.' Why, even the very name is racist. The Federation is no more than a homo sapiens only club."[27] This is important because in the 1980s, when *The Next Generation* arrived on TV, *Star Trek*'s vision of an idealistic future presented in the 1960s already looked old-fashioned and quaint in the shadow of the Vietnam War, Watergate and a growing economic disparity under the Reagan administration, even despite the looming collapse of the Soviet Union.[28]

The Next Generation premiered in 1987, at the height of Reagan-era conservatism and rampant consumer capitalism which helped define the 1980s, a decade in which Americans sought to try and reclaim their manifest destiny of the American Dream from a decade of depressed corruption and loss of faith in the state, in which neoliberalism[29] created a dominant belief in the virtue of free-market economics.[30] Roddenberry was encouraged to bring back *Star Trek*, which was doing good business at the movies with the middle-aged *Original Series* crew, but had largely lost its role as an allegorical reflection of Western society. *The Next Generation* attempted to update and recreate the idealistic paradigm that Roddenberry made a success of 20 years before, in its first season ... and it simply didn't work.

Early on, *The Next Generation* was crippled by attempting to suggest that the space-faring humans of the 24th century—approaching 100 years after the events of the *Original Series*—were the perfected apex of human society. Roddenberry famously laid down an edict that became known as "Roddenberry's Box" by *Next Generation* writers, in which Roddenberry declared there would be no conflict between the crew of the

4. The Cultural Mytharc

USS *Enterprise-D* because they had evolved beyond that sort of behavior; Captain Picard and his crew were enlightened humans who in the first season mostly spent their time analyzing strange alien beings, or imposing a patronizing will on "lesser" alien races they would encounter on their travels.[31]

Where Kirk, Spock and Bones had heart and humanity, Picard, Riker and Data were initially distant, arch and unknowable. Theirs was a future free of character, of struggle, or quite crucially *drama*. According to Ronald D. Moore, on staff for the third season of *The Next Generation*:

> We railed against that on a daily basis, found ways to get around that, found ways to get through it with varying degrees of success. I was always saying, "*The Original Series* was never like this, *The Original Series* has plenty of problems with humanity, plenty of with jealousies and bickering and even racial prejudices are alive in the 23rd century." In "Balance of Terror," Stiles is overtly prejudiced against Spock just because he is Vulcan. And that isn't the only instance of that. It made for drama and it made for conflict. It made the world work.[32]

This only began to change when the troubled first two seasons of *The Next Generation*, from a production and a creative standpoint, were stabilized by Michael Piller, who took over the writing staff for the third season. Piller creatively worked around Roddenberry and his Box, intending to start developing stories around the *characters* on the ship, and not throw characters into a situation with no consequences for them as people. Piller humanized a Utopian world, and in no small part helped fashion the style of *Star Trek* moving into the 1990s, arguably its most successful and productive decade.[33]

By the era of *The Next Generation*, as we have seen, the utopian ideal seems to have taken hold; the Federation may have been born in crisis, nurtured through years of development, but come the 24th century, humanity had worked its problems out and now saw their mission statement as carrying that vision out into space, to the thousands of worlds and civilizations ships such as the Enterprise were discovering. Yet if you examine *The Next Generation*, it didn't really do a great deal of discovering brand new worlds, not to the extent Kirk's original series crew did. Picard's world is one of colonialist fortification. Lynette Russell and Nathan Wolski argue:

> The Federation, with its mission "to seek out new life and new civilizations," has parallels with the European exploration and colonising missions of the seventeenth, eighteenth and nineteenth centuries. Space, uncharted and unknown, does not exist until the Federation charts, maps, names and ultimately controls it. Once colonised, the unfamiliar becomes familiar and is assimilated into the social structure that is the United Federation of Planets.[34]

Myth-Building in Modern Media

We need to be honest about the Federation: Is it a colonial power? Not in the context of a historical Earth antecedent like the British Empire—the Federation doesn't control and dominate races, strip them of national identity and take their natural resources. Starfleet does, nonetheless, work to bring races encountered by the UFP into their moral and philosophical orbit; *The Next Generation* considers "civilization" to be within the boundaries of the Federation. If you lie beyond that, you are open to lawlessness and savagery. You could easily become a Bajor, subjugated for over half a century by the fascist war machine of the Cardassian Empire; there is no alternate galactic system of peaceful, enlightened hegemony in *Star Trek*'s worldview *other* the Federation. You're either in the club or you're in no club at all.

If the *Enterprise-D* crew did discover new life, it tended to be a truly alien life-form, a space- or planet-bound entity,[35] or an aggressive challenge to their worldview—such as the collectivized subjugation of the Borg. In many ways, the Borg serve as the perfect antagonist to *The Next Generation*'s utopian hegemony. If the Federation's expansion beyond Earth's solar system principally concerns the colonization of planets and races who lack their resources, and have significant gains to be made in becoming part of the "Federation family," the cold, alien rationale of the Borg is in direct opposition. They are a near-primal, biological force, devoted to the assimilation of all species to achieve, as they describe it, "perfection."

The Borg were introduced to *Star Trek* in 1989, toward the tail end of the Reagan-era neoliberalist project, and their collectivization clearly serves as an externalized, alien fear of the Communist threat that had largely disappeared from the American consciousness at what would be the end of the Cold War, and the rampant spread of mass hysteria and fear concerning the AIDS virus which dominated Westerns societal anxieties across that decade. *The Next Generation*, therefore, rejects fundamentally the idea that the Borg's idiom is anything other than a direct opposition to the accepted, Federation, neo-colonialist paradigm. *Star Trek* believes humanity's freedom comes within the construct of a system of governance, however liberal and forward-thinking; the Borg represent chaos.

In the wake of Roddenberry's death, *Deep Space Nine* was created by the combined forces of Michael Piller and Rick Berman. The latter became the over-arching steward of the franchise until *Enterprise*'s 2005 cancellation.

Arguably, the credit for why *Deep Space Nine* is considered by many to be the creatively strongest *Star Trek* series goes to neither of these producers, rather the team who in Season 3 took the reins and turned the

4. The Cultural Mytharc

series into a broader, ensemble tapestry about galactic politics beyond the scope of the Federation: Ira Steven Behr and writers such as Ronald D. Moore and Robert Hewitt Wolfe. Behr had been a student of Piller during *Next Generation*'s transformative third season, and under his stewardship, the trick was repeated on *Deep Space Nine*.

The first two *Deep Space Nine* seasons oddly echoed the first two seasons of *Next Generation*, in that they lacked a sense of definition. Under the guidance of Piller and Berman, they struggled to shake off the feeling of *The Next Generation* re-heated, despite how different the setting of *Deep Space Nine* conceptually was. The show was constructed as an allegory of post–World War II France and Germany; the Bajoran people, having spent decades under the heel of the Cardassians, had kicked them off their home world and invited the Federation—acting very much as an Allied power proxy, principally the United States—to help with reconstruction efforts following the Cardassian withdrawal. This was the socio-political backbone that underpinned *Deep Space Nine* from the start.[36]

Once Behr took operational command in Season Three (as Piller stepped away from the franchise[37] and Berman focused more of his energies in developing the next spin-off series *Voyager*), *Deep Space Nine* began to develop into far more of a mythological, political and broad ensemble series with ongoing character arcs and a significant threat that would continue across the run of the show: the Dominion.

The Dominion are led by a shapeshifting race, the Changelings, who for centuries were persecuted by "solids" and subsequently developed a highly xenophobic worldview. Given their ability to transform into a duplicate of anyone, they swiftly established themselves as "gods" amongst other races and bred themselves a genetically created warrior race known as the Jem'Hadar in order to gain control over a significant portion of the quadrant via commercial and economic means, alongside brute force. The Dominion may not have aspired to a utopian worldview for all of the races under their yoke, but in communicating with the character of Odo—a Changeling sent away as an infant and the security chief of *Deep Space Nine*—they suggest that what they seek is an "ordered" galaxy in which their kind never need fear persecution again.

In the sense of establishing order over chaos, the Dominion are simply a harsher, less inclusive version of the Federation. Where the Federation has Starfleet as a militaristic peacekeeping force, the Dominion controls the Jem'Hadar through a drug-based substance. Where the Federation brings races into their collective via treaties concerning medical or knowledge benefits, not to mention military protection should they be troubled by invaders, the Dominion bolster their "dominion" by using trade and commerce—hence why they are first mentioned doing business with the capitalist Ferengi via proxies.[38] They are, in ideological respects, two sides of a similar coin, even if their ultimate aspirations differ.

Deep Space Nine, through the Changelings and the Dominion, threatens the very heart of Roddenberry's Federation Utopia: Earth. In Season Four's "Homefront" and "Paradise Lost," *Deep Space Nine*'s chief commander Sisko is recalled to Earth when the Federation president fears there has been a Changeling infiltration at the highest levels of Starfleet Command. As a story, this was largely unprecedented in *Star Trek* history. The closest the show ever came was *The Next Generation*'s oddly horrific first season episode "Conspiracy," in which leading Federation captains are taken over by a parasitic alien species that attempts to conquer the Federation. They are given short shrift by Picard and his crew, once discovered, and never heard from again.[39]

The "Homefront" storyline had much deeper consequences for *Star Trek*'s Utopian vision. Earth was meant to be past these kind of fears, an inviolate, gleaming success in the human story. *Deep Space Nine* dared to suggest that even the very heart of the Federation could be put at risk in an uncertain, suspicious and fearful world. The Communist threat, last seen in the Borg's collectivized hegemony, had returned home. "Paradise has never seemed so well-armed," Sisko remarks, concerned at the security measures instituted on Earth in the name of civil defense. The fact that the entire situation turns out to have been staged by an extremist Federation Admiral looking to stage a military coup, in order to strengthen the Federation response to a potential Dominion invasion, is an even braver twist. Sisko has to defend the Federation's liberty as the kind of organization that does not give in to such fear: "If the Changelings want to destroy what we've built here, they're going to have to do it themselves. We will not do it for them." All the while, you can't help wonder if the admiral had a point.

Once the Federation becomes involved in a full-scale war against the Dominion, *Deep Space Nine* ends up the first of two *Star Trek* shows to push this attack on utopia even further. Toward the end of the series, in Season Seven's "The Changing Face of Evil," a Dominion ally race, the Breen, launch an attack on Earth and devastate Starfleet's San Francisco headquarters. While the Dominion ultimately suffer a similar fate to Nazi Germany as part of *Deep Space Nine*'s giant World War II allegory, *Enterprise* later repeats the trick; the Season Two finale "The Expanse," a response to 9/11, sees an alien race called the Xindi attack Earth out of

4. The Cultural Mytharc

nowhere, cutting a swath out of Florida and killing millions of innocent people. Earth was no longer sacred.

One of the reasons *Star Trek* lost traction on television following the cultural trauma of 9/11 is that viewers stopped believing, as they had done in decades past, that the *Star Trek* future was attainable.

When the franchise returned in cinematic form (the J.J. Abrams-led blockbuster movies), it conquered this existential fear by looking backward, by trying to recreate the hopeful magic of the *Original Series* and reviving Kirk, Spock *et al.* for a new generation and even re-tell some of the classic stories to invoke a sense of nostalgia.[40] These movies entertain, and often capture the spirited feel of early *Star Trek*, but they shy away from the reality of where the franchise exists in the modern cultural landscape. They are afraid of looking forward.

That fear was confronted by CBS All Access' TV revival of *Star Trek*, in *Discovery*. This is a series which manages to balance that same sense of internal nostalgia with the determination to update *Star Trek* as an entity, both in the way it tells stories in Roddenberry's universe—developing aspects of its own Mytharc within the breadth of the series—but equally in the allegorical and modern parallels it chooses to spotlight. Though Season 1 was a fractured piece of work from a narrative perspective, partly down to the behind-the-scenes difficulties from a production standpoint after series co-creator Bryan Fuller walked away from the project,[41] *Discovery* chooses quite specifically to tell two key narratives which directly point to the issues we are now facing, culturally, as a species. It first worries about fundamentalism, in a similar fashion to how the prequel series *Enterprise* was concerned about terrorism, debuting as it did in the wake of the 9/11 attacks. That series, in its third year, shifted its focus away from exploration in the same context as *The Next Generation*—which it resembled across its first two seasons—and capitalized on the growing penchant for edgier, serialized storytelling, in order to depict the Xindi arc, in which the *Enterprise* goes on a season-long mission to stop a vengeful alien species from using a weapon of mass destruction to attack Earth, following a sudden devastating attack on the planet. If Starfleet were the wounded American nation, the Xindi were most definitely the al-Qaeda extremists looking to bring down accepted civilization, and in the end *Star Trek* hoped that civilization could be saved by making the radicals understand they had nothing to fear.

Discovery, thematically, looks at the consequences of that American imperialism in the first decade of this century, and how they as a nation reacted to the devastation of 9/11. Set a decade before the *Original Series*,

Myth-Building in Modern Media

Discovery taps into an untold part of *Star Trek* future history: a drawn-out war between the Federation and the Klingon Empire, referenced in the 1960s as a watershed moment,[42] and one that would segue—as the Second World War did—into a Cold War of attrition in the 1960s through to the early 1990s, before the Klingons became careful allies. This ultimately served as a perfect mirror for the Cold War anxieties of the superpowers across the latter half of the 20th century, but *Discovery* does not depict this war as a World War II allegory. It rather presents this war as a battle against radical fundamentalists who take control of a feudalist, weakened central system of rule.

The Klingon Empire we see in *Discovery* is not the battle-hardened, honor-based society of old, Cold Warriors or characters like Kor, who are essentially Japanese Ronin—warriors without masters.[43] This is a society fractured by scaremongering, by the fear that the Federation's imperialist homogeny may consume their ancient practices. They have allowed themselves to be transformed into a futuristic Isil, particularly following the death of their scion, T'Kuvma, in *Discovery*'s second episode "Battle at the Binary Stars." His death incites a fervor which results in increased Klingon aggression, a war against Federation targets which begins to transform the Federation from the exploration-focused, knowledge-gathering scientists into a fleet prepared to indulge in unethical, even immoral actions to "win the war." They are essentially a compromised America being consumed from within by their desperation to hold back the tide of fundamentalist warfare, against an enemy who wants to see their way of life destroyed.

What happens halfway into the season is the *Discovery*'s shift into what Trekkies know as the Mirror Universe. First established in the *Original Series* episode "Mirror, Mirror," and later revisited in several *Deep Space Nine* episodes and an *Enterprise* two-parter, the Mirror Universe was a clear inversion of the optimistic future world of *Star Trek*—an "evil" reflection. The humanitarian, progressive Federation becomes the tyrannical, totalitarian Terran Empire, bent on conquest rather than exploration, with a human Resistance working to bring down the imperial power structure. For decades, the Mirror Universe was an engaging (if throwaway), fun way to allow the actors in each show to play their "evil" doubles, and by the time of *Deep Space Nine* it allowed for some enjoyably pulp, B-movie action storytelling. It was never to be taken too seriously.

Discovery changes all of that. It suggests that the Mirror Universe could well be reflective of America future direction, of Western societies' future direction. *Trek* fans are now acutely aware that the Mirror Universe could well be *our* universe, and the Federation future is now the unlikely reflection. This is a sobering thought that *Discovery* plays out alongside the rise of the Trump Administration and the continued corruption of America by far-right, regressive social and economic politics, while retaining the Mirror Universe's pulp theatrics. By having the majority of the second half of its first season set in this alternate universe, the longest period any *Star Trek* series spends in the dark inversion to date, *Discovery* openly attempts to tie in the storytelling as cultural commentary. This is never more apparent than revealing the *Discovery*'s captain as a villainous agent of this alternate universe.

The signs were clear across the season that Captain Gabriel Lorca was a compromised individual, even his extreme tactical decisions in attempting to defeat the Klingon war machine, to the point that Starfleet Command—exemplified in the morally divided Admiral Cornwell—are prepared to forgive Lorca's extreme methods, and his secrets, in order to help win the war with *Discovery*'s revolutionary "spore drive" technology.[44]

In the end, it takes a ripple effect from the *Discovery*'s adventure in the Mirror Universe to help them defeat the expansion of the Klingons, an expansion which briefly looks dangerously close to challenging the Federation's existence, thereby validating the presence of a dark universe with no hope for a brighter future until, canonically, at least a century later. *Discovery* nevertheless fears the biggest danger to the Federation, and by proxy the biggest danger to America, is itself. In its willingness to compromise its ethics and belief systems to such a point that it fails to notice a dangerous, powerful enemy in its own backyard, born from the same fear the Klingon Empire are radicalized by.

Star Trek has always been in touch with its own presence as part of the cultural mythology of American society and *Discovery* is no different. The next journey it takes could well be to understand how to overcome its own enemy within.

The American Century

In 1995, the Fox Network's *The X-Files* blossomed from a cult curiosity, a strange little blend of horror and fantasy with a procedural detective drama, into a full-blown global TV phenomenon: a show that defined its decade and made household names of stars David Duchovny and Gillian Anderson as now legendary FBI Agents Fox Mulder and Dana Scully. They were soon canoodling on the cover of *Rolling Stone*, lighting up the stage

Myth-Building in Modern Media

on *David Letterman*, appearing on *The Simpsons*.[45] Soon they headlined a cinematic adaptation of the show.

From around 1995 onwards, the '90s belonged to *The X-Files*.

Something happened to the show during Season 1. Three episodes collectively known as the "Anasazi Trilogy,"[46] collecting the Season 2 finale "Anasazi" and Season 3 openers "The Blessing Way" and "Paper Clip," solidified, contextualized and broadened the main thrust of the show's storytelling which creator Chris Carter had coined "the mythology." Put simply, the mythology of *The X-Files* was the continuing storyline which underpinned Mulder's search for his sister Samantha, abducted when they were children,[47] and the extraterrestrial life he believes were behind it— alien life the U.S. government knows is real. Alien life the government conceals their existence of from the American public.

This storyline or storytelling was in no way new to the Anasazi Trilogy. Carter introduced alien abduction and the backstory concerning Samantha's abduction in the series pilot. The second episode, "Deep Throat," suggested that government insiders wanted Mulder to know the Army was secretly testing alien spacecraft.[48] The season finale, "The Erlenmeyer Flask," even posited that these shadowy government forces had access to alien DNA and were conducting experiments to breed alien-human hybrids. During Season 1, however, none of these stories seemed to directly connect to each other, bar the characters of Deep Throat and the sinister, largely silent Cigarette-Smoking Man. They certainly didn't constitute what could be considered a Mytharc.

All of that changed when, midway through Season One, Gillian Anderson became pregnant and Carter was forced to write around her (brief)[49] absence to give birth to her first child, Piper Maru. Many other shows would have simply had Scully take a vacation or visit her family for an episode or two but Carter saw an opportunity to begin what would become the series' first piece of long-form storytelling and the unexpected birth of the series' nascent mythology alongside the birth of Anderson's child. Co-executive Producer Frank Spotnitz claimed her pregnancy was "the best thing that ever happened to the series," adding: "This mythology really ended up running through the life of the series, all because Gillian Anderson became pregnant."[50]

When Spotnitz talks about "mythology," he means the narrative consequences from what ended up becoming Scully's abduction during Season 2's sixth episode "Ascension," by forces which appear to be as extraterrestrial as those that Mulder believe took his sister. Anderson wasn't out of the picture for long: Scully returned, in a coma, two episodes later

4. The Cultural Mytharc

in "One Breath," and by the ninth episode "Firewalker" the traditional status quo of Mulder and Scully again investigating the paranormal had been resumed. But what even the writers didn't realize was just how the series had changed thanks to those creative decisions. Unlike the Season 1 episodes where aliens or UFOs appeared and were quickly forgotten, there was no forgetting what happened to Scully.

As a consequence, the conspiratorial aspect of the show began to gain added characterization. The Smoking Man, particularly across the Anasazi Trilogy, became one of TV's most iconic villains and, as some have coined him, *The X-Files'* version of Darth Vader. Recurring characters such as Alex Krycek, Mulder's brief turncoat FBI partner; their boss, assistant director Walter Skinner, a man caught between a rock and a conspiratorial hard place; hard-boiled Deep Throat replacement informant Mr. X—all of them reappear, weaving in and out of Season 2 episodes both linked and not linked to the burgeoning mythology, constructing a picture of a unified narrative behind the *X-Files* investigations.[51] Then the Anasazi Trilogy began stitching the tapestry together.

Those episodes combined what we already knew of the extraterrestrial mystery, the government forces looking to cover up their existence, and various characters and storylines that were brewing over the first two seasons (Mulder's sister, his family, Scully's abduction, experiments with alien DNA). They also fused them together in the biggest, almost conclusive piece of storytelling the show had undertaken to that point. Staff writer John Shiban describes the revelations in "Paper Clip," that American citizens were being catalogued secretly through vaccination tests for decades:

> What's great about that idea is that it touches on something that everybody's done, everybody's been forced to do since we were children, get inoculated for something or other, for smallpox in this case, and to turn that into something scary is brilliant, I think, because that really means you can't trust anyone.[52]

"Paper Clip" concluded the three-part opus by blowing open the central idea that not only did our own global government community (as the episodes revealed the conspiracy involved all of the major world powers) know of the existence of alien life and were keeping the truth from the people, but that practically ever since the end of World War II had been collating and cataloguing information on American citizens as part of heinous, near-genocidal tests to create alien-human hybrids, for at this stage unknown purposes. They had even employed Nazi scientists, given amnesty after World War II, and brought them to the U.S. in these secret projects. "Paper Clip" is named after the real-life Operation: Paper Clip, a secret program: More than 1600 German scientists, engineers and technicians, such as Wernher von Braun and his V-2 rocket team, were recruited in Germany at the end of World War II and employed by the U.S. government, primarily between 1945 and 1959. Many were former members, and former leaders, of the Nazi Party. Their purpose was not just to win the accelerating battle for Cold War supremacy but also the race to land men on the Moon.[53]

With Season 3, *The X-Files* begins to embrace the idea of an all-encompassing, joined-up narrative Mytharc underpinning the series, and also to develop the idea that the show is interested in American cultural history. In very short order, it evolves beyond simply operating as a science fiction procedural crime drama with supernatural aspects and becomes about not just exposing the truth, but finding justice in the atrocities behind it. As Mulder states in Season 3's "731": "I don't need an apology for the lies, or for the fictions they use to conceal their crimes. I want an apology for what *did* happen. I want an apology for the truth."

Herein lies the crucial, central core aspect to *The X-Files* and its Mytharc—the cultural guilt of the so-called "American Century."[54] The idea that the rapid economic growth and material production of the United States following the Second World War, and the final collapse of the British Empire as its 19th century equivalent, failed to deliver on the promise of a country which, as President Franklin Roosevelt suggested in 1944 would following the war become: "the greatest material power of any Nation in the world. It will be a clean, shining America."[55]

What happened instead was a corruption of the American soul beyond anything its citizens could have imagined—a corruption successive governments worked hard to keep from the eyes of their own people.

The X-Files, in Season 3, further develops and explores the idea that the myth of the American Dream, of the land of the free, is built on what the Cigarette-Smoking Man might describe as "beautiful lies."[56] Mulder and Scully may represent the FBI, may visually reflect an idealized version of honorable protectors of the rights and freedoms of citizens, but they work as part of a monstrous collective who for decades, indeed centuries, have conspired against the very people they claim to be working for.

Darren Mooney describes the mythology of *The X-Files* as "rooted in a series of historical events. The genocide of the Native Americans at the hands of the European settlers is one such event. The Second World War represents a more recent historical trauma, one which extends even

4. The Cultural Mytharc

beyond the mythology itself."[57] After the "Anasazi Trilogy" establishes the literal sins of the fathers embedded inside Chris Carter's storytelling, having exposed Mulder's father Bill as one of the "Syndicate" of conspirators behind the larger plot to hide the existence of alien life from the public (described in "The Blessing Way" by the so-called Well-Manicured Man as "a kind of consortium" who represent "certain global interests"), Season 3 very much runs with the idea that Carter is interested in American society facing and being brought to account for sins perpetrated ever since the Native Americans were displaced from their lands and murdered by those European white settlers.

There are consistent reminders in *The X-Files* that Western societies are not the heroes of the 20th century in the way they try and paint themselves. Napoleon, the famous 18th and 19th century French military genius, is reputed to have once said "What is History, but a fable agreed upon?"[58] and this is in some sense true when we look at the world, post–World War II. It is a conflict known colloquially, certainly in much of the United Kingdom, as "the War," as if defining the second global conflict as the culmination of all historical warfare. There is a complacency inherent in the mythology of the 20th century that "the War" in which the good guys on the Allied side (America, Britain, France, etc.) defeated the "evil" Axis powers of Nazi Germany, Communist Italy, and Imperial Japan, with the Soviet Union somewhere in the middle—a complacency born out of decades of Cold War which never became "hot"; no nuclear weapons were fired at Russia or vice versa after Robert Oppenheimer invented the atomic bomb[59] and no Western territories were invaded. The proxy wars in countries such as Vietnam or Korea seemed eternally far away or distant enough to not count. They were not *the* War. *The* War, for a third time, would presumably lead to the feared Mutually Assured Destruction.[60]

The X-Files uses its Mytharc, and its fictional conspiracy, to weave in troubling, real-world aspects about American culpability in terrible crimes, crimes which may have continued to be perpetrated in secret by successive administrations. Episodes such as "Nisei" and "731" effectively tell the same story as "Paper Clip," except the heinous scientists in this case are not German but rather Japanese, tying into what would be the Japanese World War II equivalent of work undertaken by infamous Nazis such as Dr. Josef Mengele—Unit 731. As Mulder remarks in "Nisei," Unit 731 "like their Nazi counterparts they were never brought to justice."[61]

In the mythology of *The X-Files*, certain members of Unit 731, now men as aged as "Paper Clip"s' Mengele-proxy Dr. Victor Klemper, are still operating on U.S. soil on a secret government railroad attempting to create an alien/human hybrid. "731" reveals a series of horrendous "leper colonies" where test subjects in developing the science of these experiments, all on American citizens, leave innocent people exposed to leprosy (a supposedly curable disease)[62] while secret hit squads murder test subjects no longer of any use, dumping their remains in mass graves. All of this is happening in the mid–1990s on U.S. soil in *The X-Files*.

While these kind of atrocities happening in modern America, in secret, without any kind of consequence, are to many far fetched and an example of the kind of dramatic license that reminds us that *The X-Files* is first and foremost a science-fiction series, "731" not only connects to the genocidal real-life historical horror show of Unit 731 but an apology in 1994 by then-President Bill Clinton for secret radiation tests being conducted on American citizens as recently as 1974. This references ACHRE, the Advisory Committee on Human Radiation Experiments that Clinton established in 1994 which led to the release of over 1.5 million classified records which detailed how the Atomic Energy Commission had sponsored tests on hospital patients by secretly injecting them with plutonium and other radioactive materials without their knowledge.[63] This staggering revelation is one "731" weaves into the Mytharc of *The X-Files* as an example of how the conspiracies Mulder and Scully investigate are not always too far detached from the kind of terrible secrets being kept from the American people in the real world.

We find a similar example of this in Season 5's "The Pine Bluff Variant" which, while not directly connected to the ongoing mythology, is an example of an episode which thematically connects to the broader ideas about the abuse of power and corruption of American institutions inherent in the series. In that episode, a domestic-terror organization called the New Spartans are reported to have gained access to a biological weapon they are intending to spread via bank notes under the cover of an audacious bank robbery, with Mulder sent undercover by the FBI thanks to recent, public anti-government comments the Spartans heard him make while on a panel in the episode "Patient-X"—which very definitely *is* a mythology episode tied into the broader ongoing arc. What Mulder and Scully ultimately learn is that the New Spartans are essentially in league with forces inside the Federal government for what is a bio-weapons test for military applications on U.S. soil. Despite how in 1969, then-President Richard Nixon banned the U.S. production of biological weapons,[64] again they appear to have been developed in secret over the ensuing decades by the military-industrial complex, who are now using the FBI and a domestic-terror organization as the cover for their own abuses against the American people.

4. The Cultural Mytharc

What we see consistently inside the mythology of *The X-Files* is a creeping terror that we have already lost control of our world, that there is no hope for a bright and prosperous future for mankind. It is this very core principle which underpins for *The X-Files* precisely what is meant by the Mytharc, or what fans and producers came to describe as "the mythology" or the "alien mythology." The Mytharc is not simply introduced as an ongoing story arc, rather it very quickly evolves into a quest to save not just our world, but our very soul.

Storytelling often tends to operate in cycles, particularly those straying into similar thematic territory, and *Fringe* is the perfect example of a series which existed as a modern example of a previously successful property, in this case *The X-Files*.

J.J. Abrams discusses just how formative an influence on his work Chris Carter's series was:

> "I remember the excitement. The relief. The sense of possibility that Carter's show provided. It wasn't just that the genre was back on television. It was that a truly *great* genre was back on network television. *The X-Files* TV series was more than wonderfully entertaining, more than clever social commentary, more than chilling, and creepy, and thought provoking—it was encouraging. To all aspiring writers. 'There is hope,' it said."[65]

Fringe, the third major series created by his Bad Robot stable after the modest hit *Alias* and the rampant cultural phenomenon that was *Lost*, not only takes a significant stylistic cue from *The X-Files* but also from very early on chooses to embrace the idea of a Mytharc in a broader sense than its inspiration did. *The X-Files* backed into its mythology. *Fringe* arrives with it in tow.

Fringe differs from *The X-Files* in that it deals in more of a specific area of the paranormal: fringe science.[66] Abrams show—devised with Alex Kurtzman and Roberto Orci—never dabbles in aliens, ghosts, vampires, etc., in the same vein as *The X-Files*. Its monsters are often less malevolent specters lurking from the depths of our psyche, or creatures looking to exploit our human weaknesses, but rather frequently victims of corrupt organizations, extreme terrorist groups, mad scientists or devious corporations. Mulder and Scully's antagonists in *The X-Files* were the shadowy Syndicate of unknowable government officials. For FBI agent Olivia Dunham and her motley crew of investigators, its multi-billion dollar conglomerate Massive Dynamic who splash on billboards the confident slogan: "What do we do? What *don't* we do." Rather than the nebulous Cigarette-Smoking Man without a name and his shadow consortium working behind the scenes, *Fringe* worries about a world where a Steve

Myth-Building in Modern Media

Jobs or Bill Gates—geniuses with vast financial and scientific resources—may develop companies with the GDP of nations, be able to keep Prime Minister's on hold on the phone, and breach all kinds of data and security laws to act with more autonomy and secret power than many Western governments are capable of. Massive Dynamic is Google meets the Tyrell Corporation[67] from *Blade Runner*, and their enigmatic CEO William Bell is the post–*X-Files* equivalent of the Cancer Man paymaster.

The series also comes loaded for bear with a clear Mytharc construct in "the Pattern." As described to Dunham in the "Pilot" by serious official Philip Broyles,[68] the Pattern is the loose term for fringe events across the globe that appear to be connected, as part of a design; a plane crash after a virus infects the crew,[69] bus passengers frozen in preserved amber,[70] an earthquake revealing a strange beacon of unknown origin.[71] The Pattern works as a storytelling device for *Fringe*'s Mytharc as it allows the writers to tether what for *The X-Files* would have been stand-alone "monster of the week"[72] stories into a broader narrative. In "Bound," for instance, scientists reverse-engineering the common cold into a slug creature which ejects from the mouths of its victims, which turns out to be directly linked to Dunham's kidnapping the episode previously. The Pattern is only referenced specifically for the first two seasons, long enough for *Fringe* to metamorphose into a fully-serialized show for its final three seasons, but the Mytharc by that point has been comprehensively established.

Much like *The X-Files*, *Fringe* works hard to connect its Mytharc to our main characters in order to provide personal stakes. The Pattern, early on, seems to frequently link back to the fringe experiments some two decades ago by Dr. Walter Bishop, a troubled genius who spent much of the last 20 years in a mental institution, a man who frequently flits between doddering, aged eccentric and a mysterious Victor Frankenstein meets Nicola Tesla[73] who has forgotten or repressed a lot of his experiments. Walter serves as the emotional and narrative heart of the series, even as the show creates a fresh take on the will they/won't they professional dynamic between his shady son Peter Bishop and erstwhile lead Olivia. In the end, as the Mytharc reveals the existence of a parallel universe with alternate versions of our main characters locked in a secret conflict with "our side," everything comes back to Walter's work.

This is arguably something that has emerged as the concept of the Mytharc has taken root in storytelling—personalizing the broader conflict or threat in the drama. *The X-Files* arguably became a cultural phenomenon when it personalized Mulder and Scully for the audience, increasing their familial stakes and making the secrets and lies in Mulder's own

4. The Cultural Mytharc

family history the core of the show's Mytharc, but this was to some degree a consequence of production realities as we have discussed. *Fringe*, in its very DNA, bakes the idea that the Pattern, Walter's work, the Observers,[74] Massive Dynamic, etc., are all a cohesive part of the Mytharc in play, and it gives *Fringe* a stronger level of narrative unity than we saw in Abrams' previous shows *Lost* or *Alias*, or indeed we saw in *The X-Files*.

We see an evolution of many of the ideas put forward in *The X-Files*. The aforementioned "monsters," the victims of the titular fringe science, are experimented on in much the same way as alien beings or nefarious government organizations did to human beings in Carter's show. *Fringe* lacks the supernatural ambiguity of *The X-Files*, a show which would deliver upon the audience monsters similar to the spinal-fluid sucking woman in "Midnight"; in *Fringe* we often discover who is behind these aberrations of nature. Contrast this with an episode such as "Hungry," in *The X-Files*, or the double-header of "Squeeze" and "Tooms," stories featuring monsters who consume human brains or kidneys for sustenance and biological survival; there are no direct revelations as to where these abnormalities came from. *Fringe* may not explain conclusively *how* a woman can spontaneously combust with any degree of scientific accuracy, but it wants the audience to believe scientists—men—have the technology and means to create such an aberration, as opposed to it being a natural or genetic phenomenon science cannot currently explain. Everything in the world of *Fringe* is part of the Pattern.

This as a result feeds into the manner in which *Fringe* constructs its Mytharc. Many may remember the first season of *Fringe* as being fairly stand-alone, given how serialized the show becomes particularly from Season 3 onwards, but this isn't really the case. If the paranormal events depicted in *Fringe*, on the edge of scientific reasoning, are part of a Pattern, then so too is the manner in which Abrams and show runners Jeff Pinkner and JH Wyman construct the storytelling. Season 1 introduces all manner of mythological story aspects that will factor into even the series' endgame five seasons hence—Walter's mysterious work, Olivia being experimented on as a child, the master plan of William Bell, the enigmatic Observers, Peter's origin, alternate realities, super abilities. Weaved in often as part of more stand-alone cases for the division to investigate, each episode ultimately factors in some way into the grand design of the Mytharc. Very rarely does *Fringe* give you a truly stand-alone story, divorced from the mythology, as *The X-Files* did.

Fringe of course came to exist in a different era from the show it was most inspired by, indeed in a strange space other shows with mythological storytelling such as *Sons of Anarchy*[75] or *Terminator: The Sarah Connor Chronicles*[76] inhabited; a post–*Lost* world where serialized storytelling was taking shape and where cable television was on the rise with less restrictions on content and the length of seasons to be viable for network syndication,[77] yet a world *before* the explosion of prestige cable TV thanks heavily to *Game of Thrones* and the proliferation of streaming services which utterly changed the paradigm. *Fringe*, and some of the aforementioned shows, were among the first to experiment with running times longer than the standard 42–45 minutes on network television[78]; in the early seasons, *Fringe* episodes would regularly clock in at around 50 minutes, and while not a vast amount more time in real terms, structurally it had an effect on how *Fringe* told its stories. It had more breadth to capture moments of character, or spend more time on a particular plot aspect than *The X-Files* as an example may have done. *Fringe*, were it made today, would almost certainly be on a streaming service and be much more serialized, plus around 10–13 episodes, from day one.

Though thematically and in terms of concept a modern update of *The X-Files*, in truth *Fringe* very quickly determined its own course away from its chief influence, wearing the Mytharc running through the series much more deliberately on its sleeve than Carter's series ever did. With the return of *The X-Files* three years after *Fringe* concluded, updating and reimagining its own Mytharc for the purposes of the post-truth era, the mythology of *Fringe* with hindsight feels positioned between two moments of American cultural history—the post-terrorism growing fear of technological consumption as the West looked to dominant mega corporations for entertainment and escape from the darkness that 9/11 brought home, and the rise of authoritarianism under the guise of liberation for the oppressed masses.

In *Fringe*, the monsters and threats were innocents who had been corrupted, victimized and experimented upon. How little it realized what it feared would later be reflected in a climate where human rights and freedoms are being trampled on day by day, but rather by the very government forces *The X-Files* always feared. Perhaps, in that sense, these two bedfellows are more alike than either may know.

After *The X-Files* was cancelled in 2002 following its ninth season, the place of its genre-defining mythology was placed under scrutiny. The final ever episode (at that time), "The Truth," cut a direct iconographical appearance of President George W. Bush which would have connected his real-world Republican party, in the wake of 9/11, to the alien conspiracy of "super soldiers" who had infiltrated the structures of American gov-

4. The Cultural Mytharc

ernment as part of their colonization plans.[79] By 2008, when the second movie *I Want to Believe* arrived, Chris Carter vaguely nodded toward the same President on the eve of Barack Obama's successful election as a Democrat,[80] but he avoided any attempt in his storytelling to tether *The X-Files* close to the cultural force it stood as in the 1990s.

While fans had long been hoping for a third movie which would concentrate on the alien mythology, considered maddeningly unresolved after "The Truth," the rise of nostalgic revivals of popular TV series led to *The X-Files* itself being gifted a comeback on the small screen, during a period of significant political and social upheaval as Obama's progressive, if divisive on home soil Presidency gave way to the shock victory for Donald Trump's absorption of Republican politics and command of the Oval Office. If Carter's series debuted in the wake of the Cold War, at the point American anxieties were growing about the sanctity of the rule of law, then *The X-Files* returned at a point it once again could have relevance and speak to the developing cultural anxieties in the West of the 21st century.

Carter chooses to frame the entire sixteen episodes produced over first a six-part 10th season and a ten-part 11th season, around whether we can trust what we see and hear to be true. The Mytharc morphs away from the labyrinthian tale of an alien hegemony seeking to destroy us, with human collaborators, into the panicked fear of "deep state"[81] as relayed to Mulder in "My Struggle" through Alex Jones-esque "shock jock" Tad O'Malley, reconceptualizing the conspiracy as a very human, male "new world order" who subjugated alien interlopers following the 1940s Roswell incident rather than cleve to their God-like dominance, as part of a systematic plot to take control of American society and later the world. Carter weaves everything from drone strikes to cyber hacking into Mulder's realization that the truth he sought, and believed he had largely unmasked, could well have been a smoke screen all along.[82]

Quite a number of hardcore *X-Files* fans were naturally infuriated by the revival seasons attempt to wipe the slate clean of the mythology they had followed for over two decades, but Carter does not "retcon"[83] simply out of laziness, but rather as a broader conceptual point that links to the growing veracity of the "post-truth," "fake news" era of Trump's America. Nothing, not even visual images, can be necessarily taken as fact. Narratives change depending on the political or social circumstance. Social media transforms the landscape of discourse between the masses and political figures and parties. *The X-Files* was built on the idea that Mulder would never quite reach the mercurial truth agents of the cabal such as Alex Krycek warned audiences as far back as 1996 that "There's no Truth, these men, they make it up as they go along."[84] These revival series made the point succinctly: the Truth is what we decide it to be.

This comes even more sharply into focus in how the apocalyptic events of "My Struggle II"—in which Scully races against time to halt the spread of the Spartan virus, a global contagion from an extra-terrestrial source being masterminded by the nefarious Cigarette-Smoking Man—turn out to be a vision of a devastating possible future, given to her by her immaculately born, part-alien son William. *The X-Files* toyed with the idea of a viral apocalypse across the run of its original series, indeed the entire Mytharc was underpinned by this concept, but "My Struggle III" confirms this is not the agency of an alien invader but rather the same old, untouchable white man who in the same breadth is revealed to have violated Scully in the most personal of ways by having a hand in her son's procreation.[85] *The X-Files* reflects our own democratic slide toward a dystopian, totalitarian future dominated by old, regressive, hateful, white men with no respect for female agency, by having the unknowable aliens no longer interested in conquest. The bigger threat is from ourselves.

Carter suggests a magical salve in "My Struggle IV," which as it stands could be the final episode of *The X-Files*, through the character of William. Carter posits that William could end up protecting mankind in the face of viral oblivion, or indeed plots by alternate conspirators to transport the wealthy, privileged elite off a planet we are destroying through climate change. In reality, no such potential superhero (or super villain) exists. *The X-Files* ends without the same amount of hope and faith either "The Truth" or *I Want to Believe* conclude with. It offers Mulder and Scully a way out of a dark, nihilistic future in which no one may be able to prevent our own destruction, but does nothing to suggest we as a culture may be able to do the same. We may already be halfway there.

If there is one episode of *The X-Files* revival which makes the point about how culturally we are forging our own narrative, it is Darin Morgan's comedy episode "The Lost Art of Forehead Sweat." It concerns the "Mandela Effect," a psychological theory of misremembering key facts and historical points, stemming from the belief among many that Nelson Mandela was dead when he was in fact alive, thanks to the spread of misinformation which became convinced among many as fact. *The X-Files* approaches the idea from a humorous perspective by suggesting Mulder and Scully, in their decades working together, always had a third partner called Reggie who they forgot existed—to the point the episode digitally inserts the character in classic episodes, to great comic effect—but it cuts

4. The Cultural Mytharc

to the core of our bigger cultural problem—do we only remember what we want to?

> "There is an ancient Indian saying that something lives only as long as the last person who remembers it. My people have come to trust memory over history. Memory, like fire, is radiant and immutable while history serves only those who seek to control it. Those who douse the flame of memory in order to put out the dangerous fire of truth—beware these men. For they are dangerous themselves and unwise. Their false history is written in the blood of those who might remember and of those who seek the truth."[86]

So says the character of Albert Hosteen early on in *The X-Files'* Season 3 in 1995. It could almost be Chris Carter speaking out to us from the television screen.

It appears to be a warning we are forgetting.

Breaking the Wheel

Game of Thrones changed television.

Several of the TV series we have examined so far in this book could lay claim to that charge. *The X-Files* chiefly helped birth an age of prestige television which came into its own across the next ten years. the *Star Trek* spin-off series brought a credibility and fandom to the kind of science-fiction that television had not truly, comfortably engaged with since the 1960s. *Lost* became addictive, high-concept, serialized long-form television which broke through into the mainstream, even if it eventually finished as more of a cult curiosity.

Game of Thrones, however, might have been the first true TV phenomenon to fuse peak, water-cooler, mainstream discourse across the world with not just high-concept storytelling but enormously high-budget production values. HBO's fantasy saga pushed the envelope in almost every conceivable way.

David Benioff and D.B. Weiss nonetheless understood, from the very beginning, that holding true to the central mythology at the heart of George R.R. Martin's adapted book saga, *A Song of Ice and Fire*, was crucial to successfully bring his enormous[87] tale to the screen. The clue has always been in the title of the book series—*Game of Thrones* is about the coming together of two distinct, opposite elements in a world being driven by massive changes on a sociological, economic and political scale. The ice is the "bastard" son of a noble Lord, Jon Snow. The fire is the youthful princess of a realm sundered when she was a babe, Daenerys

Myth-Building in Modern Media

Targaryen. They lie at the heart of the Mytharc which drives the heart of the entire story.

Though Martin's book series may ostensibly be high fantasy with grounded, earthy human trappings, the vast narrative of Westeros, both in book and TV form, very much concerns the influence of a developing capitalist system of governance over a long-standing feudal political ideology which is crumbling under the weight of thousands of years of stagnant sociological development. The saga, described at its most basic, is the power struggle between a series of noble houses and the encroaching threat of a supernatural, undead, mythical enemy. Yet, first and foremost, it depicts a complex web of alliances, relationships and betrayals connected to the same quest of knowledge and prophecy, and as a result rippling beneath *Game of Thrones* are a great deal of cultural comparisons to our world today.

Chiefly, the world of Westeros lies on the edge of numerous cultural breakthroughs. The character of Daenerys, the exiled princess of a crushed, historical ruling regime, grows from a slave wife sold into bondage to a barbarian tribal race[88] to the driven ruler of numerous powerful cities, backed by her three powerful dragons, who for some time forsakes her determination to restore the power of her family to the Seven Kingdoms of Westeros. "I'm going to break the wheel," she states to Tyrion Lannister, in describing all of the main, ancient houses as "spokes on a wheel."[89] Her mission to free slaves from the cities of Yunkai and Astapor, which she conquers with a liberated, eunuch army of former slave soldiers called the Unsullied, becomes a multi-book and multi-season long back and forth covering a number of cultural and sociological concerns, many of which come back to an economic source.

Westeros is not just a political powder keg but an economic one. The backstory to the events in the TV show and the first book, *A Game of Thrones*, concern a major political event called "Robert''s Rebellion,' in which the leader of a noble house banded together with a number of other houses and warriors to overthrow a tyrant king.[90] Much of Martin's writing holds a cynicism about high fantasy and legend; the Rebellion is often painted as a saga of good and evil, fought between clear heroes and villains, when the truth is a great deal murkier. Robert's entire campaign was funded, in order to pay the soldiers and mercenaries who helped liberate the realm, by the richest man in Westeros—Tywin Lannister. The same man who has one of his soldiers commit infanticide against the deposed regime, not to mention rape and murder.[91] Money talked and Robert's entire new regime as King is propped up, when the story starts, by Tywin's financial clout.

4. The Cultural Mytharc

By the fourth season of the show, we discover that Tywin's pockets aren't perpetually overflowing. His gold mines in the rich Westerlands dried up years ago and the wars depicted in earlier seasons, houses against houses following a sinister conspiracy in the halls of power,[92] were funded by Tywin through assistance from the Iron Bank of Braavos. Few characters in *Game of Thrones* are particularly self-aware about their own lives or circumstances, driven by passions or lusts for power, nor are they particularly fulsome in their knowledge of changing sociological tides in their kingdom, but Tywin understands that the Iron Bank is an institution that underpins everything:

> "One stone crumbles and another takes its place and the temple holds its form for a thousand years or more. And that's what the Iron Bank is—a temple. We all live in its shadow and almost none of us know it. You can't run from them, you can't cheat them, you can't sway them with excuses. If you owe them money and you don't want to crumble yourself, you pay it back."[93]

Consider what Tywin is saying, in a rare admittance of weakness, to his daughter Cersei. Even in a land such as Westeros, ostensibly a world of great and noble houses with armies and myths and legends, there exists an economic backbone on which the entire system rests. The Iron Bank are a great deal more openly sinister than equivalent financial institutions in the modern world, or even historically, given how they hire assassins—the creepy Faceless Men of Braavos—to often assassinate wealthy figures who do not pay back what they owe, but the very fact the Iron Bank exists at all seems at odds with a feudal system whereby Lords and Kings rule and democracy is just an idea. Democracy, equally, has always been a consequence of pure economic capitalism, brewing down into so-called "trickle-down economics."[94] It was only at that stage that real world nations and powers stopped battling each other for land and resources.

Westeros is not there yet. But as the saga of *A Song of Ice and Fire* edges forward, so does Martin's story move itself ever closer to an equivalent point to the Italian Renaissance or perhaps the Age of Enlightenment or Reason,[95] with characters such as Samwell Tarly re-discovering lost knowledge in the Citadel of the Maesters from ancient times, long ignored by houses continuing the wheel—as Daenerys refers to it—of feudal rule going. Westeros is often compared to a Medieval system[96] but the story sees the fundamental precepts of that system being challenged—by dwindling economic resources and a growing reliance by the Seven Kingdoms on solid, economic institutions, plus the encroaching emancipation of women thanks to a powerful, and empowered, female figurehead. This doesn't even factor in the White Walkers.

Myth-Building in Modern Media

They serve a similar function as the Xenomorph does to the *Alien* saga. While that external, natural threat may break down the late-stage capitalism within that film series mythology,[97] the White Walkers could alternatively serve to act as a trigger for a democratic, post-feudal system of rule. An undead army spearheaded by an ancient group of original settlers of the land, the White Walkers' goal appears to be complete hegemony of a land robbed of them unduly in antiquity, and many believe the conclusion—in book form—to *Game of Thrones* will answer the question audiences have been asking for years: who will sit on the Iron Throne once the Walkers are, presumably, defeated? The answer, quite possibly, and unlike the answer the series eventually gave, will be no one. The enforced union of humanity against the threat to their way of life also will perhaps serve as a realization that feudal rule and a monarchist system is not a world they should return to.[98]

It could well serve as an impossibility when it comes to natural resources, given the absence in the Seven Kingdoms of currency to prop up the divine right of Kings. The capitalist system of democracy, in which the people of Westeros elect a chosen government working not for the pleasure of nobility but for the people themselves, may well coincide with an Age of Enlightenment and rejection of religious idols, which are prevalent in Westerosi's feudal society. The burgeoning of democracy throughout the 19th and 20th centuries pointedly coincided, largely globally, with a decrease in religious worship and reliance on the Church as a symbol of political power. A free market under an elected government uniting all Seven Kingdoms into one realm, one *country*, could well serve to liberate the people of Westeros in a different way than Daenerys Targaryen has always considered.

Before that happens, the mythical aspects of *Game of Thrones* must come to bear, as Martin's story—brought to the screen by show runners Benioff and Weiss, has lain the foundations within the show's own Mytharc since "Winter Is Coming," the first episode of Season 1. Much like the real conflict of *Lost* is the ideological battle between Jacob and the Man in Black, or the Shadows ancient wars with the Minbari and Vorlons underpin the united human/alien struggle in *Babylon-5*, *Game of Thrones* is a story all about the White Walkers aforementioned crusade to destroy the realm of men, and how the feudal system that perpetrated their ancient destruction has grown ignorant of their existence and power. Myth and legend, as in many mythologies we have discussed, returning to exact itself on those who have forgotten their own history.

At the heart of the Mytharc, much like in *Sons of Anarchy*, lies the

4. The Cultural Mytharc

destiny of a son. Jon Snow, as with many characters in Martin's saga, begins as the lowly, shunned "bastard" of a noble man of influence, sentenced to servitude at the Wall[99] as part of the Night's Watch, an ancient organization now considered an antiquated example of a mythical world that never even truly existed. By the conclusion of the penultimate season, Jon is King in the North and a challenger to the entire Iron Throne, with the audience aware of a fact he is not—that thanks to a complex bloodline and a decades-old conspiracy of silence, Jon is in fact the rightful heir of the Iron Throne.

Game of Thrones, in terms of its narrative, has always worked differently from several of the other principal Mytharcs we have examined. We, as an audience, frequently are one step ahead of many characters in Martin's expansive ensemble, many of whom hold only their own pieces of a grand, globe-spanning sequence of events that affect entire civilisations. We know the White Walkers are planning to invade the lands of men, and indeed of the veracity of their existence, from early on, whereas a principal character such as Cersei Lannister only discovers this fact in "The Dragon and the Wolf," the finale of Season Seven. We know of the legends of the "Long Night," a mythical battle against the Walkers in distant antiquity, and the prophecy of a savior reborn who will destroy them, as happened thousands of years earlier. We are able to assemble pieces of the mystery and the puzzle in ways many of the characters cannot, or never will.

Compare this to a Mytharc such as *The X-Files* or *Alias*, where we discover key aspects of the Syndicate conspiracy or Rambaldi's quest, as our protagonists discover them. Viewers knew from the end of Season 6, and theorized correctly long before,[100] that Jon Snow was the secret child of slain Prince Rhaegar Targaryen and Lyanna, the sister of Ned Stark, the man he grew up believing his biological father; up to Season 8, the final season, Jon still remained unaware of his birthright, knowledge which would affect not just his own psychology was a noble man who has fought to prove that nobility all his life, but perhaps the very fate of Westeros. He already is an analogous Christ figure in the quasi–Judeo Christian savior mythology of Martin's saga, having died and been reborn potentially to save us, but one of the few remaining mysteries is just who the prophesied "Prince Who Was Promised" would be.

There has always been a deliberate delayed gratification in the Mytharc storytelling of *Game of Thrones*. Audiences have for several seasons successfully guessed key plot developments and twists yet, uniquely, they often feel rewarded rather than cheapened by guessing Jon's lineage, or his romance with Daenerys. Not since *Lost* has a mythology existed which has bewitched online fandom with thousands upon thousands of detailed, complex theories about what aspects of Martin's enormously dense, Tolkien-esque backstory and internal universe mythology mean, particularly given the multiple tomes he has written over the last two decades which allowed many audiences, for five seasons of *Game of Thrones*, to patiently await plot points they knew Benioff and Weiss would adapt. From Season 6 onwards, once the show caught up with and moved past the book series something still entirely unique in the world of multimedia fiction, audiences started to see several of their fan theories beginning to pay off.

This has always placed *Game of Thrones* in a fascinating position in how its Mytharc plays out to the audience. The 8th and final season in the summer of 2019 served as first conclusion to *A Song of Ice and Fire*—first given Martin could possibly write a deliberately different conclusion to his books, especially given the show has always course-corrected slightly away from adapting everything he wrote. Audiences were given certain plot aspects they expected; Jon learned the truth about his lineage thanks to Bran Stark; they saw the White Walkers ravage parts of Westeros; they witnessed Daenerys reach Kings Landing. Yet many were left disappointed with the six phenomenal hours of high concept, blockbuster television, with surprises and revelations—Arya slaying the Night King, Daenerys becoming a city-burning tyrant—seen as betrayals of key aspects expected by the Mytharc in play. Jon never quite became Azor Ahai in the way fans expected, even if there was thematic resonance to choices he is forced to make in the final episode.

Game of Thrones may successfully survive the test of time in that, whether the Mytharc delivered everything fans wanted or not, they will come to appreciate given they waited so long to see these characters reach the end of their journeys, and the level of gratification on those journeys for audiences was so high, they may retroactively accept and appreciate the choices the show runners ended up making at the conclusion of the series.

Though as we have seen with many of the Mytharcs discussed, such acceptance is often far from a given.

5

Mytharcs That Never Were

Thus far, we have discussed the Mytharcs which came to life and flourished, but what about the ones that never had the opportunity to bloom?

Since the success of *The X-Files* and *Babylon 5* in establishing the template of the in-show mythology, many series have tried to replicate their alchemy. Some are successes, such as *Lost*, *Game of Thrones* and *Sons of Anarchy*, but some swiftly vanished from the popular consciousness. Particularly around the heyday of *The X-Files* and later *Lost*, series which broke free of their esoteric or science fiction trappings to become global TV phenomena, a multitude of television shows were expressly designed to capture the essential building blocks that made those shows critical and commercial winners—many of which constructed in their very DNA a working Mytharc around which the shows pivoted.

The following examples are series which tried to replicate or honor those templates, but often thanks to early cancellation, failed to bring their mythological world-building to bear.

Millennium, Harsh Realm, The After

For a man who created one of the most popular and prevalent television examples of the Mytharc in practice, Chris Carter has been surprisingly unable to make subsequent attempts as such small-screen storytelling stick the landing.

Millennium, the second series from Chris Carter launched in 1996, featured Lance Henriksen as former FBI profiler Frank Black,[1] an intense consultant to murder investigations able to "see what the killer sees." Despite the fact that *Millennium* retroactively ended up as a spin-off series to *The X-Files*, inhabiting the same universe,[2] Carter's show charted its own course over three seasons which evolved into very different beasts. *Millennium* developed its own Mytharc, following a first season very much angled as a supremely dark crime investigation drama about the psychology of its protagonist, which felt distinctly stand-alone. It was Season 2, as the show pivoted heavily on Glen Morgan and James Wong taking over as show runners, when *Millennium* embraced a sense of its own mythology.

Millennium stands out in this sense because said Mytharc essentially begins and ends in one deeply esoteric and oddly contained season, in which Morgan and Wong throw everything from Frank's visions, angels and demons, secret societies, cults, occult symbology, ancient religious artifacts, Nazi occultism and even killer viruses into a connected, overarching narrative regarding the Millennium Group, a mysterious organization preparing for the Biblically prophesied End Times come the year 2000. While Frank's arc takes him from Group initiate to a crusader to bring them down, *Millennium* embraces a Mytharc whereby the Millennium Group operate as the central MacGuffin that facilitates the show's own mythology.

Millennium's mythology does not dominate the entire series (cancelled, many would say, before its time after a critically nonplussed third season in which the show's direction again changed under new show runners).[3] That's a testament to its uniqueness and how intriguing a production the series had, with different voices placing their stamp on a dark world of pre-millennial paranoid unease that Carter originally created. If the show had had a more consistent tone and if it ran longer, there may have been more of a consolidated sense of mythology running through it.

Harsh Realm, also created by Carter in the 1999–2000 TV season, was adapted from graphic novel source material by James D. Hudnall and Andrew Paquette.[4] It attempted to arrive loaded for bear with an internal Mytharc structure more than *The X-Files* and *Millennium*, which grew into their mythologies, making it all the more ironic that it was cancelled just a few episodes into what was a truncated 22-episode first season, and only the first three episodes airing as planned, with the remaining six produced airing on the FX Network six months later.

Playing off Carter's fascinations with emerging technology,[5] authoritarian control and societal anxieties, *Harsh Realm* had the highest concept of Carter's three shows to date. Thomas Hobbes,[6] a retired Army officer, is recruited by the military to enter a virtual reality program called Harsh Realm which has been seized by a rogue general, Omar Santiago, who may be able to threaten the real world from inside. Hobbes enters an entire virtual playing field, allowing Carter and his writers to tell a narrative mixture of moralistic journeyman tale exploring the same American anxiety and guilt demonstrated often in *The X-Files*, conspiracy thriller

5. Mytharcs That Never Were

and mystery mythology, shot through with anti-war and anti-technology polemic.

Harsh Realm felt conceptually flawed from the outset, despite familiar names from Carter's Ten Thirteen production company both in front of and behind the camera. It lacked the budget to truly bring tales set during VR recreations of World War II, for instance, to life strongly, nor was it aided by the release of *The Matrix* in the same year which had the scope, budget and stylistic touches to immediately render *Harsh Realm*—which trod similar ground—inferior. Audiences were unengaged by the characters and nature of the story, which was perhaps too fluid conceptually to ground audiences who quickly understood what *The X-Files* and *Millennium* (at the outset) *were*.

Consequently, *Harsh Realm* ended before it really ever began, leaving behind the seeds of a Mytharc which teased larger philosophical and sociological ideas that Chris Carter never had the space or time to explore. If not one of the great lost TV Mytharcs, it will always remain one of the more intriguing as to where it may have all headed.

Two years before Carter returned with a revival of *The X-Files*, he was set to make a return to TV with *The After*, a typically ambitious project which conceptually feels like a culmination of everything the creator had developed in the 1990s. An enigmatic post-apocalyptic drama about a group of strangers forced together after an "event" which changes the world, *The After* only ended up as far as a pilot episode produced by Amazon.

Carter's plan was for the series to run a total of 99 episodes, to match the 99 "cantos" in Dante's famous poem "The Divine Comedy," which would have served as his model for the mythology behind the show. The pilot introduced, almost jarringly, the idea that a demonic presence existed in this post-apocalyptic landscape, which seemed at odds with the adult themes, coarse language and nudity which Carter played with, perhaps appreciating the freedoms of the streaming era in terms of content as opposed to the network TV he had made his name on. Carter wanted to ultimately bring his interpretation of Dante's 'Inferno' to television: "It might have taken us 11 years to make 99 episodes, in my mind. But I wanted to do 'The Inferno' or, as I should say, all of Dante. That was my approach: to try to mimic the 99 cantos. It was a tough sell. It was eight characters in Hell, basically. I think that's the reason we parted ways."[7]

If *The X-Files* had established Carter's propensity for a Mytharc driving his storytelling, and *Millennium* put forward his fascination with the duality of Heaven and Hell, then *The After* would have been the payoff for both of these anxieties. This would have put his previous Mytharc, in terms of reach and grand complexity, potentially in the shade had he managed to pull it off. It was not to be, and Carter later was philosophical about it:

> I think there was just a difference of opinion about the direction of the show. ... It was eight characters in Hell, and I really didn't do a bible for the show because I wanted to discover what that was about.... [I]t would have been an investment for them, if they were going to do eight episodes, of $40 million. I can understand their reluctance, and I still think I had eight great episodes.[8]

We may never know what Carter might have done with *The After* and an ultimate artistic expression of Hell on Earth.

Earth: Final Conflict

Launched in 1997, *Earth: Final Conflict* garnered advance publicity for the fact that it was an unproduced series idea from *Star Trek* creator Gene Roddenberry, developed after his death by his widow Majel Barrett-Roddenberry.[9]

Known for a complex narrative structure around a serialized format, *Earth: Final Conflict* works to combine ideas previously extolled in *Star Trek* with the trending zeitgeist for *X-Files*–inspired paranoia. The concept sees Earth visited by the Taelons—an advanced, seemingly benevolent race who offer to help unite the nations of the planet with technology to help them advance as a species—with "Companions" who arrive to work with each different nation. But through the investigations of initial protagonist William Boone,[10] a Companion "protector," it becomes clear that the true Taelon plan is anything but benevolent. So becomes a series-length battle between the Taelons to control humanity, and fight a resistance movement called the Liberation.

Earth: Final Conflict had a Mytharc structured around the Taelon plan but very quickly became a victim of rampant cast changes as actors left the show or new characters were devised. A brace of science fiction ideas—everything from AI implantation to biological engineering—were thrown into the pot, and many had no narrative payoff. In this sense, the show fails to achieve what *Babylon 5* managed, by and large, to do—despite similar production problems—by constructing its mythology with enough "trap doors" and unassailable tentpoles that the story could weather such changes. In reality, Roddenberry's series could and should have been a much bigger success.

5. Mytharcs That Never Were

It arrived at the right time for a resurgent proliferation of network science fiction, with *The X-Files* and the *Star Trek* series at the height of their popularity, not to mention *Babylon 5* and *The Outer Limits* receiving strong critical notices. *Earth: Final Conflict* inverts the *Star Trek* "future history" notion of the Vulcans—the benevolent, wise old alien race, coming down to humanity to help shepherd them to a brighter future—combining that concept with the latent *X-Files* paranoia that, should we be visited by an advanced alien species, their intentions would be hostile to the anxious American psyche of the '90s (as opposed to the hopeful mindset of the '60s).

While the show therefore ran for five seasons and over 100 episodes, it failed to strike a chord and linger in the memory, with an unformed and fluid Mytharc which did or said little that other series were not giving audiences elsewhere.

Dark Skies

Dark Skies was gifted of a concept many producers would die for. Taking the clearest cue from *The X-Files* yet, Bryce Zabel and Brent V. Friedman's series was an ambitious concept that never had the chance to reach its potential or tap fully into the conspiracy theory zeitgeist *The X-Files* had fomented. It lasted only one season, from 1996 to 1997.

Set in the 1960s, *Dark Skies*' protagonists were young Congressional aide John Loengard and his girlfriend Kim Sayers,[11] forced to go on the run when they discover evidence that Majestic-12, a secret government agency, is in league with an alien race called the Hive to invade the planet. The high-concept twist with *Dark Skies* was how it combined this alien plot with real-world UFO arcanum: the Roswell crash in the late 1940s, the rumored Majestic-12 group in the U.S. government, the assassination of President John F. Kennedy and the inclusion of known historical figures such as J. Edgar Hoover. Zabel and Friedman, much like J. Michael Stracyznski with *Babylon 5*, had a five-season plan which would have taken the characters and the Hive plot from the 1960s through to the turn of the millennium for a final confrontation. This was a show, much like *Earth: Final Conflict*, built from the ground up to appeal to the viewers who were lapping up everything about *The X-Files*.

Dark Skies is one of the best examples of a show which had a Mytharc and a grand narrative plan but simply could not get off the starting grid. Perhaps it was just *too* like *The X-Files* without having the magical alchemy of Carter's characters or lead actors. Perhaps also, conversely, *Dark Skies* suffered from being all about the alien invasion and mythology every week; *The X-Files* had the breathing room to tell different, more self-contained stories. *Babylon 5* also had a diverse enough cast and a rich enough universe for the Mytharc to not overwhelm the series. *Dark Skies*, being a post-modern fusion of the 1960s series *The Invaders* and *The Fugitive*, yet riven with the same anxieties as *The X-Files*, was perhaps simply not abstract enough or built with enough variety to capture the same audiences.

Though now somewhat lost to the mists of TV shows time forgot, *Dark Skies* remains interesting for the fact that not even a strong conceptual idea of its internal mythology and narrative structure could save it from premature cancellation, proving that successful TV shows and movies built on that mythology do not solely connect with audiences on this basis. *Dark Skies* may have had the building blocks, but it lacked the magic inside the formula.

Heroes

Another major TV series that didn't quite live up to the promise of its own mythology: Tim Kring's *Heroes*.

It is easy now to forget just how huge *Heroes* was in the mid–2000s, just a year or two after *Lost* had launched and was cementing itself as the TV phenomenon of its decade. *Heroes* was *everywhere*. Season 1 contained an alchemy specifically built off the success of *Lost*, and the trend set by series such as *Alias*, *24* and *Prison Break* over the previous few years: a mixture of high-concept storytelling, focused serialization, a clear Mytharc behind the narrative, a wide ensemble cast and numerous examples of "stunt casting" (there were recurring appearances by Christopher Eccleston, Robert Forster, Malcolm McDowell, Richard Roundtree and George Takei). Crucially, *Heroes* was the first TV series to do something that has now come to dominate the medium and indeed cinema: tell an original superhero story specifically in the style of a comic book arc.

Each of *Heroes'* four seasons were given subtitle monikers (Season 1 being "Genesis," Season 2 "Generations," etc.), and each was designed by Kring to act as one told story. Indeed, originally the plan with *Heroes* would have matched the original plan for *24*: tell one story in one season and then use a whole different cast each year under the same format, in more of an anthological style. In both examples, this plan was abandoned when the original characters became too popular with audiences.

5. Mytharcs That Never Were

In *Heroes*, characters such as Claire Bennet with her catchphrase "Save the Cheerleader, Save the World," and her father Noah "the Company Man" Bennet, and likable geek Hiro Nakamura, leapt into the pop-culture consciousness around this period as much as Jack Bauer from *24* and John Locke from *Lost* had done.

Heroes also was a little ahead of its time. Just two years after it launched, at a point when Kring's series was suffering critically and in the ratings, the nascent Marvel Cinematic Universe began with 2008's *Iron Man* which re-launched Robert Downey Jr.'s career and, with more than a little help from the acclaim lent to Christopher Nolan's *The Dark Knight* in the same year, transformed the Hollywood cinematic landscape over the ensuing decade and subsequently had a knock-on effect on TV. Without them, we never would have had the "Arrowverse" with shows such as *Arrow*, *The Flash* and *Supergirl* all part of a shared continuity, nor the Netflix-fueled Hell's Kitchen TV corner of the Marvel Cinematic Universe featuring *Daredevil*, *Jessica Jones et al*. *Heroes* was there first and should have been incidental to launching the modern trend and obsession for superhero mythology. But Kring's show is remembered more these days for how it crashed and burned rather than how it may have pioneered.

One factor that could have worked against *Heroes*, ironically, was its refusal to incorporate a cohesive, long-form Mytharc in the vein of *Fringe*, which began around midway through *Heroes'* run and, as we've discussed, built its entire infrastructure around a sense of its own narrative and mythology entwined. Kring has talked about how he wanted to learn from the shortcomings of another major series of the time: "A big complaint for *Lost* was that you had to wade through too many shows before something happened. The apocalyptic event in *Heroes* will be resolved in Season One, and we'll move on to something else in Season Two."[12] This tactic ended up backfiring, as did reusing many of the popular characters from Season One, partly due to a Writers Strike in 2007[13] which led to a truncated Season Two, but also the fact audiences felt short-changed by a Season One finale that didn't resolve anything.

In an era when Marvel built a ten-year, multi–billion dollar franchise on open-ended stories, this seems unfair to *Heroes* but these mixed messages and changes in approach and narrative sent viewers packing, and prevented all the show's mythological aspects—genetics, legacy, prophecy, cosmology, time travel and history—from coming together as part of a broader tapestry. Kring may have been right about *Lost*, about how audiences struggled as much as embraced a mythology which often meandered and course-corrected. But *Heroes* never successfully managed to capture *Lost*'s eventual momentum and broader mythological constructs the older it got, slipping away eventually to cancellation long after the hype had disappeared.

Heroes may go down in history as one of the great Mytharcs that never was, in truth, not to mention an unsung pioneer for the modern age of superheroes.

Flashforward, The Event, Alcatraz

Following the dynamic success of *Lost*, even after it moved away from the high-concept dramatic premise into arcane levels of mythic symbology and science fiction, networks looked to replicate the alchemy of that series. An example was in *Flashforward*, adapted from a 1999 novel by Canadian author Robert J. Sawyer. It saw the entire world undergo a simultaneous "flash forward" of human consciousness six months into the future for two minutes and six seconds—in which planes fall from the sky, cars crash, etc., as the entire human race exists briefly in their own future.

Flashforward in theory had all of the aspects to make a successful Mytharc wrapped up in a high-concept drama. There was source material to draw on, an interesting (if admittedly weird science fiction) hook to draw an audience, experienced writers and show runners in Brannon Braga[14] and David S. Goyer, a strong cast including Joseph Fiennes, John Cho, Jack Davenport, Alex Kingston and Dominic Monaghan (late of *Lost*), and a tone balancing mystery, action, human drama and even philosophical musings on life and death, given one character who saw nothing in their flashforward must grapple with the possibility they may not even have a future.

Yet it lasted only one 22-episode season, existing in the space between the emergence of cable and streaming services and shorter, more expensive television seasons, and the aging network model. A revolving door of show runners and writers,[15] plus an unexpected four-month hiatus in the middle of the season, were considered factors for dwindling viewership, but in reality *Flashforward* struggled to capture the magic that existed in *Lost*, its chief influence, simply because the entire mystery revolved around an event which was so inconceivable that it rapidly became impossible to reconcile as the narrative moved further down a conspiracy thriller rabbit hole.

Compared to the simplicity of a plane crashing on a mysterious deserted island, *Flashforward* lacked the long-term hook to retain viewers.

5. Mytharcs That Never Were

The same was demonstrably true of the ironically titled *The Event*, from show runner Nick Wauters, which after one 22-episode season became infamous among viewers for being about everything and nothing.

The Event was so named as a direct reaction to the kind of "event television" *Lost* became with its high-concept sci-fi trappings, lacking the awareness that Lindelof and Cuse's show backed very carefully into the stranger mythological aspects, as opposed to front-loading them. *The Event* was designed, from the outset, to plunge audiences into a well of mystery while, simultaneously, rebuking the oft-suggested idea that the show runners of *Lost* had no idea where they were heading with their own Mytharc. As executive producer Evan Katz stated, "Everything is designed to answer questions so you're not frustrated or feeling like we're making it up as we go along."[16]

The pilot episode, "I Haven't Told You Everything," established multitudes of plot lines revolving around a software engineer and his girlfriend embroiled in a conspiracy (which had distinct remnants of *Dark Skies* and the earlier 1960s storytelling it took a cue from), the U.S. president, a mysterious group of people in Alaska, and a missing passenger airliner. As a piece of television, it infuriated as much as it intrigued: Much like *Flashforward*, it established a premise that required viewers to be more interested in the aspects of the burgeoning Mytharc than the characters involved.

The Event is perhaps best remembered in hindsight of how *not* to construct high-concept television.

Following the end of *Lost*, J.J. Abrams' production company Bad Robot began looking for the next high-concept mystery series. Abrams turned to one of the *Lost* writing alumni, Elisabeth Sarnoff, to develop *Alcatraz*, a series which theoretically would have fused the traditional police procedural series with a historical mystery, thereby heaping a mythology onto the show's back. It lasted one season of 13 episodes, airing to significant fanfare and very quickly disappearing into the ether.

Set in present-day (2012) San Francisco, the series revolves around the famed American prison. In 1963, over 200 prisoners and 40 guards vanished without a trace, only to reappear one by one 50 years in the future, with no clue about the time they have missed and a propensity to return to their violent ways. Sam Neill plays an enigmatic FBI agent (formerly an Alcatraz guard) who brings in a spunky young female detective and an expert on the now-closed Alcatraz prison (played by the unlikely figure of Jorge Garcia (a.k.a. Hurley from *Lost*) to help him track down the out-of-time inmates and return them to prison, all while solving the mystery of why they vanished in the first place.

Myth-Building in Modern Media

In theory, a premise like this should have paid dividends. *Alcatraz* had flickers of *Fringe*—another Bad Robot series that was about to conclude around that time, with an unlikely team trying to unravel a paranormal mystery while engaging in detective work—while the Mytharc behind the week-by-week "catch the bad guy" concept utilized the flashback formula popularized by *Lost*, sketching in events in *Alcatraz* 1963 by exploring the prison-based backstory of whatever criminal was being hunted that same week. It was as if Abrams was combining all the storytelling elements constructed across *Alias*, *Lost* and *Fringe* (his company's three biggest successes) and bringing them to bear here.

Yet *Alcatraz* simply couldn't find an audience. Despite the gravitas of Sam Neill and a narrative fusing period '60s drama and mystery with the "cop show" element audiences enjoyed elsewhere, it failed to strike a chord in the way a show with a similar concept, *The 4400*, managed to do with its characters, or engage audiences in the necessary way to have the mystery and the mythology pull it through.

6

The Future of the Mytharc

We have seen across this book the development of the Mytharc over the last 50 years, particularly in the last 25 since pioneering series such as *The X-Files* and *Babylon 5*. Try and imagine 25 years from now, quite where the Mytharc will be.

Media is changing on an almost daily basis. Television is being forced to adapt to a world where people are watching broadcast TV fewer and fewer times every week. The younger generations are no longer bred on a diet of TV soap operas, high-concept dramas and televised films; they are raising themselves through the evolving mediums of YouTube, Vevo and dozens of other online sites which fuse the social media experience with new forms of narrative and reality brewed up into a hard-to-define concoction.

For younger generations, reality TV has become the new soap opera in terms of the digestible mode of understanding narrative. Series such as *Keeping Up with the Kardashians* and *Geordie Shore*, while appearing to many reared on nuanced, scripted storytelling to be cheap, empty-headed and vulgar, nonetheless provide a level of narrative which younger generations embrace. Reality has become a misnomer in these terms; these shows may feature real people not portraying fictionalized characters, but to those who digest them, the filmed extensions of their lives are just as much story as any manner of *Game of Thrones* epic or sprawling Marvel Cinematic Universe. The rules are simply different.

This, in many respects, is just the beginning of a media renaissance which looks set to propel jointly technology and storytelling into whole new realms of possibility.

Many of the creators, whether they be show runner auteurs, writers or directors whose work we have discussed in this book, were able to see over the next hill creatively in terms of where narrative may emerge in reflecting the trends and fears of society in the future as well as the day they were made, and they imbued their Mytharc storytelling with all of them. With *The X-Files* and *Millennium*, Chris Carter had an innate sense about our existential trauma as we entered the 21st century and how difficult we found escaping the dark shadows of our past. J. Michael Stracynski with *Babylon 5* wondered if we could escape the yoke of authoritarian control in the future, while Damon Lindelof, Carlton Cuse and J.J. Abrams with *Lost* and *Alias* wondered how useful we may find faith in an increasingly disconnected world.

Who are the creators looking over the hill beyond the one these auteurs imagined? What are they seeing? And how might their grand epics be informed by their vision?

Television

While the traditional models of delivery have not disappeared, with American and British networks such as ABC, Fox and the BBC, and the means of production within these institutions remain the same, demand has changed. Networks are now beginning to engage with how people want to watch television—CBS, for instance, with their pay-per-view service All Access, which has found success off the back of the launch of *Star Trek Discovery* locked behind a paywall.[1] The rise and proliferation of streaming services pioneered by Netflix, and increasingly matched by Amazon, have led to storytellers having greater freedoms and finances to bring their visions to life than they may have had in the days of being at the mercy of brands, advertisers and ratings.[2]

Television has, consequently, grown more and more daring, pushing the boundaries of how to tell stories. Not just in terms of content but when it comes to varying lengths of episodes, engagement with social media, and just how show runners and auteurs engage with popular culture, and challenge and reflect where we are as people.

It means television shows are now often *events* in the same manner tentpole cinematic releases are, as opposed to another season which airs in the same September–May pattern that existed in American network television for decades. The final season of *Game of Thrones*, almost two years after the last, was as big a cultural storytelling moment as any 2019 cinema release. And if there is one series which has captured the popular storytelling consciousness in recent years, while simultaneously dividing people as to its inherent quality, it is *Westworld*.

Many people believe *Westworld* originated as a novel but, in fact,

6. The Future of the Mytharc

author Michael Crichton only ever wrote a screenplay, one he also directed.[3] It depicted a near-future society where the burgeoning "theme park" which took hold in the 1970s (and has now grown to enormous proportions in dozens of countries[4]) evolves into a high-end experience for the wealthy to take part in a "Western" narrative story in which the other parts are played by robotic automatons, controlled by the Delos corporation who own the park. "Westworld" suggests that the Old West setting is not the only part of this structure.[5] All have the same construction: Theme park guests can play gunslingers, knights, gladiators, etc., and "kill" as many robotic androids as they wish, with abandon, as part of the game. Crichton's story is all about the artificial intelligence within the robotic androids gaining a level of sentience and "fighting back" against the human gamers in Westworld, rising up as an unstoppable, powerful force.

Since 2016, *Westworld* has undergone a hugely successful reimagining thanks to HBO and producers Jonathan Nolan and Lisa Joy-Nolan. It is fast becoming one of the most intriguing and layered conceptual science fiction dramas of the modern era. The Nolans work hard in the new version to capture and expand upon Crichton's original ideas about human exploitation and dehumanization of machines. A recurring line, when humans ask whether the "hosts" (as the androids are now called) are modeled after real people: "If you can't tell, does it matter?"[6] This cuts to the heart of the message within *Westworld*: What constitutes humanity, in the day and age of rapid technological development, is increasingly relative. Just because the human-looking machines are not conscious of their exploitation, does that make their dehumanization morally acceptable?

In both iterations of *Westworld*, the world beyond these "game parks" is a clear example of continued near-future elitism, particularly in the 2016 version. The cost of experiencing Westworld is around $40,000 a day. Even taking into account inflation by the 2050s when the series is set, that remains a gargantuan sum of money that only the super-rich could afford. Westworld, therefore, becomes privatized for the "upper echelons" of society, which makes the eventual spark of consciousness we see in primary host characters Dolores or Maeve even more satisfying as they strike back at the wealthy dilettantes enjoying the park at their expense. These are women who have been murdered, raped and tortured—repeatedly—to satisfy the whims of the game players, and their consciousness is swiftly sparked by some level of understandable vengeance. *Westworld* may begin in some level of utopia, but it may end the victim of a machine-organized dystopia.

Westworld is an example of cultural dehumanization, reflecting the modern propensity to abuse not just women but minority groups. The strongest factor to the Nolans' adaptation of Crichton's original concept lies in what has been described amongst fandom as the Hosts becoming "woke."[7] This means, in essence, the android, machine creations inside Westworld and the five other entertainment parks adjoining it, gaining a sense of their own consciousness. They no longer cleave to the established, programmed "narrative," and begin thinking for themselves and understanding that they have been created to service the whims of wealthy gamers.

The Nolans' series is intentionally ambiguous as to what being "woke" means, but they establish the character of Dr. Robert Ford, one of the original creators of the Hosts and of the Westworld narratives, as the God figure in the machine. Ford—played by Anthony Hopkins as an example of the wizened, white-haired, enigmatic male Christian deity—seems to intentionally engineer several of the Hosts to a point of awareness which goes beyond their programming, thanks to guiding the "damsel in distress" Dolores Abernathy through a "maze" of understanding, which awakens what could be a built-in program that serves as equivalent to the "spark of life" given by God to humanity. It is no accident that Michelangelo's famous fresco "The Creation of Adam," with God reaching out from the heavens at the heart of the Sistine Chapel, is present in Ford's office.

The mythology behind *Westworld* explores many of the spiritual and cultural cornerstones about our society that the most successful Mytharcs over the last 25 years have done. It leads the way in the current climate when it comes to an unfurling mythology on TV which has captivated audiences, leading to a surfeit of online discussion, after show breakdowns and a multitude of podcast breakdowns episode by episode which people find an unmissable addition to the viewing experience. Each season has thus far only been ten episodes, giving the show that continued air of "event television."

Perhaps weary of how some of the most recognized and established television series of the last quarter-century have ended up with relatively unwieldy mythologies, many television shows of the modern era choose to focus their lens much more on the character journey of the protagonist or ensemble. The Marvel-Netflix series,' for example, could not be considered as having a Mytharc or ongoing underlying narrative mythology, despite how the protagonists of *Daredevil, Luke Cage, Jessica Jones et al.* shared the same universe and would overlap occasionally into each other stories, not to mention being part of the wider Marvel Cinematic Universe.[8]

6. The Future of the Mytharc

Nonetheless, TV has not entirely given up on crafting series with a clear mystery or mythological underpinning.

Hulu's *Castle Rock* is a recent, fascinating example of how to bring a shared universe to life on TV. It combines literary and cinematic touchstones. The latest creation from J.J. Abrams' Bad Robot stable, *Castle Rock* is a hybrid combination of the imagination of the world's bestselling and most renowned horror author, Stephen King. His books have been adapted regularly over the last 40+ years, since Brian De Palma's memorable *Carrie* (1976), but *Castle Rock* places all of these books, stories, narratives and characters within the setting of one principal, fictional town in rural Maine, where the majority of King's fictions have been previously set.

Castle Rock has been described as broadly anthological,[9] which suggests the central setting may remain the constant but, should the series be a success, the characters and narratives may fluctuate. But TV history would suggest otherwise. *Heroes* was meant to fluctuate its cast, allowing for new stories in new settings to be told, but once the primary Season 1 characters struck a chord with audiences, the plan changed.[10] *Star Trek*'s return to TV with *Discovery* was first envisaged as an anthological approach to the franchise from Bryan Fuller, allowing each season to tell a different story with different characters in different corners of the centuries-spanning *Star Trek* timeline, but this idea also vanished into the ether.[11] If *Castle Rock* continues, and if the main Season 1 characters are well-received, chances are that show runners Sam Shaw and Dustin Thomason may find a way to keep their stories alive within the larger mythology of Castle Rock the town.

Nonetheless, we are seeing a gradual evolution of the shared universe across television in a way that we have never seen before. *Buffy* and *Angel* cross-pollinated but they still worked hard to carve their own identity. The *Star Trek* series had the occasional crossover but nothing to the degree we have seen the CW's *Arrowverse* achieve with the "Crisis on Earth X" four-part story, which took place across *Arrow*, *The Flash*, *Supergirl* and *Legends of Tomorrow*. Captain Picard may have dropped into *Deep Space Nine* once,[12] and time travel chicanery may have allowed Captain Sisko and his crew to pop up on the *Original Series'* USS *Enterprise*,[13] but these were infrequent and incidental collisions of story and character, which the extended tie-in novel universe has worked hard to remedy. When *Millennium* backed into *The X-Files* as an unwitting spin-off,[14] both series seemed positively embarrassed at the association, despite tonally and textually treading similar ground.

Castle Rock proves that audiences are now not just expecting spin-off material from the original properties they have enjoyed, but they actively desire a Mytharc which encompasses a broader world or universe of fiction. Often these new projects are coming from a literary or expansive comic-book background.

An interesting but recently aborted example (as of writing) is the first "spin-off" series to *Game of Thrones*, tentatively known as *The Long Night*.[15] Spin-off is already a disingenuous term for a prequel series to *Game of Thrones* set to take place eight millennia before the events in Westeros we have followed for almost a decade. *The Long Night* is an example of a property expanding into a universe of fiction with a strong mythological underpinning, set as it will be during the titular events of the Long Night, an event in Westerosi antiquity in which the realm of men was invaded by the White Walkers and almost conquered, but for a hero named Azor Ahai who, with his flaming sword and a unified race of men, sent the Walkers back into the frozen North beyond a newly constructed Wall. By the age of *Game of Thrones*, these events have become pure myth.

When it was announced that *Game of Thrones* would conclude, HBO—aware that they had a global brand and property which became *the* television sensation of the 2010s—sought to develop a range of possible spin-off series based on various ideas from George R. Martin's fantasy universe.[16] There have long been rumors that we could see a TV series based on the history of the Targaryen dynasty, with their beautiful blonde princes and princesses riding great dragons (and we still might), but *The Long Night* would have been a clever starting point for the *Game of Thrones* franchise to sustain itself, as these events are not just myth when it comes to the characters within the series, but they have passed into a level of mythological legend amongst fans. We still do not know a great deal about the world 8000 years ago from the *Song of Ice and Fire* novels, or the TV show adaptation of that story, which means it is prime material to expand the Mytharc behind *Game of Thrones*, but tell a similar story to the show everyone came to love while charting its own course. The same undoubtedly will be said about Amazon's impending TV show version of J.R.R. Tolkien's *The Lord of the Rings*; they spent an eye-popping $250 million to procure the rights.[17]

Though it is not expected to re-tell the primary events of Tolkien's trilogy (memorably brought to the big screen in Peter Jackson's epic adaptations), there is no indication yet to as whether Amazon Studios' adaptation will become part of a broader universe inside Jackson's movie adaptations, given the show's first season reputedly looks set to take place before the movies did.[18]

6. The Future of the Mytharc

There is no deeper mythology in fiction than Tolkien. A handful of novelists in the last century have matched or closed the gap on what Tolkien achieved with his series, in terms of the construction of a mythology, with numerous Mytharcs built into the saga. A TV adaptation, with the billion-dollar budget, seems to perhaps be the culmination of peak TV's rise to compete with cinema, when it comes to cultural events of narrative and storytelling. The Mytharc has always existed on TV, but now TV has the means and capability to render it with the scope and grandeur of the cinematic experience.

Where, then, does this leave the realm of cinema? It is already a medium, when it comes to mythology in storytelling, learning a few key lessons from its small screen counterpart.

Cinema

If the prevalence of the Mytharc has demonstrably existed in TV for over half a century, can the same be said of its bigger brother, cinema?

For many years, indeed for many decades, the answer would have been a short, sharp no. The first 30 or 40 years of motion pictures barely even embraced the idea of sequels, of any kind of continuing story arc with the same characters. Despite the first sequel being made as early as 1916 with *The Fall of a Nation*,[19] a follow-up to D.W. Griffith's controversial *The Birth of a Nation*, it was the 1930s before Hollywood began to flirt with the idea of movies that would feature the same characters. Many ended up being Frankenstein and Dracula creature features,[20] or romps by comedy veterans such as Abbott and Costello, and Bob Hope, Bing Crosby and Dorothy Lamour in their *Road to...* series.

The seeds were sown for what would become the cinematic franchise with ongoing series such as *Planet of the Apes, Night of the Living Dead, The Pink Panther*,[21] the *Rocky* saga, the *Police Academy* films, and the *Halloween* series.[22] Sequels continued the story arc, or perhaps the character arc of the protagonists, but these nascent franchises never thought broadly in terms of creating a narrative mythology behind their ongoing series of pictures.

Two franchises have begun to change that paradigm, with a third struggling under the weight of following in their footsteps.

Early in this book, I discussed how the birth of the comic book was one of the defining moments of the Mythos in storytelling, and the nature of the narrative crossover which would be embraced over the subsequent decades across different forms of media. It is fitting therefore that the Marvel Cinematic Universe, a celluloid force of nature which has transformed the landscape of the Hollywood blockbuster, is the first example of the Mytharc as we know it on TV adapted for the big screen.

Before 2008, when Marvel Studios under the aegis of producer Kevin Feige took their first tentative steps toward what we would come to know as their Cinematic Universe, superheroes in cinema had their peaks and troughs in terms of success. Since Richard Donner's *Superman* (1978), which spawned the first legion of sequels featuring Christopher Reeve,[23] the superhero movie has existed in the form of various franchises of varying degrees of success. The Tim Burton–Christopher Nolan *Batman* movies, the Sam Raimi *Spider-Man* trilogy, even the Wesley Snipes–fronted *Blade* films, all of them led the way for adaptations of many of the biggest and boldest Marvel and DC Comics characters over the last 40 years. Some worked, some didn't. Some are beloved, many aren't. They all, however, cleaved to the format of storytelling in cinema nobody dared to challenge.

Feige came along with the most ambitious idea, and amongst the riskiest ventures cinema had ever seen: a franchise not just of superhero sequels, continuing the adventures of the same character as we had seen for Bruce Wayne or Peter Parker or Clark Kent, but instead a latticework of films existing within the same overarching universe, films that would overlap with characters and narratives from film to film. Crossovers were nothing new to either the comic book or the TV world; *Star Trek*'s sequel series in particular set a trend for series which would occasionally overlap and share continuity, even with the TV shows and movies.[24] But this model of storytelling did not exist on the big screen. Franchises were based on sequels, many of which worked to financially and creatively best the other. Superman and Batman did not appear in the same films—even if attempts to do just that existed long before the birth of the Marvel Cinematic Universe.[25]

What Marvel posited was something much greater in the grand scheme of narrative storytelling in cinema. *Iron Man* (2008), the Marvel Cinematic Universe's first installment, introduced the gimmick of the post–end credits sequence[26] and in doing so introduced, via a cameo from Samuel L. Jackson as Nick Fury, the promise of the Avenger Initiative. To fans of Marvel and the world of comics, they knew what this meant: that *Iron Man* was the beginning of a road that would eventually lead to 2012's legendary *The Avengers*, a.k.a. *Avengers Assemble*[27]—bringing together the heroes who Marvel would introduce alongside Iron Man, in

6. The Future of the Mytharc

this case the Hulk, Black Widow, Hawkeye, Thor and Captain America. The post-credits tease functioned in the same manner as a TV cliffhanger, leaving audiences excited and anticipating what was to come, even if the next film that continued the promise of this would not be a direct *Iron Man* sequel. *The Incredible Hulk* (2009) featured a similar post-credits scene with Iron Man himself, Tony Stark, reaching out to try and bring Bruce Banner into the Avengers fold as Fury had done with him.

The gamble almost didn't pay off. *The Incredible Hulk* was not well-received critically and suffered enough production problems that star Edward Norton refused to play the Hulk in *The Avengers* and beyond.[28] *Iron Man 2*, despite director Jon Favreau and the main cast returning, including a beefed-up role for Jackson's Fury and the introduction of Scarlett Johansson's Natasha Romanoff-Black Widow, was critically pilloried as being a bloated take on "Demon in a Bottle," one of Marvel's most lauded comic book runs of the 1970s.[29] Feige's so-called "Phase One" of the grand plan of a cinematic universe was perhaps salvaged thanks to better notices for Kenneth Branagh's *Thor* or Joe Johnston's *Captain America: The First Avenger*. But arguably the world of cinema did not sit up and take notice of the Marvel Cinematic Universe until Joss Whedon's *The Avengers*, a film which remains revered a decade on while remaining one of Marvel's biggest hits. *The Avengers* truly gave birth to a new dimension of storytelling.

But it was a dimension that TV had been working with for decades. Feige, after *The Avengers*, revealed that the first major ongoing narrative—the first, we can quite confidently say, Mytharc—of the Marvel Cinematic Universe would comprise three Phases that ultimately would build to a confrontation of galactic proportions with the uber-villain we glimpsed in the post-credits scene of *The Avengers*: Thanos, known in comics as the Mad Titan. After ten years of storytelling, this came to bear in 2018's *Avengers: Infinity War* and 2019's *Avengers: Endgame*; a story which completed the first Mytharc in the Marvel Cinematic Universe and will propel forward the next era of storytelling. When Feige talks about Phases, however, he is in fact talking about a cinematic term analogous to the tentpole structure of plotting a TV series riven with a mythological backbone.

Up to *Avengers: Endgame*, the Marvel Cinematic Universe has comprised over 11 years a total of 23 movies. Historically, TV seasons have comprised anywhere between 20 and 26 episodes per season. This is less common today with the rise of cable and streaming, with rising production costs designed to compensate for the death of mid-budget storytelling resulting in development houses such as HBO, Netflix and Amazon producing 10- to 13-episode seasons. But when *Iron Man* debuted and the

Myth-Building in Modern Media

Marvel Cinematic Universe plan was roughly mapped out, Feige designed the first Mytharc structure of the Marvel Cinematic Universe around the equivalent of one, relatively serialized equivalent season of storytelling. This one simply took 11 years as opposed to 23 weeks. If you examine the structure of the Marvel Cinematic Universe across its first Mytharc, you can see the clear similarities with the plotting mechanisms of a season of television.

The first Marvel Cinematic Universe Mytharc is slowly and steadily introduced across the first Phase, to the point that by the end of Phase One—roughly equivalent to the first narrative turning point around six or seven episodes into a TV season—several key aspects have been established. The first Avengers team has been assembled by S.H.I.E.L.D. and an initial clash of personalities established between Tony Stark (a.k.a. Iron Man) and Steve Rogers (a.k.a. Captain America). *The First Avenger* establishes the Tesseract, an alien device of incredible destructive power which we first see in the 1940s being used by the Red Skull. Then in *The Avengers* Loki, the mischievous brother of Thor, uses it to unleash an alien army on New York, an army being controlled ultimately by Thanos, who we only glimpse as the "big bad" lurking behind the scenes. This is very much a Whedon trope used in shows such as *Buffy* and *Angel*: a major villainous force the heroes would face and destroy. As Kevin Durand states: "While Buffy confronts various forms of evil during each episode, each season of *Buffy the Vampire Slayer* had its own 'big bad' villain who dominates throughout the season. The power of the 'big bad' always threatens to end the world, but Buffy ultimately overcomes him or her in the season finale."[30] If *The Avengers* is equivalent to the early turning point in the season, Thanos remains the distant villain farther down the road.

Marvel comic book readers have always remained one step ahead in terms of how the Mytharc operates, knowing that Thanos' ultimate goal is to bring together the Infinity Stones—pieces of creation that existed at the dawn of time with the Big Bang that Thanos intends to unite in the Infinity Gauntlet, a glove he can use to wipe out half of the universe and start again. Phase Two begins introducing new characters and narratives which lead to the reveal of Infinity Stones—the Tesseract being the first one. More appear in films such as *Guardians of the Galaxy*, which features Thanos in a supporting capacity and introduces a personalized aspect to his character, *Doctor Strange* and Joss Whedon's 2015 sequel *Avengers: Age of Ultron*, which brings down the curtain on Phase Two by introducing, again in the post-credits sequence, the Infinity Gauntlet and Thanos' intent to wield it. He remains a looming "big bad," slowly being revealed as

6. The Future of the Mytharc

a character, but still in the shadows as an ominous force to come. This would roughly be analogous to the twelfth or thirteenth episode of a season, introducing key character points, narrative problems and key mythological constructs which take us closer toward the season finale.

Alongside these major events in the Mytharc, there have been several TV spin-offs which have weaved in and around these pictures. Most notably, ABC's *Marvel's Agents of S.H.I.E.L.D.* was constructed across Season 1 around the fallout from *The Avengers* and the events of *Captain America: The Winter Soldier* (2013). In an unprecedented synthesis of a cinematic and TV universe, what happened in *The Winter Soldier* had a direct effect on the events of *Agents of S.H.I.E.L.D.* to such a degree that the entire show was forever altered around it[31]; in fact, the very genesis of the series was designed to connect to the bigger Marvel Cinematic Universe. The show eventually charted its own course but it remains linked to the broader Cinematic Universe via cinematic characters dropping in: Fury, Cobie Smulders' Maria Hill, Jaime Alexander for two stints as Asgardian Lady Sif, plus major connections to the Kree alien race who featured in *Guardians of the Galaxy* and also played a part in 2019's *Captain Marvel*. Links to the cluster of Netflix-developed New York–based shows do exist but they are far more tangential, with only the odd "Easter egg" reference here and there.[32]

Ultimately, Marvel Studios have worked hard to replicate the format of a wide, interlinked comic book universe on the big screen across these 23 films and numerous TV shows with differing amounts of connections to the broader Mytharc, but as a season analogy the Marvel Cinematic Universe's first three Phases operate less like a cable-streaming era serialized drama, and much more akin to the network shows with a broad backstory and mythology of old. The Mytharc does not play a part every week in *The X-Files* and the same is true of the Marvel Cinematic Universe; *Avengers: Age of Ultron*, which left the future of the superhero team very much in limbo, was followed by *Ant-Man*, another origin story which was almost entirely stand-alone in nature, bar a guest appearance of the Falcon and a post-credits sequence which connected to the next big advancement in the Mytharc, *Captain America: Civil War*. The Marvel Cinematic Universe's narrative structure works by delaying gratification, and layering and building plot elements and character arcs which factor into the broader mythology. By *Civil War*, Ant-Man played as key a part in the bigger story being told as many of the other heroes we had been following for much longer.

Like any successful Mytharc, the Marvel Cinematic Universe's success has only been as strong as the character journeys key to the bigger master plan of Thanos and the threat of the collected Infinity Stones. While there is no one central protagonist in Marvel's shared universe, it is hard to imagine this story having broadly played out without Robert Downey Jr.'s Iron Man. Besides launching the universe, Tony Stark's journey has taken him from arrogant philanthropist sailing on the fame of being a superhero, through to regretful genius who almost destroyed the world with artificial intelligence meant to protect it, and later whose family history leads to a central conflict with Steve Rogers and the dissolution of the Avengers as a unit. It runs through the Marvel Cinematic Universe. Alongside that, Chris Evans' Captain America has had a parallel journey; the World War II hero trapped in ice for 70 years, who becomes leader of the Avengers, takes down a secret Nazi threat at the heart of modern S.H.I.E.L.D., and later has a conflict with Tony Stark over Ultron, the Sokovia Accords at the heart of *Civil War*, and finally the personal aspect of his best friend Bucky Barnes' dark history with the Stark family. Steve Rogers has been as crucial to these first three Phases as Tony Stark. They are the lynchpins of the Mytharc.

Centrally, while the broader threat has always been Thanos' genocidal plan to restore balance to an over-populated universe destroying the natural resources of existence, the Mytharc is really about the importance of teamwork. The Avengers, these heroes with their powers that echo the mythological ancestors of antiquity, are always weaker when they're apart. Captain America's trilogy of films, with *Civil War* serving as much as a semi–*Avengers* picture as a Captain America–focused story, are all about friendship. In *The First Avenger*, Steve loses Bucky on a mission. In *The Winter Soldier*, he discovers he was reprogrammed as a H.Y.D.R.A. assassin for decades, and finally, in *Civil War*, he sacrifices his new friendship with Tony Stark to save the life of Bucky and help restore him to the man he used to be. *Civil War* frames this personal conflict around the bigger, much-publicized clash between the "good guys." Based on the Mutant Registration Act idea of the *Civil War* source comic, Anthony and Joe Russo's film plays off the tragedy in *Age of Ultron* with the similar Sokovia Accords which put the assorted collection of Avengers on ideologically different sides of a battle for their right to existence. *Civil War* acts analogously to around the sixteenth or seventeenth episode of a TV season, where the threat looms largest and the characters are further apart than ever before.

When Thanos finally begins his quest to unite the Infinity Stones and threaten the entire universe in *Infinity War*, the Mytharc has built to

6. The Future of the Mytharc

the point of conclusion. New aspects which will carry through into the next era of the Marvel Cinematic Universe have been put in place; characters like T'Challa, King of Wakanda, in *Black Panther*, introducing an advanced "future city" which would serve as a base for a future Avenger team; worlds such as the magical dimensions in *Doctor Strange* which open up entirely different realms, beyond deep space, as in the *Guardians of the Galaxy* films and *Infinity War*; and seeds of future plotlines, such as the Kree-Skrull War featured in the penultimate film of Phase Three, *Captain Marvel*, and suggested that the next era of the Marvel Cinematic Universe could adapt the famed "Secret Invasion" comic book run.[33] While this is all speculation, from a narrative perspective the Marvel Cinematic Universe is preparing to close off one Mytharc and is laying foundations for the next, much like an ongoing TV series establishes aspects in Season 1 they intend to play out in Season 2.

In that respect, the Mytharc storytelling of the Marvel Cinematic Universe perhaps best reflects a synthesis of Joss Whedon's *Buffy-Angel* season structure. Whedon ensured one season had a plan, had a villain, had clear character arcs, and seeded idea that could play out the next year while having the freedom to start relatively fresh. The Marvel Cinematic Universe looks set to be going the same way. The Mytharc surrounding Thanos, of the core unity of a team of heroes who can only succeed if they work together, and the central friendship of Iron Man and Captain America, paid off in *Avengers: Endgame*. Yet that isn't the end of the story for the first cinematic franchise in film history to not just create a continuing story but rather a continuing universe. The Marvel Cinematic Universe, and the mythological storytelling within, will simply evolve with the assumed Phase Four into something else entirely, much as the precedent of comic runs often do.

Along the way, the Marvel Cinematic Universe will leave a legacy that others are already rushing to emulate. But, as the DC Comics attempt at a cinematic universe has shown us in recent years, that elusive quest for a successful Mytharc is not as easy as Marvel makes it seem.

DC Comics should have got there first, by rights.

The Marvel Cinematic Universe was created with characters that mainstream audiences outside of the United States simply did not know in the way they knew the DC headliners (Batman, Superman, Wonder Woman, etc.). These were characters who over the decades had fronted hugely successful comic book blockbuster franchises or enjoyed success on the small screen with TV series going back to the 1950s and 1960s.[34] The fact it took years for the DC Extended Universe to take shape is an indication of why, ultimately, the attempt to create a Mytharc that could rival the Marvel Cinematic Universe has largely failed.

When *The Dark Knight Rises* concluded the Christopher Nolan Batman trilogy, and with the success of the Marvel Cinematic Universe following *The Avengers* proving the shared universe could work conceptually, DC Films realized they needed to compete in a marketplace that was embracing the idea of storytelling across shared media which was more than the sum of its parts. Their approach was to not try and replicate the model of the Marvel Cinematic Universe, starting slowly and working up to *The Avengers*, but capitalizing on the fact that they had the two most famous characters in their ranks by beginning with the team-up fans had always wanted: Batman *and* Superman in the same film.

Batman vs. Superman: Dawn of Justice was designed specifically to introduce not just the seeds of a Mytharc but to explicitly lay out key beats of a broader story that would ripple across the DC Extended Universe (as it was so named); indeed, *Man of Steel*, made by the same director Zack Snyder in 2014, was retroactively considered part of the mythological canon the DC Extended Universe, having introduced Henry Cavill's take on the Clark Kent–Superman origin story via the lens of Christopher Nolan (who also served as executive producer). *Man of Steel* would be described as darker,[35] certainly in comparison to the previous litany of *Superman* movies.[36] *Man of Steel* was "Superman Begins," nodding to Nolan's successful reboot of Batman in his 2005 beginning of what would become the *Dark Knight* trilogy, *Batman Begins*.

The climax of Snyder's *Man of Steel*: Following an explosive battle between Superman and his nemesis General Zod, which destroys most of the fictional city of Metropolis with significant human casualties, Superman executes Zod in the middle of City Hall. It is hard to believe that Superman would ever take a life, even that of an alien terrorist such as Zod.[37] Even Nolan ensured his dark and distinctly grounded take on Batman never saw Bruce Wayne's tortured hero kill. Snyder nonetheless carried this darker interpretation of Superman into, technically, the first film of the nascent DC Extended Universe, *Dawn of Justice*, intending to deliver a legendary conflict from the world of comics: Batman vs. Superman.

Dawn of Justice courted an equal amount of fan and critical controversy through how thematically and stylistically gloomy the picture was.[38] At its core, the conflict between Batman (depicted here by Ben Affleck as a middle-aged Bruce Wayne) and Superman is based on an ideological fear, tapping into modern American anxieties about the "other." Batman, wealthy and powerful but ultimately human, buys into the American fear

6. The Future of the Mytharc

that Superman may be less a Christ-like savior and more of a danger to humanity, after the human cost of the Metropolis battle which the opening of *Dawn of Justice* depicts allegorically as a 9/11-style attack on American life—as seen through the eyes of Bruce Wayne in one of the film's most effective scenes.

While this context makes sense, the revelation that this Communist-era hysteria in American politics about the presence of Superman is being whipped up by Lex Luthor, here a younger, brattish billionaire, a super-villain Mark Zuckerberg[39] if you will, attempting to capitalize on the fear of Superman to gain knowledge from an extraterrestrial source that will increase his own power, weakens the nature of the eventual battle between Batman and Superman. As proven by the fact that the mention of their shared mother's names is what quells their antipathy, if both men had just sat down and talked, they could have avoided the entire conflict. Snyder's narrative structure feels less interested in establishing a cogent reason for their conflict, and Superman's ultimate heroic sacrifice to stop Kryptonian monster Apocalypse, than in establishing key points of the Mytharc that will play out in the planned *Justice League* sequel and ripple across a presumed "Phase One" of DC Extended Universe films that were already being announced as *Dawn of Justice* arrived.

By the time Snyder's film premiered, audiences already knew a litany of DC Extended Universe films were to come. The aforementioned *Justice League*, which would feature a team-up of famous DC heroes who would then ripple out into their own movies; *Wonder Woman*, the long-overdue big-screen origin story of Amazonian warrior Diana Prince, who is introduced as played by Gal Gadot in *Dawn of Justice*; *The Flash*, featuring super-fast forensic photographer Barry Allen, despite the fact the Flash already has a successful TV incarnation over multiple seasons of the CW's "*Arrowverse*"; as played by Ezra Miller, he is also introduced albeit briefly in *Dawn of Justice*; *Aquaman*, the King of Atlantis as portrayed by Jason Momoa; and *Cyborg*, a science experiment gone wrong as portrayed by Ray Fisher. All of these characters are glimpsed in *Dawn of Justice* thanks to files recovered and watched by Diana Prince, despite them having no bearing on the story at hand.

A key example of Snyder's approach to the DC Extended Universe Mytharc comes via a scene witnessed by Bruce Wayne as he is visited from the future by the Flash. The scene screams post-credits sequence in the Marvel style yet appears roughly halfway through *Dawn of Justice*, where Bruce sees a vision of a post-apocalyptic future set in a desert environment where, as a battle-worn Batman, he battles and consumes a legion of flying alien creatures who appear to be dominating Earth. It is a sequence purely designed to tease the events of *Justice League* and even later films, with little context to the main narrative of *Justice League*; to understand the scene, audiences had to research articles online which had picked apart details from the comics which the film borrowed from, in this case the army of alien villain Apokolips and the symbol of Darkseid, already being suggested as the DC Extended Universe's equivalent of Thanos as the distant arch-enemy of the cinematic universe.

To understand just how differently the DC Extended Universe is utilizing its Mytharc here as opposed to Marvel, we should try and imagine if during the first or second *Iron Man* movie, Tony Stark had received a vision of the future via, perhaps, Dr. Stephen Strange of the events on Titan during *Avengers: Infinity War*. Consider how confused audiences would have been or how starkly (if you'll pardon the pun) it may have contrasted with *Iron Man*'s origin tale. While the DC Extended Universe is afforded the luxury of Batman being much more of an established character in cinema than Iron Man, with *Dawn of Justice* not being his origin story,[40] the Apokolips vision nonetheless does little except take the audience out of the story. It is telling that when Marvel did something similar, thanks to the fairly pointless vision quest Thor undertakes in *Avengers: Age of Ultron*, much of it was cut by director Joss Whedon at the behest of studio executives[41] and what remained, now we have seen *Infinity War*, lacks a sense of cohesion in terms of continuity and narrative.

Snyder, in attempting to explode the Mytharc aspects of the DC Extended Universe at the very beginning of the story, makes it conversely difficult for audiences to buy into the narrative. Marvel's Marvel Cinematic Universe works conceptually because it layers characters and storylines steadily atop one another, building the patchwork while managing to tell singular character stories for each of the heroes. The further into the Marvel Cinematic Universe, the more heroes may intertwine (take Tony Stark in *Spider-Man: Homecoming*, or the Hulk in *Thor: Ragnarok*) but principally the core narrative remains central to whatever character is front-loading the film. *Dawn of Justice* and particularly *Justice League*, by trying to embrace too much mythology too soon, floundered at the first hurdle and alienated audiences who were previously excited that the creatively rich DC universe may receive the same interconnected world-building we saw Marvel Comics deliver.

Ever since *Justice League*, which during production was itself scaled back from two intended blockbusters to just one film, as well as suffering production troubles,[42] DC Films has rallied in an attempt to course-correct

6. The Future of the Mytharc

and scale back on the Mytharc interconnectivity of their upcoming films. *Wonder Woman* looks set to chart its own course under director Patty Jenkins when it arrives in 2020. *Aquaman* under James Wan largely divorced itself from the larger DC Extended Universe following Momoa's introduction as Arthur Curry in *Justice League*. The Flash's big-screen take starring Ezra Miller has gone through half a dozen directors but remains on track to be made (as of writing), as does Matt Reeves' take on *The Batman* (which no longer features Affleck). *Cyborg* looks to have suffered as the casualty of a universe which conceptually stalled out the gate.

What the DC Extended Universe experiment, and its partial failure, seems to have proven, is that the cinematic Mytharc and universe is much harder to make work. A disastrous beginning for Universal's so-called Dark Universe in Tom Cruise's *The Mummy*, for instance, may have put paid to an attempt to devise a Mytharc around the company's legendary collection of movie monsters.[43] The DC Extended Universe may one day return, perhaps keeping the existing films within the same canon, more likely pressing the reset button and starting from scratch. They may be wiser to follow the Marvel model: build a mythology one film at a time, rather than expect the mythology to carry you.

A franchise which has played the middle of these two attempts at a mythological underpinning is the very saga which helped birth the cinematic sequel.

Cinema can now be defined as pre– and post–*Star Wars* (much as perhaps TV can be defined in a similar manner regarding *Star Trek*), given how writer-director George Lucas adapted the Flash Gordon comic book tales and adventure serials he watched in his youth as a kid and developed his own swashbuckling, revisionist re-imagining of the fantasy saga. Millions of pages have been written on *Star Wars*, what it means, what it was trying to do and its legacy, but it's hard to calculate how important a cultural moment Lucas' film was on Western societal culture and consciousness following austerity, Vietnam, Watergate, Nixon and a steady move away from broad, bravura escapism. But there is, behind the artifice, a metaphysical backbone which underpins the mythology of *Star Wars*: the Force.

Along with the Jedi, an ancient order of mystical knights, essentially, the Force has become as synonymous in popular-culture as any spiritual or religious real-world principal. The underlying Mytharc at the heart of *Star Wars* concerns "balance" in the universe, about how good and evil must be weighed on a philosophical, cosmic scale in order for humanity to survive. These are principles we will see repeated in TV shows such as *Lost*, and even the later blockbuster phenomenon *Avengers: Infinity War*. The Force can be used by both the Jedi (good) and their opposite, the Sith (bad); the emperor himself turns out to be a Sith in disguise all while operating as a Senator and later chancellor of the Republic, before beginning a genocide which sees the Republic morph into the Empire. That balance, certainly in the Original Trilogy, is eventually achieved by Lucas' hero Luke Skywalker, but only after his journey within whereby he is almost corrupted. His balance restores the equilibrium in the galaxy by the end of *Return of the Jedi*.

Lucas enhances the message of *Star Wars* by the prequels, which were released at the turn of the 21st century, and just on the cusp of the modern American tragedy, 9/11. Where the original series suggested the emperor was an external source of evil who corrupted the goodness of the galaxy, the prequels very much paint a world in which Palpatine, the man who would become the emperor, was himself corrupted by a previous mentor based on a dark religion, in the same manner the prequels show Anakin Skywalker suffer the same fate and become Darth Vader. That was the entire point of exploring the *Star Wars* world decades before *A New Hope*, in order to show the tragic fall of *Star Wars*' signature character. It furthers the idea of corruption from within, but the blame can be pinned on an external source of evil. Much like Anakin, Palpatine presumably was not always evil, he was just more easily corrupted.

The route to salvation, for Lucas, was more of an ephemeral idea you sense he perhaps had stopped believing in by *Revenge of the Sith*, the final prequel film in the trilogy. Where in *Return of the Jedi*, Luke rejected the Dark Side in order to help the Rebellion restore democracy and peace to the galaxy, Anakin in *Revenge* is consumed by the darkness and as a result the world around him slips into fascist rule. This was, of course, a backstory Lucas already had envisaged in the 1970s, when he wanted *Star Wars* to restore a level of hope and escapism into the American cultural consciousness. *Revenge* (2005) is more reflective of a world slipping again, post–9/11, further toward the kind of American cynicism in ruling institutions they felt in the 1970s.

By the advent of the newest phase of *Star Wars*, the sequel trilogy (and subsequent franchise), we had very much arrived in that world. Disney's acquisition of LucasFilm[44] and announcement that *Star Wars* would return to continue the story, post–Jedi, came just a few years before the presidential election of Donald Trump and a growing cultural unease about freedom of the press, freedom of speech, and the sanctity of

6. The Future of the Mytharc

American institutions. *The Force Awakens* arrived at the tail end of the Obama presidency and restored the status quo evident in the first *Star Wars* film; the peaceful new Republic has crumbled, the Empire has risen once again into the re-badged First Order, and the Rebellion has reformed into the Resistance. New names, same game. Fascism once again rising from the ashes. History we are dooming ourselves to repeat.

While *Star Wars* has never expressly embraced what would be considered a Mytharc in the same terms as shows such as *The X-Files* and *Babylon 5*, it has subsequently emerged as part of a broader cinematic concept of a connected, interlaced, shared universe.

Since Disney's 2012 acquisition, not only has the original six-film saga continued with 2015's *The Force Awakens*, 2017's *The Last Jedi* and 2019's *The Rise of Skywalker*, Kennedy and LucasFilm have attempted to create a broader universe with *Rogue One*: It takes a line from *A New Hope* and from it constructs the darker, edgier tale of a group of rebel spies and mercenaries who steal plans for the Death Star in hopes of helping the Rebel Alliance destroy it. *Rogue One*, though an entirely solitary story with many characters who do not survive the conclusion, directly leads into the very first scene of *A New Hope* with a seamless guile.

With the subtitle banner *A Star Wars Story*, *Rogue One* and the less successful *Solo* (which tells the prequel story of how original trilogy legend Han Solo came to pilot the Millennium Falcon), LucasFilm and Disney have attempted to tell what they termed "anthology" stories within the *Star Wars* fabric. The central Mytharc remains the so-called Skywalker Saga of the nine primary episodic films but these ancillary stories have been designed to tell tales within the bigger universe that fans may always have wondered about. *Rogue One* and particularly *Solo* suffered troubled productions, however, and thanks to a particularly underwhelming box office performance by *Solo*, Disney has pulled back from rumored future anthology films featuring Obi-Wan Kenobi and Boba Fett, perhaps conscious of franchise fatigue.[45]

Nonetheless, *The Last Jedi* director Rian Johnson is developing his own trilogy set in a completely different area of the *Star Wars* universe, suggesting that the plan for *Star Wars* to expand and continue beyond the presumed end of the original nine-episode Skywalker story continues apace. Plus Jon Favreau has developed the first live-action *Star Wars* TV series, *The Mandalorian*, which for the first time has tethered the franchise to the small screen, outside of popular animated series *The Clone Wars*, *Rebels* and now *Resistance*.[46] Given the franchise remains the biggest, most recognizable and perhaps the most popular brand in cinema, if ever a mythological world could be developed across cinema, it would be through the *Star Wars* universe.

What these examples show is that while cinema may have been traditionally the preserve of sequels and prequels, with a film series usually outstaying its welcome by the fourth or fifth installment, entertainment is now embracing the idea of large-scale, continuing mythological cinematic universes. Television and cinema are feeding into one another with increasing regularity and the next Mytharcs could transcend these formats, interlacing between big and small screen year on year.

They may even stretch into the interactive sphere, with video gaming continuing to embrace cinematic mythology and television narrative influences like never before.

Video Games

In 2018, Telltale Games closed their doors and filed for bankruptcy after 14 years as one of the most significant video game developers of the previous decade.[47]

It was founded by a trio of developers, Kevin Bruner, Dan Connors and Troy Molander, who had left LucasArts following the company's decision to discontinue the production of video games in the adventure genre.[48] There, these man had made their name with the *Monkey Island* series, *Day of the Tentacle, Sam and Max, Indiana Jones and the Fate of Atlantis* and *Grim Fandango*—examples of a subgenre throughout the '90s and part of the 2000s which for my generation, growing up at the birth of the video game console, were as key to the formative storytelling experience as any number of TV shows and movies. Telltale had been designed to do just that: tell tales, not just allow audiences to play games.

While at first they revived certain LucasArts properties with built-in fanbases but which wouldn't necessarily capture a wide audience, such as the aforementioned *Sam and Max* and *Monkey Island*,[49] Telltale eventually expanded to take in licenses such as *Jurassic Park, Back to the Future* and in 2012 the title which helped Telltale break out into the mainstream: *The Walking Dead*. What they did with these adaptations of famous cinematic, comic-book (soon adding *Batman* to their roster) and television (including *Game of Thrones*) properties was not simply to take the original properties and turn them into video games, but rather use them as an opportunity to tell stories within those same universes—whether a sequel, as with *Back to the Future*, or a story which operated akin to an

6. The Future of the Mytharc

ancillary, side-quest narrative that non-fans could enjoy without a cavalcade of backstory but built-in fans would eat up as part of that same universe of storytelling.[50]

This is an example of how video gaming and mythological world-building and storytelling are continuing to merge as one greater example of cross-media narrative, including cinema, comic books, television and literature.

The genesis of this comes from developers such as LucasArts. With their original games, they challenged the preconceptions of video gamers across the 1980s and 1990s, after Nintendo and Sega originally dominated the market with their original consoles the NES and Master System, were used to this sub-culture involving primarily simplistic forms of entertainment. First person shooters, platform games, puzzlers, many of them with a functional level of story (Mario must rescue Princess Toadstool from King Koopa) designed to facilitate the game play. LucasArts, and developers such as Hideo Kojima who for Konami in 1998 became one of *the* most famous names in gaming with his first entry for the *Metal Gear Solid* franchise, started to transform video gaming. No longer were games *just* games. They were stories. They were sagas.

Metal Gear Solid games are still being released, even though Kojima has stepped away from making them,[51] and every one cleaves to an in-universe Mytharc which has steadily been unfolded since the original game, one which ties deeply into politics, religion and American conspiracy theory. *Snake Eater*, the third *Metal Gear* game designed for the PlayStation 2, was a Cold War–set prequel which for gamers frustrated given a heavy proportion of the game involved cinematic cut scenes advancing story. Kojima has been known to include cut scenes in *Metal Gear* games that can run anything up to 15 minutes before gamers can continue playing. Games such as *Snake Eater* and *Guns of the Patriots* are arguably story first, gameplay second, and Kojima is perhaps the closest thing the video game world has ever had to a narrative auteur, their own Chris Carter.

Perhaps the next significant forward jump in the fusion of mythological storytelling and world-building in gaming came from a French-Canadian company called Ubisoft and their ongoing *Assassin's Creed* saga.

In 2007, *Assassin's Creed* arrived as a stand-alone adventure for the PlayStation 3 in which you played Altair, a man in eleventh century Jerusalem who was also an Assassin—not in modern terminology as a killer for hire, but from the ancient tradition of the "Hashashin," an order of warriors who across history have protected the world from the aspirations of an order who seek to control and subjugate humanity, here in the first game defined by the Knights Templar. Though the game at times was stodgy, it had enough mythology driving the concept that Ubisoft soon found an appetite for sequels, and in short order an entire franchise was born. *Assassin's Creed* swiftly began to serve as an example of secret history within fiction, and this allows for an entirely different kind of mythology to exist within the precept of a world we *do* recognize.

The crux of the franchise was that each game would take place in a different time frame but connect to the same, overarching mythological narrative. In *Assassin's Creed II*, set in Italy during the Renaissance, it becomes clear that there existed in prehistory a supremely advanced race of humans who became known as the "Precursors," some of whom likely inspired mythological gods in subsequent civilizations. The Precursors' aims are nebulous but they leave messages and clues inside artifacts, tombs and pieces of their technology, which directly connect to Assassins thousands of years hence. *Assassin's Creed* revolves around bloodlines and uses modern technology known as the Animus to allow modern Assassins to re-live long-ago events that their Assassin ancestors lived.

This turns out to be the central tenet of the gameplay; *Assassin's Creed* games are not simply set in Ancient Egypt or Victorian London, etc., they are the construct of "genetic memory" which modern technology uses to recount hidden events of the past, to expose the secret history of the Assassins and the Templars spanning thousands of years. *Assassin's Creed: Origins* (2017) suggests that this battle for prehistoric secrets dates back before the very reaction of "Assassin" or "Templar," beyond Christian religious practice and into polytheistic Egyptian worship and paganism, fueled even further with 2018's analogous Ancient Greek setting for *Assassin's Creed: Odyssey*. It is a secret conflict, often determining the world's destiny, which has played out in a hidden war between two distinct ideologies: freedom and control.

The *Assassin's Creed* games build their mythology from the standpoint of an alternate version of history, just one that most of humanity never knew existed. In this world, the Biblical story of Eden existed as a pre-historical rebellion of human, *homo sapien* slaves against the Precursor civilization who used powerful, mind-controlling technology to subjugate them. In the late 1400s, Rodrigo Borgia, a.k.a. the corrupt Pope Alexander V, attempts to use an Apple of Eden—one of these technological marvels—to take control of the world. Templar machinations and attempts to find Precursor technology influence the very creation of the United States during the War of Independence, which we see play out in *Assassin's Creed III*. The examples are legion—major global events,

6. The Future of the Mytharc

featuring key figures in history, all secretly connected to the Assassin-Templar war to control humanity's destiny.

Given the success of the franchise from a gaming perspective, *Assassin's Creed* inevitably branched out into other media. The year 2017 saw a cinematic adaptation, or perhaps continuation may be more accurate; Justin Kurzel's film very clearly holds to the same continuity as the games, with in-film visual references to game adventures, and *Origins* later in its arcanum within the game directly references the events at the climax of the *Assassin's Creed* movie. Similarly, a whole range of tie-in novelizations, including new stories, not to mention still-ongoing comic adaptations featuring a range of different time periods in history, are all part of the same shared universe. *Assassin's Creed* has become a tapestry of stories building and constructing a secret alternate history around a world we believe we know.

Crucially, *Assassin's Creed* as a franchise holds true to the same mythological continuity, despite whether you're playing games on a PS3 or PS4, reading novelizations or comic books, or watching the movie tie-in. It is the one franchise to cross-pollinate different forms of media, after starting life as a video game, and remain successful for over a decade. No other franchise, even those which have had financially successful cinematic adaptations such as *Tomb Raider*, have succeeded in this approach.

Video gaming remains one of the keys to the future of the Mytharc in storytelling, as the form continues to evolve and tether ever closer to different formats of entertainment.

Before it became insolvent and ceased development in October 2018, Telltale Games had been planning games which tied into franchises including the hit Netflix series *Stranger Things*[52] and *Guardians of the Galaxy*, one of the key components of the Marvel Comics universe, which theoretically could have seen the company making all kind of games linked directly to the Marvel mythology. Just because they ultimately could not remain a going concern does not mean other developers will not try and create similar video gaming experiences, aware increasingly of the financial and creative rewards of shared continuity across different forms of media.

At the end of November 2018, the mobile strategy game *Star Trek: Fleet Command* launched. Mike Johnson, one of the writers of the IDW Publishing tie-in comics to the *Star Trek* reboot universe, revealed that it would feature characters expressly created for the comics, despite those stories being canonically loose.[53] More frequently, examples of ingrained franchises and mythologies sharing story threads between games and other forms of media are becoming apparent.

Myth-Building in Modern Media

The question is, where is all of this heading, in terms of how we interface with narrative? Not just in terms of how the Mytharc may sustain itself beyond television or even cinema.

Though now one of the grand masters of storytelling across the late 20th century into the 21st, Steven Spielberg, in his adaptation of Ernest Cline's populist, dystopian sci-fi novel *Ready Player One*, showed that he was more than capable of imagining what leaps we may take in how we imagine and digest narrative in the future. This near future world sees an ostensibly free human population, particularly that of the United States, willingly opting into a simulated salve for their own societal woes.

Cline's story takes place in the 2030s and a world in which most of humanity, suffering from economic collapse thanks to the rise of corporate entities and the ineffectiveness of government organizations to distribute resources equally, have abandoned stewardship of the world for the OASIS—a simulated, online virtual reality whereby everyone becomes an "avatar," a virtual representation of themselves created to look like and sound like whoever they want. People put on a headset, establish an online connection, and while sitting in their living rooms they can play out an entire universe of possibilities in a virtual world where *any*thing is possible. The OASIS is the ultimate extension of innovations such as Google Glass and PlayStation VR fused with the omnipresence of pervasive social media applications.

Ready Player One suggests that many of the established functions of modern society have been channeled through the OASIS; services can be bought or sold, kids go to school on learning "planets" (such as Ludus in the novel) and even prostitution and sexual gratification appear to be on the table. All people need to do in the "real world" is fulfill the basic biological functions—eat, sleep, use the bathroom. Everything else the OASIS can provide, from entertainment to learning and social interaction. Cline suggests our modern obsession with technology, of transforming the landscape of human interaction with our world from the tangible to the ephemeral, will lead us to sunder our control of the natural world and simply allow the promise of utopia to decay around us. If a simulation can provide our perfect, idealized world, then why invest the much harder effort into creating that in the real world?

The fact that Cline's story focuses on youth underscores the sense of hope behind the mythology of his world that Spielberg, naturally given his creative sensibilities, writ large on his cinematic canvas. Wade Watts, the young protagonist gamer who goes after the Easter eggs in the OASIS that are key to the story, comes from a depressed environment; he lives in "the

6. The Future of the Mytharc

stacks," with impoverished Middle Americans now living in stacked trailers which resemble makeshift tower blocks.[54] Through the OASIS, and his partnership with the strident female gamer Art3mis, Wade seeks a very utopian, socially inclusive ideal hidden at the core of the digital world.

While *Ready Player One* is fiction, it could also end up as prescient as William Gibson's *Neuromancer* was in how we interface with the online world. Is it too great a stretch to see one of Cline's most intriguing concepts, Flicksynchs, one day become reality thanks to the advent of VR technology? Flicksynchs, in the novel, is an innovation of sinister corporation GSS which sees them buy the rights to classic TV and movies and turn them into a game where people would play the lead role in their favorite story, within the confines of the OASIS.[55] Who wouldn't relish the chance to play Sean Connery's James Bond, smoking casually in the casino in *Dr. No* and uttering his immortal introduction? Or Ellen Ripley in *Aliens* in the cargo loader delivering the line, "Get away from her. you bitch!"? These innovations, these fusions of narrative and gameplay, the kind of which we see in *Ready Player One*'s dystopian future outlook, could easily become reality with the right fusion of technological advancement and business acumen.

It is also worth pointing out that *Ready Player One*'s hero Wade has an online avatar named Parzival, named after the Knight immortalized in Richard Wagner's 19th century opera, hunting the Holy Grail. Parzival's quest could well be the ultimate narrative Mytharc, reflecting that search for meaning in all of us, a search destined to continue into a century filled with uncertainty as to where our own story may be headed.

7

Finding the Mytharc

Across this exploration of the Mytharc, principally in television, we have seen all kinds of examples as to how mythological storytelling drives the stories, and importantly the character journeys, of the tales we enjoy.

Character remains the most important of these alchemical elements to the Mytharc. Why else do we engage with a story if not to undertake a journey with characters we care about? We engage with the Monomytharcs of characters such as Fox Mulder because of that connection and attachment, created in that space between what we see and what is written on a page by a creator. All characters are, in their own way, the act of a god. All writers, no matter what branch of media they are writing for, are the creators of that character's journey. Some are from the pen of one creator, others the pen of many, but if often the Monomytharcs of Mulder, or Frank Black or Jack Shephard, are tied up with faith and a search for truth or meaning, perhaps we seek these kinds of characters as part of our own journeys.

There is a reason many of the stories we have examined come back to some kind of divine force or higher power. Everything from the aliens of *The X-Files* to the mystical God figures in *Lost* and *Alias*, to the superheroes of *Heroes* and the Marvel and DC Cinematic Universe, are equivalent in some respect to our search for Creation. For the writers penning these works, from the Chris Carters and J.J. Abramses, to the super-producers such as Kevin Feige and Kathleen Kennedy, it is about using these franchises and stories to reflect the journeys we undertake as modern humans in a complex, uncertain, fast-moving world. If we are losing the faith our ancestors had in enlightened times, these creators are handing back worlds, and characters, for us to believe in.

Mythology is what binds it all together. The myth of story plus the arc of these characters, whether its the mutiny of Michael Burnham in *Star Trek: Discovery* for the right reasons in the wrong circumstances, or the path Jon Snow in *Game of Thrones* takes from unwanted bastard to King of the North, is what we use to reflect our own beliefs, morals, hopes and

7. Finding the Mytharc

dreams. The worlds may be futuristic, historical, fantastical or unknowable, but in all of them we see ourselves. We see who we are. We see who we could be. We see who we do and do not want to be.

These stories, and these journeys, these Mytharcs, have become our modern mythology. Where the ancients looked up to the stars and created gods such as Zeus, sending lightning from the heavens, or Vulcan working in the bowels of the earth in his forge, we look to the stories we see on our screens, read in our books and comics, and play on our video games, for the same level of meaning. Our counterparts in antiquity were always looking to explain who *they* were in believing in the gods they fashioned out of stone and clay, out of imagination. We now use writing software, cameras, sets and graphics cards for the same effect. Any of us who creates a world, creates fiction, are contributing to the wider cultural story of our past, our present and our future.

Much like Mulder's search for his sister, and Parzival's search for the Holy Grail, the truth is that the Mytharc is easy to find.

It is in every single one of us whenever we allow ourselves to be swept away by these worlds, these characters and their stories. In this, we are blessed, as the Mytharc has existed since the time human beings were able to imagine, and it will be with us until the end.

Chapter Notes

Preface

1. Frank Spotnitz, Co-Executive Producer of *The X-Files*, when I asked him about this, didn't know specifically when the use of Mytharc came to be, nor what sparked its popularity: "I always felt the term was a bit grand for a television series. I guess it suggests that there is something archetypal about that storyline. I'm not sure that there is, but I guess that's better left to others to judge. I suppose it refers not just to the defined plot and characters that are in the alien conspiracy storyline, but all the themes and narrative possibilities it suggests. In the case of *The X-Files*, every time we answered a question we were sure to always ask several more. The longer the series went on, the more questions there were for which the audience expected an answer. But the continuing storyline wouldn't have been very interesting if it were simply the unspooling of a plot. There were big ideas driving the show, and our best episodes in the mythology arc—episodes like the "Redux" trilogy and "Memento Mori"—didn't just ask narrative questions, but questions about faith and belief that Chris and I were deeply interested in."
2. Neal, "TV Show Mythology," *Literal Minded*, February 2, 2010.
3. Ibid.
4. English Oxford Living Dictionaries, "Mythology."
5. J.R.R. Tolkien, "Mythopoeia" (poem).
6. E.E. Stokely, "What Is Mythopoeia?" Phantammeron, November 21, 2015.
7. John Adcox, "Can fantasy be myth? Mythopoeia and *The Lord of the Rings*," JohnAdcox.com.
8. "How was *The Lord of the Rings* influenced by World War One?" bbc.co.uk.
9. The Mayor serves as the antagonist in just one season of *Buffy the Vampire Slayer* but he encapsulates Joss Whedon's approach to each season; he would pivot every year of *Buffy* around whatever particular villain reflected the thematic story each of the main characters were experiencing. Whether the Mayor as reflective a bad father figure, the dark Angelus in Season 2 of the bad influence boyfriend, the Story Arc would see Buffy each year have to overcome and learn from these enemies, which played into her wider ongoing character arc.
10. A.k.a. Gillian Anderson's pregnancy, which forced the writers to creatively write around her absence during the early part of Season 2.
11. Joseph Campbell. *The Hero with a Thousand Faces* (Princeton, NJ: Princeton University Press, 1968, 30; Novato, CA: New World Library, 2008), 23.
12. Online Etymology Dictionary, "hero."
13. It is arguable that recent James Bond movies, featuring Daniel Craig, have attempted to buck this trend and see the Bond archetype change and grow by the end of each film. While the character does not subscribe to the Monomyth as such, the Bond by the end of *Casino Royale* or *Skyfall* is not the same Bond we knew at the beginning. The Pierce Brosnan and even Timothy Dalton eras flirted with such character development but Craig's incarnation is the first time we have seen James Bond develop truly from one place to another, whilst remaining true to the cinematic archetype.

Notes—Chapter 1

14. Todd Van Der Werff, and Caroline Framke, "*Twin Peaks*, Decoded for Novices and Obsessives Alike," *Vox*, May 21, 2017. https://www.vox.com/culture/2017/5/19/15660502/twin-peaks-explained-showtime-david-lynch.

15. Vince Tomasso, "Classical Antiquity and Western Identity in *Battlestar Galactica*," Tor.com, Jan. 26, 2015.

Chapter 1

1. S.T. Joshi, *A Dreamer and a Visionary: H.P. Lovecraft in His Time*, Liverpool University Press.

2. YourDictionary.com, "mythos."

3. *Ibid*.

4. OxfordDictionaries.com, "myth."

5. A fervor which Lovecraft perhaps sensed would grow into what became the Nazi regime. The Imperial German Navy officer who experiences these events, Karl Heinrich, Graf von Altberg-Ehrenstein, in his name has an air of the historic Prussian righteousness of noble aristocracy that Lovecraft hints could grow into the rabid anti-semitism and sense of manifest German destiny that drove Nazism.

6. H. P. Lovecraft, *The Complete Fiction of H. P. Lovecraft* (New York: Chartwell Books 2016).

7. As Wes House states: "A relatively straightforward detective story, 'The Horror of Red Hook' unfolds in Lovecraft's typical fashion; the deeper evil is slowly brought to light in scenes of intermixing immigrants whose neighborhood is revealed in the final act to be the literal gateway to hell. Strong anti–immigration sentiments and gaudy displays of sympathy for racist policing appear throughout, with references to immigrants that range from 'monsters' to 'contagions.' We see blacks and immigrants, the bringers of chaos in American law and order, subjected to a scientific scrutiny that perceives them as a danger to the master race." Wes House, "We Can't Ignore H.P. Lovecraft's White Supremacy: Lovecraftian Narratives of Race Persist in Contemporary Politics," *LitHub*, Sept. 26, 2017.

8. Stephen King is on record as considering Lovecraft a major influence in his work. "I think it is beyond doubt that H. P. Lovecraft has yet to be surpassed as the twentieth century's greatest practitioner of the classic horror tale. Lovecraft ... opened the way for me, as he had done for others before me ... it is his shadow, so long and gaunt, and his eyes, so dark and puritanical, which overlie almost all of the important horror fiction that has come since." Curt Wohleber, "The Man Who Can Scare Stephen King," *American Heritage*, December 1995.

9. August Derleth referred to Lovecraft's stories as the "Arkham cycle" privately, after the institution featured in several stories.

10. S.T. Joshi, *H. P. Lovecraft: A Life* (West Warwick, RI: Necronomicon Press 1996).

11. You only have to look at the aforementioned *The Evil Dead* with Raimi or even aspects of *Spiderman 3*, with Venom a comic-book example of Lovecraftian alien horror consuming the human body. Lovecraft is all over John Carpenter in everything from the creeping dread of *The Thing*, to the metatextual horror of *In the Mouth of Madness*, which in itself could be a Lovecraftian title. Del Toro has even come close to a big screen adaptation of *At the Mountains of Madness*, once to have starred Tom Cruise, but studios have often seemed wary of Del Toro's historically poor box office showings, and for the fact Del Toro would almost certainly make a Lovecraft adaptation as weird and niche a piece of horror cinema as Lovecraft's short stories. The critical and financial success of Del Toro's *The Shape of Water* may change that position in years to come, however.

12. For more: Tyler Calloway, "Marvel Vs. DC: Exposing the Fan War Myth," *Geeks*, 2017. https://vocal.media/geeks/marvel-vs-dc-exposing-the-fan-war-myth.

13. Jess Nevins, "A Brief History of the Crossover," *i09*, Aug. 23, 2011.

14. "The term comic-book was used occasionally, but not consistently, and while collectors and scholars have attached the name "The Platinum Age" to this period, with respect to DC's history, it needs to be regarded more as "The Stone Age": a primitive period of experimenta-

Notes—Chapter 1

tion." Paul Levitz is here referring more to the newspaper comic-strips which began to emerge at the end of the 19th century, but the idea of the "superhero" and a visual narrative of storytelling can be traced as far back as cave paintings dating back to 32,000 BC and the cuneiform writing system developed by the Sumerians at the dawn of pre-history. Paul Levitz, *75 Years of DC Comics: The Art of Modern Mythmaking* (Köln: Taschen, 2010), 9.

15. Joe Schuster and Jerry Siegel considered Superman, however, to be the opposite. Brian Overland discusses the concept of the Ubermensch and their reaction to it: "The Ubermensch starts by asserting that God is dead. The Nietzschean hero is self-assertive. He has replaced God with himself. This is either good or bad depending on your point of view. He's either a brave creature who can stand on his own two feet, not needing to enslave himself to another, or he's egotistical and even dangerous. The Ubermensch rejects conventional wisdom, including conventional morality. And this is where the philosophy is most controversial. He puts himself above society's ideas about good and evil. In 1933, Schuster and Siegel rethought the character of Superman and this time made him a hero—but a hero who embodied a rejection of all Nietzschean values. Though he had superhuman powers, he would use them to defend those who couldn't help themselves. It is a classic dichotomy. Nietzsche's Superman would say that might creates right ... that the truly free man breaks free of conventional morality. The comic-book Superman holds to the more conventional idea of might for right." Brian Overland, "Origins of Superman: Nietzsche and the Man of Steel," BrianOverland.com, 2013.

16. Paul Levitz: *75 Years of DC Comics: The Art of Modern Mythmaking*, 56.

17. Remarkably one of the earliest examples of a comic-book television crossover would be in the popular 1950s comedy series *I Love Lucy*, starring Lucille Ball, in which George Reeves' Superman, from popular serial *The Adventures of Superman*, helped rescue her from a window ledge in an episode from 1957 called "Lucy Meets Superman." Though not an example of shared continuity, it speaks to how comic-book characters were leading the way in developing ideas of crossing between series and platforms. Ball herself would play a quiet but crucial role in the development of *Star Trek*, one of the leading cultural mythologies of the 20th century.

18. Paul Levitz: *75 Years of DC Comics: The Art of Modern Mythmaking*, 56.

19. Superman's adventures arguably grew lighter the deeper into WW2 the American people raced, however, perhaps as an escapist counteraction to the fears and real-life battles being faced by GI's in Europe. Rather than sailing into Berlin and punching out Hitler, Superman found himself battling strange foes such as Mr Mxyzptlk. Readers arguably wanted lighter, cosmic adventure to balance out the darkness of the real world, while still believing Superman could survive their worst fears—such as an atomic blast, which by 1945 he was capable of not being killed from.

20. Such as the post-modern revisionist graphic novels in the mid–1980s from writers such as Frank Miller which recast Batman as a tortured, darker than dark hero.

21. "Westerns have earned their place at the heart of the national culture and American iconography abroad because they've provided a reliable vehicle for filmmakers to explore thorny issues of American history and character. In the enduring examples of the genre, the real threat to the homestead, we learn, is an economic system that is being rigged for the wealthy, or the search for the bad guy becomes a search for meaning in a culture of violent retribution, or the treasure of the Sierra Madre is a diabolical mirage of the American dream. In the Great Depression especially, as capitalism and American exceptionalism came under question, the cowboy hero was often mistaken for a criminal and forced to prove his own worthiness—which he inevitably did." Michael Agresta, "How the Western Was Lost (and Why It Matters)," *The Atlantic*, July 24, 2013.

22. Four episodes of which are sadly lost to the BBC's penchant for wiping tapes of shows to make room for other material, a

Notes—Chapter 1

fate which of course befell early episodes of *Doctor Who*.

23. The year 2012 saw the arrival of the 50th anniversary James Bond movie, *Skyfall*, which helped the series recover from the lukewarm critical response to 2008's *Quantum of Solace* and went on to be the franchise's first ever billion-dollar box office movie. A year later, feature-length *Doctor Who* episode "The Day of the Doctor," had cinematic production design, was released for a limited period in UK and U.S. cinemas, and celebrated 50 years of the character by featuring every single incarnation of the Doctor through a clever storytelling mechanism. It was celebrated by fans and critics alike.

24. The first ever broadcast serial in the traditional multi-part format, broadcast on the BBC between November 24 and December 13, 1963, starring William Hartnell as the First Doctor.

25. "I loved *The Prisoner*, which was a very odd sort of hybrid of sci-fi, mystery and character, and certainly there are elements of *The Prisoner* in both *Alias* and *Lost*. The prisoner was a guy constantly wondering where the hell he was. And there was some kind of agency that seemed to be in control of his destiny, and that was clearly a theme in *Alias*." Shawna Malcom, "J.J. Abrams, *Lost* Boss Tackles *Star Trek Enterprise*," *TV Guide*, Aug. 11, 2006.

26. *Lost* in particular feels heavily inspired by *The Prisoner*. It is set in a location the world has no idea exists and is almost impossible to both reach and escape from; there is a "Village" of technologically advanced, enigmatic people with their own agenda, often theatrically pretending to be something other than who they are for the purposes of manipulation—plus they abduct and psychologically condition them, at times to extract information; there is also a strange "security system" in the Smoke Monster which appears out of nowhere and can kill or consume people, a system which may or may not be controlled from elsewhere. *Lost* also has a unique strangeness about the philosophical ideas in play, often about determinism and free will, which stand out from TV in the 2000s as much as *The Prisoner* stood out in the 1960s.

27. Patrick McGoohan: "As long as people feel something, that's the great thing. It's when they're walking around not thinking, not feeling ... that's where all the dangerous stuff is, cause when you get a mob like that, you can turn them in to the sort of gang that Hitler had."Laurens C. Postma (director), and Chris Rodley (writer) *Six into One: The Prisoner File*, Channel 4, documentary, 1984.

28. The same could be said about the reaction aimed at *Lost* creators Damon Lindelof and Carlton Cuse after *Lost*'s finale "The End" aired, a conclusion that many felt was an unsatisfying ending which left too many questions open ended, though it is without doubt far more resolved than "Fall Out" ever was.

29. Chris Gregory makes the comparison between *The Prisoner* and early 1990s American TV series *Twin Peaks*, arguing that both are the result of a very clear, defined "auteur" at work, in that show's case noted surrealist filmmaker David Lynch. "Like McGoohan, Lynch was attempting to subvert the conventions of the major forms of prime-time television, in this case the soap opera and the detective story. Behind the banal surface of life in Lynch's "typical" American small town lie subtexts of murder, perversion, corruption, madness and conspiracy." Chris Gregory, *Be Seeing You: Decoding the Prisoner* (Luton, England: University of Luton Press, 1997), 185–186.

30. *Kolchak* was remade by Frank Spotnitz in 2005, following *The X-Files* success and the birth of the Mytharc on modern television, but Spotnitz feels the prevalence of mythology may have hampered its success. He told me "I thought the mythology of "*Night Stalker*" was incredibly rich, but alas we didn't get the chance to explore it. My complaint about "mythology" is that broadcasters have, in my judgment, pushed it too hard. When we did "*The X-Files*," the "mythology" episodes were six to eight out of 24 episodes produced each season. By the time I did "*Night Stalker*," three years after *The X-Files* ended, the broadcasters were asking us to advance the mythology in every single episode. I think that creates a story tonnage that becomes very unwieldy awfully fast. I much prefer taking a "slow burn" approach."

Notes—Chapter 2

Chapter 2

1. It is odd that Mulder, in the historical lore of *The X-Files* universe, never met or interacted with *Millennium*'s protagonist Frank Black, who would have been profiling at the FBI on very similar violent crime cases in the 1980s around the same time. Mulder, when they finally do cross paths in Season 7's "Millennium," has certainly heard of Frank's reputation, but they almost certainly would have inhabited the same space at the same time, even if they never actually worked a case together.

2. Interestingly, however, Mulder is not the first agent to investigate these cases in the FBI. Season 5's "Travelers," a story which acutely parallels insidious alien control with 1950s Communist paranoia, reveals an agent named Arthur Dales first looked into them after an FBI secretary placed them in a cabinet marked "X" because she ran out of room in the "U" drawer for Unexplained. In a nice piece of metatextual casting, Darren McGavin plays Dales; an actor who originally portrayed Carl Kolchak in the 1970s series that principally influenced Chris Carter in making *The X-Files*, who was originally asked to play Mulder's father, and went on around the same time as "Travelers" to play Frank Black's father Henry in *Millennium* episode "Midnight of the Century."

3. Roche feels very much in the Thomas Harris mould of serial killer popularized by his books including *The Silence of the Lambs*, and films such as *Manhunter*; indeed actor Tom Noonan, who portrayed Roche, played the role of the "Red Dragon," Francis Dolarhyde, in Michael Mann's 1986 adaptation of *Manhunter*.

4. Though not as intentionally apocryphal as the similar flashback story in Season 4, "Musings of a Cigarette-Smoking Man," "Unusual Suspects" theory about the cause of Mulder's paranoia is never confirmed nor picked up on again, but it feels like an extension of the same influence that chemicals in the water of his apartment building in "Anasazi" do to Mulder. In one respect, it explains Mulder's inmate obsession with conspiracy but in the same breath feels as much of a nod and a wink as the appearance of Richard Belzer as *Homicide: Life on the Street*'s ubiquitous detective John Munch.

5. The aforementioned "Travelers" suggests that Mulder may have at some point before he met Dana Scully, around 1990, been married; that episode sees him pointedly sporting a wedding ring. This is nothing Mulder ever discusses in the show, or to Scully, but many fans came to believe Mulder may briefly have been married to the character of Diana Fowley, introduced in "The End"; the first FBI partner of Mulder's to investigate X-Files with him and secretly part of the Syndicate group of conspirators. Though the show strongly suggests Mulder & Diana have been previously intimate, to this day Mulder's youthful marriage remains a key character mystery.

6. Joseph Campbell. *The Hero with a Thousand Faces*, Princeton, NJ: Princeton University Press, 1968, 48.

7. Almost. It is replaced on various occasions with lines and slogans which reflect themes and ideas within particular episodes, such as "Apology Is Policy" in "731," "Everything Dies" in "Herrenvolk," and "This Is The End" in "My Struggle II."

8. We never meet one of them, Charles. He is only briefly seen in childhood flashbacks in "One Breath" and heard via phone in "Home Again."

9. In this case, it is revealed by the end of "End Game" that this Samantha was one of many clones created by cloned alien doctors living in secret from their extra-terrestrial overlords.

10. *The X-Files*: Paper Clip, 3X02.

11. Joseph Campbell. *The Hero with a Thousand Faces*, (Princeton, NJ: Princeton University Press, 1968), 59.

12. *The X-Files*: Anasazi, 2X25.

13. Joseph Campbell. *The Hero with a Thousand Faces*, (Princeton, NJ: Princeton University Press, 1968), 64.

14. *The X-Files*: The Blessing Way, 3X01.

15. Joseph Campbell. *The Hero with a Thousand Faces*, Princeton, NJ: Princeton University Press, 1968, 97.

16. The word "MacGuffin," coined by the English screenwriter Angus MacPhail, describes an object which serves as the function driving a narrative but which does not end up being the *point* of the

Notes—Chapter 2

story; the Ark of the Covenant in *Raiders of the Lost Ark* or the Rabbit's Foot in *Mission Impossible III*, for example. Alfred Hitchcock popularized the term in his 1935 film *The 39 Steps* and described it thus: "It might be a Scottish name, taken from a story about two men on a train. One man says, 'What's that package up there in the baggage rack?' And the other answers, 'Oh, that's a MacGuffin.' The first one asks, 'What's a MacGuffin?' 'Well,' the other man says, 'it's an apparatus for trapping lions in the Scottish Highlands.' The first man says, 'But there are no lions in the Scottish Highlands,' and the other one answers, 'Well then, that's no MacGuffin!' So you see that a MacGuffin is actually nothing at all." *Framing Hitchcock: Selected Essays from the Hitchcock Annual*, Detroit: Wayne State University Press, 47–48.

17. The greatest irony in this conversation is how it is heavily implied that the Smoking Man allows Jeremiah to go in exchange for the man using his power to cure the lung cancer he is dying from. He may try and convince Jeremiah he is nothing, but he relies on his God-like power for survival and is mercurial enough to accept it.

18. *The X-Files*: Talitha Cumi, 3X23.

19. *The X-Files*: Herrenvolk, 4X01.

20. *Ibid.*

21. Cambridge Dictionary, "apotheosis."

22. In truth, Mulder's roughly ten-episode disbelief in aliens, before he once again believes, stands as probably the most ineffectual character point in his arc, and in the Mytharc running alongside his journey as a whole. By this point, Mulder has witnessed his sister be abducted by aliens, almost died at the hands of a retro-virus from acidic green blood, glimpsed countless UFO's and alien creatures, encountered shape-shifting beings, cloned child versions of his sister and has been infected by an oily black virus capable of possessing a human host… and yet one long conversation at the DOD convinces him for half a season that extra-terrestrials don't exist. It would work had we not spent four seasons witnessing Scully's rational scientific rigor proven wrong at every turn, with Mulder's faith in the supernatural and unknowable validated week after week after week. The Mytharc is one of the few aspects of *The X-Files* that was never in doubt, yet we are asked to believe Mulder may have considered his entire journey to this point a falsehood.

23. Director of "Two Fathers," along with "One Son" being the episode that concluded the Syndicate mythology that had existed for four seasons, Kim Manners stated: "I've said for years that the show really resolved itself, if you will, by accident. The whole story line of the Syndicate and the bees and the aliens and the chips in the neck, they all seemed to just accidentally fall into place and create an intriguing, mysterious storyline that eventually got so mysterious and so intriguing that Chris had to blow it up, because he couldn't deal with it anymore." Matt Hurwitz, and Chris Knowles, *The Complete X-Files* (London: Titan Books, 2016), 159.

24. *The X-Files*: Biogenesis, 6X22.

25. Joseph Campbell. *The Hero with a Thousand Faces*, (Princeton, NJ: Princeton University Press, 1968), 107, 110.

26. "No one really dies on *The X-Files*," Chris Carter is oft quoted as saying and this is especially true of the Smoking Man. He was shot seemingly dead at the end of "Redux II," pushed down a flight of stairs in "Requiem," blown up with a surface to air missile in "The Truth" (which we literally saw sear off his flesh) and is now shot repeatedly and pushed into a river by Mulder in "My Struggle IV." If the series ever does return in its current incarnation, the Smoking Man may well return with it.

27. Joseph Campbell. *The Hero with a Thousand Faces* (Princeton, NJ: Princeton University Press, 1968), 163.

28. *The X-Files*: Closure, 7X10.

29. Carter already had taken a strong cue from Thomas Harris in the character of Dana Scully on *The X-Files*, who very much was modelled after *The Silence of the Lambs*' Clarice Starling. In a level of cyclical storytelling and inspiration, Bryan Fuller's 2013 series *Hannibal*, adapting Harris' source material, would take a significant cue from *Millennium* in the portrayal of Will Graham's unique profiling "facility"– despite how Frank himself was inspired directly by Graham as a character.

Notes—Chapter 2

30. *Millennium*: Pilot, 1X01.

31. You wonder if "The Blood Dimmed Tide" might have made a fantastic alternative episode title for the premiere episode of *Millennium*.

32. *Millennium*: Pilot, 1X01.

33. This is partially inspired by the true-life experience of John Douglas, an FBI agent who became a pioneer in criminal psychology as a profiler who interviewed and hunted some of the most notorious serial killers in American history. He inspired much of Thomas Harris' work and the basis of the David Fincher-produced Netflix series *Mindhunter*, about the birth of criminal profiling.

34. A trope Glen Morgan and James Wong will actualize in Season 2's "Beware of the Dog," which John Kenneth Muir also argues pitches Frank as a symbolic apostle: "In the apocryphal Acts of Andrew, the apostle Saint Andrew is called upon to expel demons in the form of dogs from an imperiled city, and that is exactly the role Frank takes on in this installment." John Kenneth Muir, "Snakes in the Grass and Snakes in the Open," John Kenneth Muir's Reflections on Cult Movies and Classic TV (blog), http://reflectionsonfilmandtelevision.blogspot.com/.

35. Joseph Campbell, *The Hero with a Thousand Faces*, Princeton, NJ: Princeton University Press, 1968, 49.

36. Inspired originally by the Academy Group, a real-life organization of retired law enforcement officials who worked as a private investigating consulting firm. Chris Carter had become familiar with Academy Group members via FBI contacts made while producing *The X-Files*, and shaped the characters of both Frank and Peter Watts around the "offender profiling" the Academy Group did.

37. The death of Bob Bletcher is a turning point for *Millennium* in a similar way the death of Deep Throat at the end of *The X-Files* Season 1 was a turning point for that show, because in both cases you never see the deaths coming, and they were characters you believed to be inviolate in relation to our protagonist, based on existing TV conventions.

38. The Polaroid Man nonetheless serves as an indicator of how the show changes course between Seasons 1 and 2; when we first meet him in "Paper Dove," he shows few of the overtly prophetic, doom-laden, deliberately "millenniumistic" (to borrow from "Jose Chung's 'Doomsday Defense'") characteristics we then see in Doug Hutchison's portrayal in Season 2 premiere "The Beginning and the End." Had Carter still been running the series into Season 2, the Polaroid Man would likely have been a very different character.

39. "We were approaching the millennium and, when you started looking at it, every religion had this kind of apocalyptic literature, Also, there was an anxiety about the millennium—which I think didn't really come into fruition until after the year 2000 had passed—but that was something interesting as well. I didn't want to bail upon what they did in the first year with serial killers—there are still serial killer episodes in year two—but there was an approaching anxiety about the next century, and it wasn't on TV." Adam Chamberlain, and Brian A. Dickson, *Back to Frank Black: A Return to Chris Carter's Millennium* (London: Fourth Horseman Press, 2012), 114.

40. Joseph Campbell. *The Hero with a Thousand Faces*, Princeton, NJ: Princeton University Press, 1968, 81.

41. As an archetypal Western hero, Carter described him as "self-reliant, quiet, capable, dangerous" and makes comparisons to Alan Ladd's *Shane* in the 1953 George Stevens film of the same name. Order in Chaos, Making Millennium Season One (DVD), 04:48–05:09.

42. Magic circles appear in numerous TV shows and movies to depict protection (indeed one made of salt is used in Frank Black's final canonical appearance to date in *The X-Files* Season 7 episode, "Millennium"). It is a circle of space marked out by practitioners of many branches of ritual magic, which they generally believe will contain energy and form a sacred space, or will provide them a form of magical protection, or both.

43. *Millennium*: Goodbye Charlie, 2X11.

44. Due to the fact the revival seasons

Notes—Chapter 2

from 2016–2018 of *The X-Files* ignore or gloss over, even in some cases "retcon" (a.k.a. retroactively alter continuity for the sake of plot) mythology points, some fans have questioned the canonicity of the shows' return and, particularly in Season 11, believe Carter seeded in clues that suggest the revival seasons could even be a dream due to narrative inconsistencies in continuity. Wendy Attwell, *"The X-Files*: Season Eleven is all a Dream and Here's Why!" setthetape.com. https://setthetape.com/2018/07/23/the-x-files-season-eleven-is-all-a-dream-and-heres-why/.

45. This is exemplified in "Owls" and "Roosters" as Nazi war criminals who escaped justice at the end of WW2 and have lived well in South America for the last 50 years, a well-popularized idea since the Simon Wiesenthal Nazi hunting case of Adolf Eichmann came to prominence in the 1960s, carried through into successful movies such as 1978's *The Boys From Brazil*, adapted from Ira Lewin's novel about Dr. Josef Mengele's plan to create Aryan clones and restart the Third Reich.

46. Legion is particularly memorable in the form of Lucy Butler, played with ethereal relish by Sarah-Jane Redmond; a beguiling woman who Frank faces three times across each season (though he shares no scenes with her in Season 2's "A Room With No View"). If Frank has such a thing as a "nemesis" in *Millennium*, in the classical sense, it is Lucy—given she murders his colleague and friend Bob Bletcher in the basement of his Yellow House in "Lamentation." "She was by turns alluring and seductive, deceiving and utterly enigmatic, and, at her most extreme, horrifyingly violent, inhumane, and covered by no moral law, acting according to her own selfish maxims and a perverse and emotionless logic." Alexander Zelenji, Back to Frank Black, 250.

47. *Millennium*: The Curse of Frank Black, 2X06.

48. *Into the Wild*, a 1996 non-fiction book by Jon Krakauer, tells the story of Christopher McCandless, a young man who rejects college, leaves his family and perishes in 1992 while hiking in Alaskan mountains. Later adapted into by Sean Penn into a successful 2007 movie, starring Emile Hirsch as McCandless, With *Millennium*'s "Luminary," writer Chip Johannessen very much adapts the story and character to depict Alex Glaser and through him, Frank's own journey into the wilderness.

49. Joseph Campbell. *The Hero with a Thousand Faces*, (Princeton, NJ: Princeton University Press, 1968), 89.

50. *Ibid.*, 178.

51. At this point, one wonders if Peter Watts undergoes his own Monomytharc across Season 2. Much like Frank in Season 1, Peter is a static character whose main function, in almost a waste of Terry O'Quinn's talents as an actor, is to deliver exposition as support to Frank's insight. In Season 3, Peter is framed as more of an antagonist, yet in Season 2, he transforms from a gifted, professional profiler into an enigmatic cultist who experiences a profound crisis of faith in line with continuing to bring Frank deeper into the Millennium Group. Peter's arc may have been abandoned largely in the restructure of Season 3, but he experiences his own calling, apotheosis and threshold across Season 2 in parallel to Frank's.

52. *Millennium*: The Time Is Now, 2X23.

53. The initial pitch presented by Damon Lindelof and Carlton Cuse to ABC most intriguingly promises the series will be "self-contained," despite the presence of a pervasive mythology. This was a claim, likely to appease network television executives at the time still concerned with syndication rights in the pre-streaming era, that would immediately be not borne out by the structure of Season 1. "*Lost* Writers Guide," J.J. Abrams, Damon Lindelof, May 5, 2004.

54. Fanlore.org, *Babylon-5*.

55. Fanlore.org, *The X-Files*.

56. Chief among them was *The Lost Experience*, which between Seasons 2 and 3 delved much deeper into the backstory of the Hanso Foundation, who were revealed to be in "Orientation" financially funding the DHARMA Initiative. The depth of the mythology and lore within this, plotted by one of the show's writers, Javier Grillo-Marxuach, was unprecedented in terms of how it connected to the

Notes—Chapter 2

broader TV narrative. Lostpedia.fandom.com, Alternate Reality Game.

57. Lostpedia.fandom.com, Official *Lost* Podcast.

58. Lostpedia remains of the most in-depth curated resources for a television series online, having been created and updated during *Lost*'s original run and maintained ever since.

59. Jack was never originally meant to be the lead character. He would have been killed instead of the pilot in the "Pilot" halfway through, leaving Kate as the protagonist, with J.J. Abrams approaching film star Michael Keaton to play a role that would have been billed as the star turn, only for the shock twist of his death in the premiere: "I said, 'I'll seriously consider it, send me the script,'" says Keaton. He said, "No, we're keeping the guy alive," and I said, "Oh, ok, well I can't do that.' Keaton says he knows he made the right decision. 'I wouldn't do it if the guy was going to be in the show every week,' he says. 'An hour show every week ... I've got stuff to do, I've got a life to lead. When would I fish?'" "Michael Keaton Reveals Why He Passed on *Lost*," Jan. 9, 2005, movieinsider.com.

60. Christopher Hooton, "*Lost* Writer Admits They Just Made It Up as They Went Along," *The Independent*, Jan. 14, 2015.

61. *Lost*: White Rabbit, 1X05.

62. *Lost*: White Rabbit, 1X05.

63. *Lost*: Walkabout, 1X04.

64. The current and exiled leader of the Others, the mysterious Island community who worship Jacob. Ben and Widmore's battle is a microcosmic version of the grander, mystical battle between Jacob and the Man in Black, which itself is part of the deeper philosophical conflict between Good and Evil at the core of the series.

65. Joseph Campbell. *The Hero with a Thousand Faces*, 74.

66. A term coined by Jack at the end of "White Rabbit" in a speech to the survivors after his own journey to accept the Call to Adventure. "It's been six days ... and we're all still waiting. Waiting for someone to come. Well, what if they don't? We have to stop waiting. We need to start figuring things out. Every man for himself is not gonna work. It's time to start organizing. We need to figure out how we're gonna *survive* here. Last week most of us were strangers. But we're all here now, and God knows how long we're gonna be here. But if we can't, live together ... we're gonna die alone." *Lost*: White Rabbit, 1X05.

67. Steven Simunic, "Why ABC's *Lost* Is Losing It," *The Daily Californian*, March 15, 2007.

68. professorstotch, "*Lost* News—Huge Damon Q&A!" Jan. 20, 2009.

69. Jack is haunted by his failed marriage to Sarah, a woman whose spine he manages to "fix" and he later falls in love with, but who leaves him for another man partly due to Jack's obsessive savior complex. Ben's use of Juliet in manipulating Jack is therefore far from coincidence.

70. Although the series only really ever truly makes its mind up about the love between Juliet & Sawyer across Season 5, which itself never really feels as powerful as the only bond that ever shines through as believable: Kate and Sawyer, who may or may not have ended up together after "The End." Until the afterlife, where Kate ends up with Jack. Maybe. Look, it's complicated, ok?

71. Joseph Campbell. *The Hero with a Thousand Faces*, 101.

72. Each season of *Lost* would be gifted a codename by Lindelof and Cuse to refer to the cliff-hanger moments at the end of each year, and "The Snake (or Rattlesnake) in the Mailbox" remains the most well cited. Only one code name directly references something from inside an episode, Season 4's "The Frozen Donkey Wheel." Lostpedia.fandom.com, Code-named finale scenes.

73. Joseph Campbell. *The Hero with a Thousand Faces*, 167.

74. Joseph Campbell. *The Hero with a Thousand Faces*, 170.

75. *Quantum Leap* was an ABC science-fiction series which ran from 1989 through to 1993, starring Scott Bakula as Dr. Sam Beckett, a scientist who becomes lost in spacetime during a government time travel experiment, each week entering the body of someone in a different time period of American history, often at a time of significant social or political change.

76. Joseph Campbell. *The Hero with a Thousand Faces*, 188.

77. Joseph Campbell. *The Hero with a Thousand Faces*, 204–205.
78. *Lost*: What They Died For, 6X15.
79. Joseph Campbell. *The Hero with a Thousand Faces*, 206.
80. It also effectively settles the debate as to quite what denomination *Lost* was. As discussed in Chapter 4, *Lost* flirts with concepts of Buddhism and Zoroastrianism over the course of its six seasons, but by the end of "The End," *Lost* removes any secular doubt: this is a Christian tale of birth, death, rebirth and life everlasting.

Chapter 3

1. Islam considers Adam, the same Adam from Biblical Genesis myth considered the first human being, is considered the first "Nabi," a.k.a. Prophet on Earth, and is looked upon with reverence. Lalljee, compiled by Yousuf N, *Know your Islam*, 3rd ed (New York: Taknike Tarsile Quran, 1981), 71.
2. This even coined him the amusing soubriquet of "Nostravinci" among the *Alias* writing staff.
3. See notes (16) Chapter 3—The Monomytharc.
4. Other direct inspirations for Abrams included the original 1960s *Mission: Impossible* series, the James Bond movies, 1960s spy series *The Prisoner*.
5. J.J. Abrams: "For me, [the Rambaldi story] ratchets up the uniqueness of *Alias*. The show is not just about spies and going after nuclear codes or whatever—it's about something weirder." Mark Cotta Vaz, *Alias Declassified: The Official Companion* (New York: Bantam Books, 2002), 98.
6. Abrams gave a well-known TED talk on the subject of The Mystery Box in which he revealed his grandfather, Harry Kelvin, ignited his interest in mystery through his love of taking apart electronic devices and showing his grandson. Abrams would later, when making his 2009 reboot of *Star Trek* on the big screen, name a Starfleet vessel and subsequently an entire parallel universe "Kelvin," partly in honor of his late grandfather. J.J. Abrams, "The Mystery Box," 2007, ted.com.
7. "There was definitely a time somewhere around the middle of the show where the mythology of the Rambaldi device and the plot mechanics started to overwhelm the character telling. We identified that and course-corrected and made the last season-and-a-half, two seasons back to what the bulk of the story was about: emotion and character, with the plot servicing that rather than the other way around." Jeff Pinkner, "*Alias* Oral History: Jennifer Garner, Series Creator J.J. Abrams and Cast Mark Spy Drama's 10th Anniversary," May 4, 2016.
8. Abrams has long argued he always envisaged, to some extent, the idea of a gigantic Red Ball over a city as some kind of doomsday device, which we eventually see in Season 4 finale "Before the Flood," but *Alias* rarely feels like it has a singular plan of quite how its reaching its destination. The Red Ball was forgotten about for over two seasons, and its ultimate use doesn't end up serving as a conclusion to the series, rather a tee-up for an even more confusing final act.
9. Forty-seven is a key number Abrams revisits time and time again in his TV series and movies. There are 47 shapeshifters in *Fringe*. A scene in *Mission Impossible: Ghost Protocol* takes place on Pier 47. In *Star Wars: The Force Awakens* a thermal oscillator is located in Precinct 47.
10. *Alias*: The Prophecy, 1X16.
11. Imagine the X-Files department if Mulder had money and resources.
12. "Q&A" also serves as *Alias*' first and only "bottle episode." The term "bottle episode" refers to an episode placed in a season which uses clips from previous episodes, or sets the action in one specific place, in order to save the production staff money and/or allow actors a break. They have become much less common as network television has started to give way to cable and streaming series with fewer episodes and larger budgets.
13. It doesn't help, of course, that her CIA father breaks the rules every five minutes and her mother was a KGB spy who now runs a major, global crime syndicate, but that's neither here nor there!
14. This terminology has extra resonance in *Alias* for another specific reason—that in Season 1 the shadowy villain

Notes—Chapter 3

in direct opposition to Sloane and the Alliance cabal he works for is known as The Man, who is in fact Sydney's mother, Irina Derevko.

15. This is specifically mentioned in the two-part episode of *Millennium*, "Owls" and "Roosters," which seeks to connect the Annuit Coeptis to Freemasonry and the suggestion that the Founding Fathers of American society were Masons.

16. The Great Seal of the United States, state.gov.

17. *Alias*: Before the Flood, 4X22.

18. *Alias*: Countdown, 2X20.

19. The contents of which we never actually see. The inference is that it was a letter to Sloane from Rambaldi which directly tells him what to do next, which turns out to be build the machine compiled from 47 (there's that number again) of his innovations, Il Diree a.k.a. The Telling, which itself reveals to Sloane the means to find Nadia. The best interpretation of what Rambaldi tells Sloane in the letter is that he has a daughter; this would carry the import actor Ron Rifkin gives upon reading it, and partly explain some of Sloane's subsequent comments and actions.

20. Sloane undoubtedly has a deeper river of humanity than the Smoking Man, however, who rarely shows any indication he cares about anything but his own self-interest. He actually tries to murder his son Jeffrey Spender and later subjects him to horrific experimentation. Sloane, rather, genuinely does change and become a good man for a while, if a mercurial one, and though his actions cause Nadia's death, he does not kill her intentionally. It is hard to forgive Sloane's actions, and Sydney never really does, but his villainy is not a clear, straight line.

21. Which, literally translated, means "a formal alliance with God."

22. Sister to Irina and aunt to Sydney and Nadia. Later in the life of *Alias*, the writers create two Derevko sisters in order to fill the void of Lena Olin's protracted two-season absence as Sydney's mother.

23. This further ties *Alias* to the same sense of American legacy in terms of the Nazis as *The X-Files*, weaving the fictional mythology of Rambaldi into the mythologized Nazi search for the occult, which has influenced dozens of mediums since the Second World War when it comes to narrative, principally in cinema with the *Indiana Jones* series.

24. There is a sense that by the end of "Resurrection," the closing episode of Season 3, and the Season 4 episode which told this story, the writers changed their plan for what the Sphere of Life meant and would do. Its purpose in "Before the Flood" remains maddeningly unclear. It also likely was the reality of production factors and a writing staff who heavily course-corrected at the end of "Resurrection," to the point the ominous final moment of Season 3—in which we're meant to believe loveable Jack Bristow may well be a bad guy—is carefully skirted around, mainly to facilitate explanations as to Lena Olin's consistent absent as Syd's slippery mother Irina.

25. Prophet Five feel more like *The X-Files*' Syndicate than any other mysterious villainous organization the show has yet given us. They are ostensibly compared with the Alliance across the first two seasons but they had more in common with the James Bond SPECTRE organization. Prophet Five seem deliberately like a group of old, white men inside austere rooms with tentacles in global government and crime, influencing an apocalyptic agenda.

26. "We weren't as true to the characters," Abrams said of Season 3. "They became pawns in a plot-driven story." Bill Keveney, The many aliases of J.J. Abrams, Jan. 4, 2005, *USA Today*.

27. *The X-Files* creates its own Mytharc in how it deals with Gillian Anderson's real-life pregnancy, and later chooses to introduce a baby into the narrative as a means to develop a brand new Mytharc. *Alias*, conversely, never seems to know quite what to do with Syd's baby, despite in "The Horizon" attempting to introduce a level of mystery around it. Considering the earlier prophecy regarding Rambaldi's rebirth in a child, it is strange *Alias* does not choose to try and incorporate Garner's pregnancy into this aspect of the Mytharc.

28. And a bad one at that. Irina seems intent on firing missiles at Washington and London simply because she *can*. Does she intend on becoming an immortal ruler

Notes—Chapter 3

of an aggressive Russian power in the wake of the West's destruction? Like so many aspects of *Alias*' Mytharc from a character perspective, this is never clear.

29. One wonders if Ubisoft's game series *Assassin's Creed*, which arrived the year after *Alias* ended in 2006, took a cue from *Alias*' use of this in making the access of genetic memory to channel secrets of their ancestors a key component of its concept.

30. The character of Jeremiah Smith. For more on him, see Chapter 3.

31. Episodes which existed outside of the ongoing mythology. Standalone tales which often featured monstrous characters or villains, so named after the third episode of Season 1 "Squeeze" introduced the series' first monster, the immortal (in more ways than one) Eugene Victor Tooms.

32. Darren Mooney, "*The X-Files*: Talitha Cumi," review, themovieblog.com.

33. This, of course, does not track with the alien invaders collaborating with the Syndicate, certainly in terms of motive. It begs the question as to whether a multitude of alien races or species had visited Earth with differing agendas, in this instance a conservation concern rather than mass destruction.

34. This is partly a production reality of a show at its peak, come Season 4, which is not likely to have Mulder discover the truth about everything he's been seeking when the show has plenty of life left in it.

35. Chris Carter, Frank Spotnitz, Kim Manners, Vince Gilligan, Darin Morgan, John Shiban and Dean Haglund (commentary), "The Truth Behind Season Four," The X-Files: *The Complete Fourth Season*, DVD box set.

36. An entity most commonly associated with the United States that refers to the connection between a nation's defense industry and the military it supplies. "Redux" provides a complete "alternate history" (within the alternate history of *The X-Files*) in which Mulder comes to believe the conspirators have been developing biological weapons by experimenting on innocent citizens, as part of a systemic means of global control. Chris Carter will eventually return to similar themes in "My Struggle" in Season 10.

37. Darren Mooney even theorizes that Mulder becomes reflective of meta-textual awareness within this "awakening": "Mulder finds himself confronted by the logic of the real world, as opposed to the internal logic of *The X-Files*. In brushing against the idea that aliens are nothing but fictional constructs and his entire life has been a made-up story, Mulder seems to touch upon the idea that he may be a fictional character himself. His life is not his own, it is orchestrated by outside forces. In essence, his life has been written and plotted, and pieced together." Darren Mooney, *The X-Files*: Gethsemane (Review), https://them0vieblog.com/2015/04/06/the-x-files-gethesemane-review/.

38. *The X-Files*: Redux II, 5X02.

39. *The X-Files*: Redux II, 5X02.

40. It is a subtle arc but an arc nonetheless for Scully. "Beyond the Sea" presents her as faithful but the potential link between a Death Row murderer to her father on the other side troubles her, as do the anxieties presented at the end of "Revelations" after she believes she was destined by God to protect a young boy exhibiting signs of stigmata. After the murder of her sister Melissa and the lack of justice for her killers, not to mention her cancer diagnosis, it feels earned by "Redux II" that Scully would believe she had misplaced her faith and seek it in her greatest time of need.

41. At the behest of Mulder working on information provided by the Cigarette-Smoking Man, no less. This "miracle" cure and the Smoking Man's fairly creepy tether to Scully as a result would be revisited in Season 7's "En Ami," and much later in "My Struggle III" in Season 11, which stoked significant fan ire. That, however, is another story...

42. *The X-Files*, The Sixth Extinction, 7X01.

43. The alien creature who crashes in a UFO in Season 1's "Fallen Angel" resembles the Predator more than anything else; a transparent blur that can cut through laser grids.

44. Memorably seen in Season 2's "Duane Barry," but they also appear (in slightly more satirical terms) in Season 3's "Jose Chung's 'From Outer Space.'" The

Notes—Chapter 3

Grey itself will reappear in a host of episodes across the run of the series in various forms and guises.

45. This is first suggested as far back as Season 2's "Colony," and clarified in arch terms in "Talitha Cumi."

46. Michael Shermer nonetheless argues the ancient aliens theory is based on a scientific fallacy: "Ancient aliens theory is grounded in a logical fallacy called argumentum ad ignorantiam, or "argument from ignorance." The illogical reasoning goes like this: if there is no satisfactory terrestrial explanation for, say, the Nazca lines of Peru, the Easter Island statues or the Egyptian pyramids, then the theory that they were built by aliens from outer space must be true." Michael Shermer, How Beliefs in Extraterrestrials and Intelligent Design Are Similar, Scientific American.

47. A character named Gibson Praise, played by Jeff Gulka, who would go on to be something of an elusive "Rosetta Stone" in Mulder's search for the truth and only appear when the plot particularly required him to.

48. "Having searched everywhere for confirmation of the feared and desired conviction that "they're here," in other words, that extra-terrestrial life exists, Mulder finds that he himself is partly alien to the core of his being. In *The X-Files* mythology, the dividing line between the human and the alien begins to blur, and in fact (as the show has begun to suggest towards the end of the sixth series) the distinction between the two has always been blurred from the very beginning of life of Earth. We have met the alien enemy, and it is us." Dr. Peter Knight, *Conspiracy Culture: From Kennedy to* The X-Files (London: Routledge, 2001), 178.

49. It speaks to the nature of death and rebirth that the beginning of *Prometheus* shows the Engineer give his own life in a ritualistic sense to merge his DNA with the primordial soup that existed at the dawn of time. For new life to bloom, another must be extinguished.

50. The journey to Mulder's "brain disease" across the Biogenesis trilogy is nebulous to say the least. The trigger appears to have been his infection in "Tunguska" in Russia with the Black Oil, the aforementioned alien life force, which he survives thanks to a Russian vaccine. This is only vaguely alluded to, however, and it is left to audiences to truly try and connect the mythological and narrative dots.

51. Ancient apocalypse literature goes as far back as the Assyrians, who were according to Riley Winters: "A powerful Mesopotamian culture that lasted for roughly two thousand years. A tablet was found dating back to sometime between 2800 and 2500 BCE that bears the first known prophecy of the end of days. According to the translation, it claims that the earth was in its final days in those years, and that the world was slowly deteriorating into a corrupt society that would only end with its destruction. Though it is not known who wrote this inscription, and where specifically the tablet came from, it is a fervent example of how far back in human history apocalyptic prophecies (of the end of) world began." Riley Winters, "How it Ends: The Ancient Roots of Doomsday Prophecies and End of the World Beliefs," *Ancient Origins*, July 15, 2018. https://www.ancient-origins.net/history/ancient-roots-doomsday-prophecies-and-end-world-beliefs-002571.

52. The Tree of Knowledge appears in many of the religions which existed on the alien spacecraft Scully discovers. The Biblical story in Genesis concerns the original sin that leads to the fall of man, while in Judaism the fruit of the tree represents the union of good and evil as a combined force when picked. Islam removes the "knowledge" from the derivation and replaces it with "immortality," but the story of God's warning about the fruit remains similar.

53. A pair of much weaker episodes than the Biogenesis trilogy, they nonetheless serve as a coda which combines the ancient aliens aspect of the Mytharc to the "new Mytharc" surrounding Scully's baby, as it concerns a religious cult who discovered another craft in Canada and abduct William believing he is either destined to save humanity or lead the returning aliens to destroy it.

54. Darren Mooney argues that these episodes, the culmination of the new Mytharc introduced alongside "Mulder

Notes—Chapter 3

replacement" John Doggett (played by Robert Patrick), for the eighth season, is decidedly *anti-religious*: "At first glance, "Essence" and "Existence" play out as a repetition of the classic nativity story, with Scully giving birth to her miraculous son in the wilderness. But there is something quite subversive in how "Existence" incorporates those familiar elements. For the first time, Mulder acknowledges that this is not a virgin birth; although guided to Scully by a light in the sky, it is implied that Mulder was chasing an alien ship. Mulder and Scully agree William is a more generic sort of miracle. William is not the messiah, but a child born of the love of a man and a woman." Darren Mooney, *Opening the X-Files: A Critical History of the Original Series* (Jefferson, NC: McFarland, 2017), 149.

55. This feels like a searing, and timely, warning about the dangers of climate change coded into "My Struggle IV." If even an alien force we cannot begin to fight believe our world no longer worth invading and conquering, should we be taking a look in the mirror at what we've become?

56. The show was also co-created by Jeffrey Lieber, who had no direct involvement in the series' development beyond the concept, which was originally a very different idea pitched to ABC head Lloyd Braun called "Cast Away," taking a cue from the well-received Tom Hanks starring, Robert Zemeckis film of the same name in 2000. Lieber envisaged his take as a *Lord of the Flies*–style story, a: "realistic show about a society putting itself back together after a catastrophe." David Bernstein, "Cast Away," *Chicago Arts & Culture*, July 23, 2007.

57. Quite a few have tried. Lostpedia. fandom.com, Bibliography.

58. *Game of Thrones*, of course, has an immense literary tapestry from its source material books and world-building to build off, whereas *Lost* started with a television pitch alone.

59. Exemplified by the still-active online resource Lostpedia and its message board forums, which would scrutinize and analyze every facet of each episode of the series as they debuted.

60. Although not the first time we see Jacob, the episode in which Ben takes Locke to see Jacob is called "The Man Behind the Curtain," an allusion to *The Wizard of Oz* which is even mentioned inside the episode.

61. For more on Jack's journey, see Chapter 3.

62. Q is essentially the mythological trickster God from folklore, a galactic Loki played by John de Lancie. A being of limitless power, Q appears to the crew of the USS Enterprise-D in *The Next Generation* primarily (plus he occasionally drops into spin-off series *Deep Space Nine* and *Voyager*) and taunts them with his omnipotence, often attempting to display and prove human failure through the Enterprise crew members.

63. Egyptian mythology repeatedly appears in *Lost*. The symbols on the countdown timer in the Hatch are hieroglyphs. Ben uses a secret door covered in hieroglyphs to summon the Smoke Monster in "The Shape of Things to Come." We see ancient tunnels which lead to an Egyptian chamber in "Dead is Dead" and the Temple on the Island is most likely of ancient Egyptian origin.

64. The Man in Black has appeared frequently across popular culture. *Men in Black*, the 1997 science-fiction blockbuster starring Will Smith and Tommy Lee Jones, plays off the urban legend of the "men in black'; sinister government agents who in UFO folklore visit people who witnessed possible extra-terrestrial craft or were abducted by them, to keep their mouths shut. Johnny Cash, one of the greatest singer songwriters in American history, was often referred to by this moniker (thanks to his all black dress sense); *Westworld*'s principal antagonist goes by this name and Stephen King popularized it in his books, *The Dark Tower* series and *The Stand*, as the name of a mythological Devil figure also known as Randall Flagg. "Stories of 'men in black' have parallels to strange people who visit those who have come into contact with monsters. Peter Rojcewicz sees both resemblances and differences between the descriptions of the men-in-black and more traditional appearances of the devil. He raises the question

Notes—Chapter 3

of whether the visits of the men-in-black can, at times at least, be considered a kind of psychological drama." James R. Lewis, *The Gods Have Landed: New Religions from Other Worlds* (State University of New York Press, 1995), 218.

65. *Lost*, Across the Sea, 6X14.

66. Based on comments made by Lindelof and Cuse, we can reasonably assume the episode takes place around the time of Christ, but no precise date is given.

67. *Lost*, Across the Sea, 6X14.

68. In Greek mythology, Gaia is considered the ancestral mother of all life, bearing the Titans themselves who would go on to form the polytheistic Olympian pantheon of Gods. In this sense, if we consider the Island along similar lines, the character of Mother could almost be a twisted, symbolic inversion of the healing Goddess.

69. For a show obsessed with "rules," quite why Jacob can leave the Island and the Man in Black cannot is never made particularly clear. In "There's No Place Like Home Part 3" there is the suggestion he appears on the freighter in the guise of Christian, and even in the same guise perhaps appears off-Island in "Something Nice Back Home." Who knows?

70. See Chapter 3.

71. *Lost* is a show built on interconnectivity. From Season 1, Lindelof and Cuse go out of their way to tie many of the crash survivors pasts together; for instance, the father of the brother-sister Boone and Shannon ends up being brought into the same hospital Jack works after a car crash, the same crash involving Jack's future wife Sarah. The show increasingly suggests this is the work of Fate, stitching these people's destinies together on their journey toward the Island.

72. Jen Chaney makes the point that sitcoms over the last two decades in particular have depicted the flawed side of parenthood: These days on television, parents are stupid at home regardless of their economic status. That's not because they have abdicated their family for the world, but because they either need or want to work, have a strong desire to be defined by more than the fact that they are mothers or fathers, and are more fully fleshed-out humans who do what humans do: screw up. They're not simply parents, they're also people still trying to figure stuff out. The idea that parents want to do more than just parent is far more universally accepted, in real life and on TV, than it was even 20 years ago, and that certainly has had an impact on the way parental figures are written and portrayed on sitcoms." Jen Chaney, "The Rise of the Messed-Up Parent on TV," *Vulture*, Jan. 19, 2018. https://www.vulture.com/2018/01/the-rise-of-the-messed-up-parent-on-tv.html.

73. This goes back to the Fate idea, something that drives *Lost*'s Mytharc. It becomes clear first in the Desmond time travel mini-arc, which begins in "Flashes Before Your Eyes" in Season 3, where the all-knowing Eloise Hawking suggests time cannot be changed and "whatever happened, happened." This goes on to inform the entire pre-destination paradox of the character Daniel Faraday and Season 5, which even has an episode called "Whatever Happened, Happened." The characters in *Lost* are repeatedly made aware they have no free will and that everything in pre-determined. Ironically, the only character with that free will, in terms of their manipulation of events on and off the Island, is the Man in Black.

74. "Earning the 'woke' badge is a particularly tantalizing prospect because it implies that you're down with the historical fight against prejudice. It's a word that arose from a specific context of black struggle and has recently assumed a new sense of urgency among activists fighting against racial injustices in Ferguson, Sanford, Baltimore and Flint. When Black Lives Matter activists started a website to help recruit volunteers to the cause, they called it StayWoke.org. 'Woke' denotes awareness, but it also connotes blackness. It suggests to white allies that if they walk the walk, they get to talk the talk." Amanda Hess, "Earning the Woke Badge," *New York Times Magazine*, April 19, 2016.

75. There is a consistent sense that Jacob has grown tired of life, tired of waiting for his successor. He does not fight his death in "The Incident pt 2" in any way.

76. *Lost*: The End, 6X17.

77. The ritual seems to suggest acceptance of the guardianship of the Heart, of

Notes—Chapter 3

the Island itself. Jacob recites the same Latin phrase Mother said to him thousands of years previously to Jack: *"Nam non accipimus hoc quasi vulgarem potionem, sed ut ille sit quasi unus mecum"* which translated into English means, "Because we don't accept this as a simple potion, but so that he shall be as one with me." The phrase may be less important than the drinking of sacred water as later Jack passes on the guardianship to Hurley successfully without reciting it.

78. The name Jacob, however, is repeatedly invoked with the same grandness as the word God throughout the series, and Jacob's absence until the final season adds to the distant mystique of the character. The name Jacob was undoubtedly no mistake by Lindelof and Cuse, as it explictly references Genesis 27:36, having "supplanted" his elder brother by buying his birthright. "And he said, Is not he rightly named Jacob? for he hath supplanted me (יַעְקְבֵנִי) these two times: he took away my birthright; and, behold, now he hath taken away my blessing."

79. This was, of course, the final taunt in *A New Hope* of Obi-Wan to his former protege Anakin Skywalker before he is indeed cut down, becoming a spiritual guide as part of the Force to Luke Skywalker. Jacob, in Season 6, fulfils a similar role to a number of the characters as they battle the Man in Black. *Star Wars* allusions are all over *Lost* generally; indeed Season 5's "Some Like It Hoth" is a deliberate pun which details a key plot point for Hurley connected to *The Empire Strikes Back*.

80. As did, cheekily, the credits at the end of the series finale titled, appropriately, "The End."

81. *Lost* is as unsubtle about this as it is muddled. The man who delivers the revelation of this, through Jack to the audience, is his father. His name? Christian Shepherd. Jack, naturally, takes the longest to become "woke" to the fact he is essentially dead and is reuniting with the most important people in his life. This takes place in a Christian church. *Lost* begins as non-denominational and ends as a fully Christian parable, even if it avoids specific religious terminology. The inference is clear. Yet on a character level, it is inconsistent. Certain key people in the lives of the main characters are missing. The show tries to push onto us meaning which, in some cases, just doesn't exist, or feels cheap. It is as inconclusive an ending as you may expect from *Lost*, one which ends the chapter in life to begin the same one after death.

82. *Lost,* The End, 6X17.

83. Jack coined the phrase "Live together, die alone" as early as Season 1's "White Rabbit," as a catchphrase for the series' themes it repeatedly bears out in the Mytharc and structure of the series.

84. While the Swan is the most key station, otherwise known as the Hatch where a significant amount of Season 2 takes place, the other stations all play key roles in some form or another across the series—the Flame, the Arrow, the Orchid and so on.

85. Time travel is key to the entire structure of *Lost*. The whole narrative essentially takes place over fractured time periods, whether the flashbacks (many of which sketch in mythological details, particularly later in the series) and flashforwards, and in key storylines from Season 1 onwards which suggest the Island exists out of time. Writer David Fury admits it was going to originally be more explicitly referenced early in Season 1: "There was an exchange (pitched by J.J. when he and I broke the story) in an early draft of "Solitary" when Rousseau tells Sayid she had been part of a research team. Sayid asks her what they were researching. She replies: "Time." The network saw that draft and asked us to remove the line. They were very timid about anything that smacked of Sci-Fi during the first season." Lostpedia.fandom.com, "The Lostpedia Interview: David Fury." https://lostpedia.fandom.com/wiki/The_Lostpedia_Interview:David_Fury.

86. The Frozen Donkey Wheel was the only "codename" applied to the *Lost* seasons which directly referenced an actual element from within the show itself. See Notes Chapter 3 (72) for more on *Lost*'s season codenames.

87. "Exotic matter is a hypothetical kind of matter that has both a negative

Notes—Chapter 3

energy density and a negative pressure or tension that exceeds the energy density. All known forms of matter have positive energy density and pressures or tensions that are always less than the energy density in magnitude. In a stretched rubber band, for example, the energy density is 100 trillion times greater than the tension. A possible source of exotic matter lies in the behavior of certain vacuum states in quantum field theory (see Casimir effect). If such matter exists, or could be created, it might make possible schemes for faster-than-light travel, such as stable wormholes and the Alcubierre warp drive." Exotic matter, davidddarling.info.

88. encyclopedia.com, "Dharma."

89. Albert Grünwedel, *Buddhist Art in India* (London: Quaritch, 1901), 67.

90. Which according to producers Cuse and Lindelof reveal the word "underworld"—a clear reference to the Smoke Monster's usage and passage through ancient tunnels on the Island, likely created by the Egyptians in antiquity.

91. The derivation of "Taweret" roughly means "she who is great" or simply "great one." considered a common pacificatory address to dangerous deities. Geraldine Pinch, *Magic in Ancient Egypt* (London: British Museum Press, 1994), 39.

92. Mother is a Smoke Monster remains very much just a theory, with no precise evidence to suggest this is the case, but the implication is that one middle-aged woman (however psychotic) slaughtered and burned an entire camp of men in scenes which are quite reminiscent of what the Monster was known to do. It is difficult to ignore the parallels. But, as with everything else when it comes to Mother, every answer would just lead to another question....

93. The first notable example would be *The Next Generation*'s Season 3–4 bridging episodes "The Best of Both Worlds," a seminal *Star Trek* story in which Captain Jean-Luc Picard is assimilated into one of the deadly Borg. The only significant follow up this gets on television is in "Family," the episode directly after the two-part story.

94. Ryan Britt, "Is This the Smoking Gun Proving *Deep Space Nine* Ripped Off *Babylon 5*?" Tor.com, Feb. 26, 2013. https://www.tor.com/2013/02/26/is-this-the-smoking-gun-proving-deep-space-nine-ripped-off-babylon-5/.

95. As *Deep Space Nine* was considered an unconventional series, it was born in times marked by a Presidency that was in and of itself unconventional. "It is probably the case that few Clinton historical retrospectives will get very far before noting that this was only the second American President to suffer the disgrace of impeachment. It is evident from the presidency of his successor that any harm Clinton did to the institution of the presidency was, all things considered, rather meager, as the younger Bush has amassed an extraordinary degree of power in that office. But the damage done to Clinton's place in history is far more pronounced and probably permanent. Future historians will likely evaluate not just what Clinton did, but also what he did not accomplish, because he was tied-up in a second-term struggle for political survival. It is this consideration of "what might have been" that may be Clinton's greatest obstacle to gaining historical stature." Russell L. Riley, *Bill Clinton: Impact and Legacy*, UVA Miller Center.

96. "I mean, how it was presented to the country initially is how it continues to be referred to today, which is an affair, the Lewinsky affair. But by virtue of using that word, one assumes it was in some way an actual relationship of sorts—romantic, physical, whatever, it was a relationship—which couldn't be farther from the truth. What it was was a series of encounters to address a physical need, a use of a young girl, and then the sort of cold, hard dismissal of her on any human level." Amy Chozick, "Clinton Scandal of '90s Resurfaces with Papers," *New York Times*, Feb. 10, 2014.

97. "By far, the end of the Cold War is the dominate event of the decade and, indeed, the later half of the twentieth century. From a geo-political standpoint, the most significant factor to emerge is the preeminence of the West collectively as the dominant world power. In military terms, the West is the coalition forged by the United States to confront Saddam Hussein

Notes—Chapter 3

in the Gulf War. That war demonstrated the superiority of Western military technology and ended America's self-imposed, post–Vietnam restraint from an active and interventionist foreign policy." Frederick C. Cuny, "Humanitarian Assistance in the Post-Cold War Era," *Frontline*, July 1993.

98. *Wagon Train* was a TV series that aired on ABC between 1957 and 1962, depicting the adventures of a wagon train as it makes its way from St. Joseph Missouri across the Mid-Western plains and the Rocky Mountains to California, plus the trials and tribulations of the series regulars who conducted the train through the American West. "Roddenberry's model, though, was *Gulliver's Travels*: social, political, even philosophical commentary disguised as adventure. Yet instead of Swift's savage indignation, Roddenberry had an unsentimental optimism. His earthlings of the future were the same old unstable compounds of good and evil, but they hadn't destroyed themselves, and darned if they'd let ornery aliens push them or anybody else around. Good to hear, especially with Vietnam and the arms race going on." "Gene Roddenberry's Wagon Train to *Star Trek*," *Newsweek*, March 3. 2016.

99. Like the monotheistic faiths mentioned above, these are all still practiced today in the early 21st century.

100. On Aug. 2, 1943, while flying B-17E-BO, 41-2463, "Yankee Doodle," out of Espiritu Santo, the plane Roddenberry was piloting overshot the runway by 500 feet (150 m) and impacted trees, crushing the nose, and starting a fire, killing two men, bombardier Sgt. John P. Kruger and navigator Lt. Talbert H. Woolam. Roddenberry was absolved of any responsibility in the official report. Alexander, David, Star Trek *Creator: The Authorized Biography of Gene Roddenberry* (New York: Roc, 1995).

101. It is only in Peter David's tie-in novel, "Q-Squared," that Trelane is explicitly tied, canonically, into the Q Continuum. In TOS, Trelane remains indicative of an idea Roddenberry would go on to explore in Q twenty years later in *The Next Generation*'s pilot episode "Encounter at Farpoint."

102. Khan's master plan is the perversion of a terraforming project called, haughtily, Genesis. Writer Nicholas Meyer fills the picture with religious allusions; the newly formed planet Genesis having its own Edenic innerspace, Spock's sacrifice and rebirth in this Garden of Eden, or at least hints of it that will play out in sequel *The Search for Spock*, and Kirk's own personal rebirth over the course of the film. Meyer appears much more sympathetic to this Christian parable than Roddenberry was.

103. He is also, again in tie-in fiction, linked to the cosmic Q continuum. He is in fact 0, an inter-dimensional being of immeasurable power, who in the Q-Continuum trilogy threatens the entire universe. Again, *The Final Frontier* merely paints him as a warped, unsympathetic allegory of the Old Testament Biblical almighty.

104. This theme ripples across the entire run of the series, from the Bajoran reconstruction efforts following the withdrawal of their fascist occupiers Cardassia in the early seasons, to the genocide perpetrated (ironically) on the Cardassians later at the end of the Dominion War.

105. Kirk's character skirts the Monomyth, particularly in the three-arc movie story of *The Wrath of Khan*-*The Search for Spock*-*The Voyage Home*. He sacrifices himself and his potential future in order to go on a dangerous quest, to an unknown land, in order to save the life of Spock. It's a religious transformation in many ways for Kirk, one of personal rebirth—he grows younger, in many respects, over these movies, even while William Shatner is visibly ageing.

106. And given Patrick Stewart has returned to the role, Picard's story is not yet over.

107. *DS9*: Emissary, 1X01.

108. *Deep Space Nine* never entirely, by default of the concept, followed this mantra as any of the other series did or have. Season 3, when the Defiant was introduced, did allow them episodes such as "Meridian" or "Children of Time," but the show primarily eschewed traditional exploration in favor of character stories or narratives that would forward ongoing plots within the series' ensemble.

109. Who goes on to be the next Kai

Notes—Chapter 3

and a recurrent, dangerous thorn in Sisko and Kira's side.

110. *DS9*: The Siege, 2X03.

111. Though a working staff writer under Michael Piller since Season 3 of *The Next Generation*, Behr became joint show runner at the beginning of *DS9* Season 3 and then full show runner for the duration of the show by Season 3's "The Die Is Cast." That could be as symbolic a title for Behr's arrival as the show could find, as from then on the series began to demonstrate a much larger narrative plan for the duration of its run.

112. *TNG* episodes such as "Sins of the Father," the "Redemption" two-parter and the "Birthright" two-parter.

113. The aforementioned "Family" is the only episode to deal with the psychological fallout from Picard's experience (despite several future Borg appearances on *TNG*), but the second *TNG* movie, *First Contact*, very much explores Picard's long-standing assimilation trauma.

114. *TNG* episodes such as "The Measure of a Man," "Datalore," "The Offspring," "In Theory," "Brothers." and the first movie, *Generations*.

115. *Voyager* flirted with a long-term recurring story arc in Season 2 with a veritable Cold War against the Kazon, a tribal group of alien antagonists, but later opted for recurring appearances of successful villains across seasons which forwarded their narratives—the Hirogen, for instance, in Seasons 4 and 7, or introducing the Borg at the end of Season 3 who would reappear sporadically up to and including the series finale "Endgame."

116. *DS9*: Shadows and Symbols, 7X02.

117. *DS9*: What We Leave Behind, 7X26.

118. "Once I had the locale, I began to populate it with characters, and sketch out directions that might be interesting. I dragged out my notes on religion, philosophy, history, sociology, psychology, science (the ones that didn't make my head explode), and started stitching together a crazy quilt pattern that eventually formed a picture. Once I had that picture in my head, once I knew what the major theme was, the rest fell into place. All at once, I saw the full five-year story in a flash, and I frantically began scribbling down notes."

Straczynski, J. Michael (January 24, 1995). "Re: ATTN JMS: Why Accelerate t," The J. Michael Straczynski Message Archive, originally from AOL.

119. Otherwise known as the primary "Dominion War" arcs—firstly between "A Call to Arms" and "The Sacrifice of Angels," in which the Dominion occupy the station, and finally the serialization of the final conflict between "Penumbra" and "What We Leave Behind," which even counting *Enterprise*'s fairly serialized Season 3 and *Discovery*'s equally serialized first two seasons, remains among the longest stretch of truly serialized, inter-connected episodes *Star Trek* has ever produced.

120. Episodes which took place in the "evil" Mirror Universe, first established in *The Original Series* episode "Mirror, Mirror"—Season 2's "Crossover," Season 3's "Through the Looking Glass," Season 4's "Shattered Mirror," Season 6's "Resurrection" and Season 7's "The Emperor's New Cloak." *Enterprise* would then get in on the action with the two-part "In a Mirror, Darkly" before *Discovery* devotes the latter half of Season 1 to a Mirror Universe set story.

121. Episodes which focused on the characters of Quark, Rom and Nog primarily, often more comedic tales emphasizing the silliness of Ferengi customs and society. Season 1's "The Nagus," Season 2's "Rules of Acquisition" (although it does have the distinction of being the first episode to reference the Dominion), Season 3's "Prophet Motive," and so on. Ferengi episodes, though not always successful, became a staple of *DS9*'s unique tapestry.

122. These episodes play off work began in the aforementioned *TNG* Worf episodes, in which the Klingon Empire returns in "The Way of the Warrior" to being an antagonist through Seasons 4 and 5, before circling back around as an ally.

123. A true example of a Mytharc within the broader Mytharc, the battle between Sisko and rebel Starfleet officer Michael Eddington is, even referenced in show, a play on Victor Hugo's *Les Misérables*, which takes place across four episodes in Seasons 3 to 5. Sisko is Javert to Eddington's Valjean, at least in the latter's interpretation.

Notes—Chapter 4

124. A primary example is the blockbuster Season 5 two-part episode "Dark Frontier" serving as a sequel to Season 3–4's "Scorpion," as well as *TNG* movie *First Contact*, as it reintroduces the villainous Borg Queen.

125. Matt Wright, "Ira Steven Behr Reveals How He Really Wanted *Star Trek: Deep Space Nine* To End + More." DS9 At STLV 2018, trekmovie.com, Aug. 21, 2018.

126. Frequently considered by *Star Trek* fans as the worst final episode of a *Trek* series in history, framed as it was not around the crew of Enterprise but rather *TNG*'s William Riker amidst *TNG*'s Season 7 episode "The Pegasus." It is as bizarre a storytelling choice as it sounds.

127. Matt Zoller Seitz, "The *St. Elsewhere* Finale at 30," *Vulture*, May 25, 2018. https://www.vulture.com/2018/05/the-st-elsewhere-finale-at-30.html.

Chapter 4

1. Genre in its dictionary definition is of course: "a style, especially in the arts, that involves a particular set of characteristics." But it also corresponds to a growing trend of labelling series in the science-fiction and fantasy genres, in the American TV landscape, as "genre." Perhaps more as a definition of shows which command a particularly loyal fanbase and cleave to a more detailed level of mythology that shows of other, as the definition goes, genres.

2. "It is no secret that for many years I was not exactly the biggest booster of ST. Having been in at the beginning before the beginning of the series, having been one of the first writers hired to write the show, I was wildly enthusiastic about the series as Gene Roddenberry had initially conceived it. (In fact, at the very first Nebula Awards banquet of the Science Fiction Writers of America, which I set up at the Tail O' The Cock here in Los Angeles, I arranged for a pre-debut screening of the pilot segment.) The show debuted on Sept. 8, 1966 and by December it was in trouble with NBC. The Nielsens were very low, and Gene asked me if there was anything I could do to get the popularity the show was experiencing in science fiction circles conveyed to the network. I set up "The Committee" and using the facilities of Desilu Studios, I sent out five thousand letters of appeal to fandom, urging the viewers to inundate NBC with demands that the show be kept on the air." Harlan Ellison, "Harlan Ellison's Watching" (Los Angeles: Underwood-Miller, 1988).

3. Star Trek.com Staff, Bjo Trimble—The Woman Who Saved *Star Trek* Pt 1, Star Trek.com, Aug. 31, 2001.

4. Fanlore.org, *Star Trek* Lives! (convention).

5. As of writing, there are two *Star Trek* movies in development. The next in the series after *Star Trek Beyond* featuring the "Kelvin timeline" crew from the J.J. Abrams-led reboot films, reputedly set to be a time-travel story featuring Chris Hemsworth as Kirk's father George. The other is believed to be Quentin Tarantino's next project, featuring the same crew. As it stands, nobody knows if either, both or neither of these projects will come to fruition.

6. See Chapter 4.

7. Peak TV is a term first uttered by network executive John Landgraf to describe the diversity and range of current television in the streaming era. "Like the best neologisms, this one has swiftly taken on a life of its own. When Landgraf said "peak TV," he was trying to name a problem. Nearly 400 original series aired in 2015, and that number will get higher in 2016. From Landgraf's perspective, this volume is keeping audiences from finding good series they would enjoy, and this is unsustainable on the network end of things. He went so far as to predict a future contraction in original programming. But peak TV has caught on as a description more than as a warning and that's because it's perfectly expressive. There is an insane amount of good television out there, and like Everest (and far lesser climbs), it can be genuinely overwhelming." Willa Paskin, "The TV Club, 2015," *Slate*, Dec. 23, 2015.

8. HBO, Netflix, Amazon, Hulu to name but a few, plus now Disney and in the near future Apple, both of whom could dwarf and consume the competition.

9. Given Season 1 ends with the Dis-

Notes—Chapter 4

covery coming face to face with the USS Enterprise, and the crew of Captain Christopher Pike in the era before the original pilot episode "The Cage" (before all of the characters and actors but Spock and Leonard Nimoy were replaced), *Discovery* subsequently in Season 2 told a story involving Pike's Enterprise which fits inside *Star Trek*'s all-important established canon.

10. Later, by the final *Original Series* movie *The Undiscovered Country* and *The Next Generation*, "no man" became "no one" to reflect increasing sociological strides toward gender diversity and equality. It's a wonder the franchise didn't get there sooner.

11. A la five seasons, which of course *Star Trek* never had given its truncated cancellation at the end of Season 3.

12. As reflective of the fear surrounding portraying Spock with such depth, he went from being a "half-Martian" with a "slightly reddish complexion and semi-pointed ears" to a Vulcan who the executives at NBC were so concerned about, particularly his ears, that they feared Spock may look Satanic to audiences. Gene Roddenberry, Stephen E. Whitfield, "The Making of *Star Trek*," 1991.

13. Richard Zoglin, "A Bold Vision: How *Star Trek* First Made It to the Screen," *Time*, July 21, 2016.

14. The concept existed in the original 60s series, but it often didn't stop Captain Kirk beaming down to a primitive culture and getting caught up in all kinds of trouble, despite the protestations of his second in command, Spock. It was a key tenet of Federation exploration that was abided by with more vigor in *The Next Generation* and *Voyager* by Captains Picard and Janeway respectively.

15. Referencing the famed civil rights orator's speech. "I say to you today, my friends, so even though we face the difficulties of today and tomorrow, I still have a dream. It is a dream deeply rooted in the American dream. I have a dream that one day this nation will rise up and live out the true meaning of its creed: 'We hold these truths to be self-evident; that all men are created equal.'" Martin Luther King's "I have a dream" speech, Aug. 28, 1963.

16. Terry Lee Rioux, *From Sawdust to Stardust: The Biography of DeForest Kelley* (New York: Gallery Books, 2005), 308.

17. Jeffrey C. Goldfarb, The Cynical Society: The Culture of Politics and the Politics of Culture in American Life (University of Chicago Press, 1991).

18. Darren Mooney, Opening the X-Files: A Critical History of the Original Series, 11–26.

19. Star Trek.com Staff, "Exclusive Interview: Part III, Nicholas Meyer on Today's Trek," Sept. 24, 2014.

20. *Enterprise* ultimately becomes all about narrative continuity in its fourth and final season, primarily an exercise is reconciling certain points of canon in the history of *Star Trek*—the Eugenics Wars, Vulcan pre-history, the invention of the transporter system, Colonel Green and a rise of xenophobia just before the birth of the Federation. The list goes on. Coto even wanted to bring William Shatner back to *Star Trek* a decade after Kirk's death in *Star Trek Generations*: "Shatner would have played his Kirk counterpart from the Mirror Universe, which is a whole other story. We talked to Shatner and he was ready to do it. I thought that would have had a chance of really popping in the ratings and maybe opening up a new audience to come in and say, 'Hey, wow, look what this show is doing now.' Paramount wouldn't pay the money, and so that never happened. So that's a long way of saying there was a small hope (of getting a fifth-season green light) and the Shatner idea was one small way to maybe bring in a new audience or bring back our old audience. And we had ideas for the fifth season. I've talked a lot about them (previously), but I wanted to get into the Romulan conflict and I wanted to look at things that tied into *The Original Series* that we hadn't seen before, like the floating city (of Stratos), and the story behind that. There were a number of different things we wanted to do that we were still very excited about." "Manny Coto Talks *Enterprise* and *24*," StarTrek.com Staff, April 27, 2014.

21. Much like it took a World War Three in *Star Trek* that killed billions to trigger a human unity unlike anything known across recorded history, it took

179

Notes—Chapter 4

a devastating interstellar war with the Romulans to lay down the conditions for the Federation's formation. Though sadly Enterprise was cancelled before we had chance to witness the Earth-Romulan War play out on screen, backstory and developed mythology of *Star Trek* describes in detail a long, hard-fought war Starfleet almost lost, and how Archer ends up becoming the first President of the United Federation of Planets; an organization not unlike the United Nations in how it was constructed first as a peace-keeping force, uniting various races such as the Terrans, Vulcans, Andorians and Tellarites, under a mutually-beneficial treaty of protection and safeguarding. The tenets of exploration came later. This is explored in detail in Christopher L. Bennett's not necessarily canonical tie-in novels from Pocket Books.

22. Both of which depict the fallout from the so-named "post-atomic horror" of a WW3 which decimated human society around the mid-21st century. *First Contact* looks to the future in depicting the technological event that changed human history—the first successful warp flight and subsequent first alien contact with the Vulcans.

23. This is of course a reference to Russell Watson's much lambasted song "Faith of the Heart," which draped over the credits sequence for the first two seasons of *Enterprise*. It felt like a long road getting to end of the song...

24. Essentially *Star Trek*'s parallel to the invention of the airplane and air propulsion—the single most important technological breakthrough of the 21st century which propels humanity toward the *Star Trek* future we know.

25. Interestingly, however, as the 1990s wore on, *Star Trek* began introducing the idea that while Earth may be an Edenic, post-capitalist paradise, the same wasn't necessarily true for the rest of the Alpha Quadrant, as the galactic quarter of space inside which the Federation mainly exists. *Deep Space Nine* does a great deal of work in exploring the Ferengi civilization, and very clearly making them an allegorical mirror of 20th century capitalist humanity; characters such as Quark are driven solely by the acquisition of wealth, of profit, through a galactic currency known as "gold pressed latinum." He charges people in his bar for drinks, to gamble, and to use his holographic technology as a means of relaxation or, at its most unsavory, personal pleasure. Across the series, Quark also ends up frequently involved with terrorist, crime organizations and nefarious individuals from a multitude of races, none of whom cleave to the post-capitalist ideals of humanity and the Federation. The episode "Business As Usual" sees him significantly out of his depth attempting to broker trade with powerful arms dealers. This is a long way from Roddenberry's utopia not driven by an economic need for wealth, which hovered more sharply into focus in *The Next Generation* than the original 1960s series, perhaps as a reaction in 1987 to the neoliberal ascendancy across particularly the United States and the UK of conservative governments led by hawkish leaders who believed in free market economics as the ultimate expression of national prosperity. By the 90s, even *Star Trek* seemed to understand a world without capitalism was a world hard to swallow.

26. "I think *Enterprise* was embraced, but by certainly a smaller audience. It was not embraced by a lot of people. There are a lot of different guesses one could make about why. I always felt that whoever came up with the term "franchise fatigue" was right, that there was definitely some of that. There was just too much going on at the same time. By then, *DS9* had ended, *Voyager* was still on the air, a third *TNG* movie was coming out, and there was definitely a feeling that maybe we were pushing it. "Oh, my God, here comes another *Star Trek* show." It was the fourth *Star Trek* series in a decade. The prequel idea I think was a good idea. After *Voyager* we certainly weren't going to say, "OK, now it's time for a new show. *Voyager* is going to go off the air in May and in September you're going to get a new crew on a new ship in the same century." The idea of going back and learning a little something about what went on for the very first people who were stepping out into space ... it seemed to us to be a great idea. ... The show certainly had a great start. It got very good

Notes—Chapter 4

reviews and it had a huge audience for the first half a dozen episodes and then it started to slip. I could take the blame for it. I could put the blame into the scripts. I could put the blame into franchise fatigue. I don't know why it didn't work." Nathalie Caron, "*Star Trek* Producer Reveals the Reasons *Enterprise* Failed," *SyfyWire*, Dec. 14, 2012. https://www.syfy.com/syfywire/star_trek_producer_reveal.

27. Nicholas Meyer (director), *Star Trek VI: The Undiscovered Country*, 1991.

28. Peter W. Lee (editor), Captain Picard, President Wilson and the Reagan Era, Exploring Picard's Galaxy: Essays on *Star Trek: The Next Generation*.

29. In essence, a revival of 19th century economic liberal ideas that favor privitaization, austerity, deregulation and free trade, all designed to push forward the role of the private sector in a nation's economy. "In short, "neoliberalism" is not simply a name for pro-market policies, or for the compromises with finance capitalism made by failing social democratic parties. It is a name for a premise that, quietly, has come to regulate all we practice and believe: that competition is the only legitimate organising principle for human activity." Stephen Metcalf, Neoliberalism: the idea that swallowed the world, *The Guardian*, Aug. 18, 2017.

30. Michael W. Clune, "When Neoliberalism Exploded," *Salon*, March 9, 2013.

31. A telling example involved "The Bonding," an early third season spec script from future show runner Ronald D. Moore, in which Klingon security chief Worf befriends the grieving child of a fellow officer mortally wounded in the line of duty. Roddenberry took issue with the child's grief, claiming "he wouldn't cry" because humans had moved beyond such emotional reactions to death. Finding this assertion, even for a Utopian world, preposterous, Piller re-tooled the story to be about the child, Jeremy Aster, learning it was ok to feel grief for the mother he had lost and embrace a pain he was repressing. Roddenberry felt that story did not betray the Utopian principles of the series and allowed it to be made, but this typifies the struggles *Star Trek*'s sequel series had with trying to tell dramatic stories about character in a world where humans were meant to be, essentially, perfect. Michael Piller, Fade In: The Making of *Star Trek: Insurrection*, 2003.

32. Anthony Pascale, "Exclusive Interview: Ron Moore On Breaking Out of The Box," trekmovie.com, June 12, 2008. https://trekmovie.com/2008/06/12/exclusive-interview-ron-moore-on-breaking-out-of-the-box/.

33. Michael Piller, "Fade In: The Making of *Star Trek: Insurrection*," 2003.

34. Lynette Russell, and Nathan Wolski, "Beyond the Final Frontier: *Star Trek*, the Borg and the Post-colonial," *Intensities: The Journal of Cult Media*, 1 (spring/summer 2001). https://intensitiescultmedia.com/2014/08/27/beyond-the-final-frontier/.

35. For instance the non-corporeal Koinonians in "The Bonding," "Junior" the spaceborne life-form from "Galaxy's Child," or the coalescent organism from "Aquiel."

36. Note the immediate difference from *The Next Generation*. This was not a series about a starship spreading the neo-imperialist, scientific dogma across the galaxy, but rather a stationary piece about a space station hub attempting to operate as the reconstructive vanguard of a non-Federation world, against an alien species who they had previously been at war with. Though it never actually happened in the run of the series (only in subsequent tie-in fiction), part of the deal for helping with Bajor's reconstitution was their eventual membership into the Federation. Despite this far grittier and deeper political underbelly, itself charged with a religious aspect given Bajor's highly devout culture, the first two seasons still attempted to tell stories that could have—and sometimes were—been ported in from *The Next Generation* writers room.

37. Piller would later return to write the third *Next Generation* movie, *Insurrection*, about the making of which he wrote a book, Fade In. He sadly died in 2005 at the age of 57 of cancer. The book was published posthumously by his widow.

38. In this case an outwardly silly race of species called the Dosi, who the Ferengi via Quark do business with in "Rules of

Notes—Chapter 4

Acquisition," but it is typical of *Deep Space Nine*'s approach to introduce such a deadly villainous organization in such a low-key way. They would introduce the Dominion's foot soldiers, the Jem'Hadar, in a similar manner in the Season 2 finale, the first act of which is played for comedy.

39. Except in non-canon tie-in media, where in the novel *Worlds of Deep Space Nine: Volume 2*, they are revealed to be a genetically engineered offshoot of the symbiotic Trill species, best known via the main DS9 character Jadzia Dax.

40. Be it *Star Trek Into Darkness* telling a mirrored version of *The Wrath of Khan*, or even *Star Trek Beyond* sundering a destroyed *Enterprise* over an alien world, a la *The Search for Spock*. Both films expressly mirror or lightly copy scenes from *The Wrath of Khan* as part of their storytelling.

41. The official line is that Fuller was too busy developing the adaptation of Neil Gaiman's *American Gods* at the same time, but given he had long campaigned to develop a *Star Trek* series, after his involvement with the franchise as far back as *DS9* and *Voyager*, fans remain sceptical this is the whole story.

42. *The Original Series* episode "Errand of Mercy" suggests at historical conflict which has created a systemic tension between both the Klingons and the Federation. *Enterprise* would later establish certain reasons as to why contact had been minimal since the mid–22nd century between the two races.

43. Defined specifically as a samurai without a lord or master during the feudal period (1185–1868) of Japan. A samurai became masterless from the death or fall of his master, or after the loss of his master's favor or privilege. There are significant parallels between the Japanese samurai and Klingon warriors, indeed Barry Till describes them as a class who "lived by an ethical code known as bushido ("the way of the warrior")"—also the title of the *DS9* Season 4 premiere which introduces Worf to the show—"derived in large part from Chinese Confucianism, bushido was based on the principles of chugi (loyalty) and giri (moral obligation or duty)—first to the daimyo, then to family and society."

Though not an exact match culturally, many of the Klingon principles of an honorable death and service to their houses reflects feudal Japanese warrior culture. Barry Till, *The 47 Ronin: A Story of Samurai Loyalty and Courage* (San Francisco: Pomegranate, 2005).

44. It is important not to understate the importance of a *Star Trek* main character Captain being revealed as the enemy, however. In each series from the 1960s onwards, the Captain has not just been the rock at the heart of the show—from Kirk to *Enterprise*'s Jonathan Archer—but they have also been an inviolate, beyond reproach example of the Federation's moral and ethical nobility. To have this bastion of a role revealed to be an insider, be the very enemy the Federation battles against, is a powerful example of *Star Trek*'s attempt to deconstruct and place itself in a contemporary context.

45. In the tenth episode of Season 8 entitled "The Springfield Files," in which Mulder & Scully investigate a sighting Homer Simpson has of an alien being in the town, who turns out to be his spaced-out boss Mr Burns, who exudes a green alien glow thanks to years working in a nuclear power plant. Duchovny & Anderson provided their own voices for the episode, as does Leonard Nimoy playing himself in a framing device which lampoons his own paranormal documentary series, *In Search Of....*

46. In the UK these episodes were known as "The Unopened File" thanks to the name of its VHS release. Similar mythology episodes across the third, fourth and fifth series had home video releases under "File" names.

47. See Chapter 3.

48. Insiders typified by the titular Deep Throat, who was named after the informant who leaked information to Washington Post journalists Bob Woodward and Carl Bernstein that helped bring down the Nixon presidency. He was subsequently named as Mark Felt, a former FBI Assistant Director.

49. In real terms she is only absent from the series for one episode, "3," in which Mulder falls in with a sexy vampire cult, thereby proving he does not function well when Scully is out of the picture.

Notes—Chapter 4

50. Matt Hurwitz, and Chris Knowles, *The Complete* X-Files, 99.

51. Though it is somewhat jarring when X does appear in non-Mytharc episodes such as "Fresh Bones," ostensibly about voodoo. Deep Throat on occasion in Season 1 appeared in episodes which also did not link to the wider mythology, such as "Ghost in the Machine," and from Season 3 onwards the prevalence of informers appearing in episodes not concerning the alien mythology significantly decreased.

52. Spotnitz, Frank, Carter, Chris, Shiban, John, Manners, Kim and Gordon, Howard among others (2004). *Threads of Mythology* (DVD). 20th Century Fox Home Entertainment.

53. Annie Jacobsen. *Operation Paperclip: The Secret Intelligence Program to Bring Nazi Scientists to America* (New York: Little, Brown & Co., 2014).

54. Generally characterized as the historical period between the mid–20th century and the present which has been dominated politically, economically and culturally by the United States, in a similar manner that British Imperialism dominated the 19th and early 20th century.

55. Donald W. White, *The American Century: The Rise and Decline of the United States as a World Power*, Chapter One, The New York Times on the Web, 1996.

56. *The X-Files*: Redux II, 5X02.

57. Darren Mooney, *Opening the* X-Files, 55.

58. Sources vary as to whether this came from Napoleon, with numerous other historical figures such as Voltaire and Ralph Waldo Emerson cited as possible originators of the phrase. "What Is History But a Fable Agreed Upon?" quoteinvestigator.com.

59. The bomb was of course infamously dropped on the Japanese cities of Hiroshima and Nagasaki by President Harry S. Truman in 1947, which signaled the end of continued Japanese hostilities and the only time, to date, a thermonuclear weapon has been launched on a foreign territory.

60. MAD (as the acronym goes) is a military strategic doctrine based on the theory of deterrence, in which the threat of nuclear weapons being used against an enemy actively prevents the use of such weapons, for fear of retaliation and the subsequent annihilation of both sides. This doctrine held true throughout the Cold War between America and the Soviet Union from 1945–1991, and still holds true in nuclear states today.

61. "Unit 731 and Unit 100 were the two biological warfare research centres set up in spite of the Geneva Protocol of 1925 banning biological and chemical warfare. Led by Lieutenant-General Ishii Shiro, 3,000 Japanese researchers working at Unit 731's headquarters in Harbin infected live human beings with diseases such as the plague and anthrax and then eviscerated them without anesthesia to see how the diseases infected human organs. Because of the Unit's secret nature, there is no complete list of the experiments that were undertaken by Unit 731." Unit 731: Japan's Biological Warfare Project, Experiments, https://unit731.org/.

62. Leprosy is indeed curable thanks to multidrug therapy, offered freely by the World Health Organization, and the number of chronic cases have dropped from millions in the 1980s to hundreds of thousands globally today, over half in India alone.

63. Advisory Committee on Human Radiation Experiments, web.archive.org.

64. "The United States shall renounce the use of lethal biological agents and weapons, and all other methods of biological warfare. The United States will confine its biological research to defensive measures such as immunization and safety measures." Richard M. Nixon, "Statement on Chemical and Biological Defense Policies and Programs" on November 25, 1969.

65. Matt Hurwitz, and Chris Knowles, *The Complete* X-Files, 18.

66. The entire premise of *Fringe* hinges on the idea of scientific study which is divorced from the mainstream, via a questionable application of a scientific approach (which the show displays weekly through Walter Bishop). Examples have included Wilhelm Reich's work on the orgone or cold fusion, though some previous theories considered "pseudoscientific" have been subsequently accepted by mainstream scientists—plate tectonics or heliocentrism, for example. "The confusion

Notes—Chapter 4

between science and pseudoscience, between honest scientific error and genuine scientific discovery, is not new, and it is a permanent feature of the scientific landscape.... Acceptance of new science can come slowly." Michael W. Friedlander, *At the Fringes of Science* (New York: Perseus, 1998).

67. The Tyrell Corporation in the fictional universe created by Philip K. Dick in *Blade Runner*'s source novel "Do Androids Dream of Electric Sheep?" is a biotechnology corporation based in Los Angeles, named after its founder Eldon Tyrell. Their principal focus is on the production of android machines known as "replicants." Their slogan could well refer to many of the "monsters" in *Fringe*: "More human than human."

68. Broyles is essentially *Fringe*'s cross between *The X-Files* boss figure of Assistant Director Walter Skinner and one of Mulder's traditional informants, in how he both monitors Fringe Division and can act as a conduit of access into Massive Dynamic.

69. *Fringe*: Pilot, 1X01.

70. *Fringe*: The Ghost Network, 1X03.

71. *Fringe*: The Arrival, 1X04.

72. The name given to episodes of *The X-Files* which would feature a "monster," or creature who the agents would have to face, be it liver-eating mutant Eugene Victor Tooms or death fetishist Donnie Pfaster. Separate from the alien Mytharc episodes, "MOTW's" became a staple of *The X-Files* style, later inherited by shows such as Superman prequel series *Smallville*.

73. Tesla was perhaps the most pioneering futurist of the late 19th and early 20th centuries, best known for his contributions to the electricity supply system, but he was famously known to be involved in patents for technologies that have endured in popular culture, chiefly the "Tesla coil."

74. One of the more paranormal aspects of *Fringe*, even for that show, the Observers appeared in every episode through the character of September; a strange, briefcase carrying bald man in a suit and hat who viewers would enjoy trying to spot in the frame every week. Ultimately, the Observers were revealed later in the series to be future scientists from a possible 27th century, keeping track of key events across time.

75. A series which aired on FX between 2008 and 2014 about a Californian motorcycle gang/organized crime organization which was steeped in inter-generational mythology. The core narrative was loosely adapted from William Shakespeare's *Hamlet*.

76. A spin-off series from the *Terminator* cinematic franchise, *The Sarah Connor Chronicles* served as an alternate sequel to *Terminator 2: Judgment Day*, set in modern day 2007 (the year it debuted), in which Sarah and her son John Connor work to prevent the launch of SkyNet. Around the time travelling, pulp science-fiction concept, the show built a mythological backstory which questioned the humanity of artificial life. It was cancelled, on a cliffhanger left unresolved, at the end of Season 2.

77. Syndication, whereby TV and radio shows are broadcast on numerous station without going through a major broadcast network, was long the golden goose for American TV networks. If a show reached 100 episodes, it could be easily sold into syndication and the network would profit from lucrative "reruns" on networks across the country. *Fringe* ended up finishing exactly at 100 episodes—just getting it past the syndication finish line. This is a major reason why many American TV series ran to over 20 episodes per season for decades and lasted roughly 5 seasons—so they would be viable for syndication.

78. Specifically, *Fringe* was part of an initiative by FOX called "Remote-Free TV," which was designed to limit the amount of commercials on a network show, which added around 6 minutes to the run time of the first season. Other shows such as *The Sarah Connor Chronicles* and Joss Whedon's even shorter-lived *Dollhouse* were also part of the experiment. It was short lived and cancelled in 2009. Brian Stelter, "Fox TV's Gamble: Fewer Ads in a Break, but Costing More," *New York Times*, February 12, 2009.

79. Frank Spotnitz revealed that not only did they hope to use the Oval Office set from in-production political series *The*

Notes—Chapter 4

West Wing, but even considered having Martin Sheen appear as West Wing character, President Jed Bartlet, thereby tying the two shows into the same continuity. This surely remains one of the lost, glorious TV moments of the 2000s.

80. There is a slightly bizarre moment where an appearance in *I Want to Believe* of a framed photograph of Bush is underscored by the signature, six-note *X-Files* theme by Mark Snow. It is deliberately telegraphed to hint at conspiracy and is decidedly, and unusually, fourth-wall breaking.

81. Described in American terms by Mike Lofgren as "a hybrid association of government elements and parts of top-level industry and finance that is effectively able to govern the United States without reference to the consent of the governed as expressed through the formal political process." Mike Lofgren, "Anatomy of the Deep State," BillMoyers.com, February 21, 2014. https://billmoyers.com/2014/02/21/anatomy-of-the-deep-state/.

82. In this sense the episode is pointed akin to the "Redux Trilogy" of Season 5, which provides a less overtly science-fiction-based counterpoint to the conspiracy Mulder believed in for decades.

83. Season 10 does arguably display elements of retcon in how Chris Carter frames the alien conspiracy as aliens more being victims of heinous human villains, as opposed to the powerful, returning alien colonizers of the first nine seasons.

84. *The X-Files*: Tunguska, 4X08.

85. This twist was among the most contentious ever devised by Carter in the series' 25-year run. Another example of retconning is in how Carter ties the events of Season 7's "En Ami," in which the Cigarette Smoking Man drugged and potentially undressed Scully, to her pregnancy in Season 8. Many fans were unhappy and deeply troubled by the connotations that resulted.

86. *The X-Files*: The Blessing Way, 3X01.

87. And as of writing, unfinished, with still the last two books, *The Winds of Winter* and *A Dream of Spring*, still to be released at an unspecified date.

88. The Dothraki, modelled broadly after the Mongol hordes popularized by the armies of Genghis Khan in medieval history.

89. *Game of Thrones*: Hardhome, 5X08.

90. These events directly inform the beginning of Martin's story, with the eponymous Robert Baratheon a bored, lazy King on a throne surrounded by potential usurpers. The tyrant king, Aerys Targaryen, is the father of Daenerys, hence her claim to a throne she believed was taken in a staged coup.

91. The terrifying Ser Gregor Clegane, a.k.a. "The Mountain," who at the end of the Rebellion rapes and murders the future Queen, Elia Martell, and murders her baby with Prince Rhaegar Targaryen by grueling dashing it against a wall. The show, thankfully, spares showing us these horrific deaths.

92. Otherwise known as the "War of Five Kings," depicted in the second of Martin's books, *A Clash of Kings* and across the second and third seasons of *Game of Thrones*.

93. *Game of Thrones*, First of His Name, 4X05.

94. Typified most clearly in the 1980s by the Reagan Administration, a.k.a. "Reaganomics." Some commentators consider the trickle-down effect as nothing more than an economic theory as opposed to hard reality. Kimberly Amadeo, "Why Trickle-Down Economic Works in Theory But Not in Fact," *The Balance*, updated Oct. 29, 2018. https://www.thebalance.com/trickle-down-economics-theory-effect-does-it-work-3305572.

95. While the Renaissance was a rebirth of artistic expression and culture after centuries of warfare and religious stoicism, the "Enlightenment" found its roots in the philosophical and intellectual movements in Europe across the 17th and 18th centuries. They came loaded with ideas of liberty, tolerance and constitutional governance which paved the way for the significant French and American political revolutions of the 18th century, and the 19th century industrial revolution kick-started in Great Britain.

96. Martin claims his chief influences were the Wars of the Roses, with the houses of Stark and Lannister sitting it for the York and Lancaster houses, but

there are suggestions that the series does not entirely represent the Medieval era as it may appear to. Stephanie Pappas, "How Real Is the *Game of Thrones*' Medieval World?" *Live Science*, April 3, 2014.

97. This may seem a strange comparison but the *Alien* saga, while operating in a very different space to *Game of Thrones*, concerns economics in as keen a way. It is a world driven by flawed, egocentric geniuses, ruling over mega-corporations that have replaced the traditional paradigm of nation states and control over the direction of the humanity, through the march of capitalism. Much like *Star Trek* used technology in order to help employ a utopian future, the *Alien* franchise does the reverse; technology becomes the vehicle in which "the Company" as they are simply known in the first two *Alien* movies, later Weyland-Yutani, manage to control populations, the workforce, and particularly the exploration and exploitation of deep space. This isn't a world where humanity work for the betterment of a unified, utopian galaxy. This is a world saved only from dystopia by the cold, hard grip of corporate hegemony.

98. This became clear in May 2019 when *Game of Thrones* concluded on television, though whether Martin's source novels, which will, in an unprecedented situation, conclude after the TV show adaptation, will follow the same path from a storytelling perspective is anyone's guess.

99. Though the Wall certainly has traces of the Australian penal colony system of colonial Britain, given many of the workers are convicts, Martin's chief inspiration was a much older historical wall: "I was in England visiting a friend, and as we approached the border of England and Scotland, we stopped to see Hadrian's Wall. I stood up there and I tried to imagine what it was like to be a Roman legionary, standing on this wall, looking at these distant hills. It was a very profound feeling. For the Romans at that time, this was the end of civilization; it was the end of the world. We know that there were Scots beyond the hills, but they didn't know that. It could have been any kind of monster. It was the sense of this barrier against dark forces—it planted something in me. But when you write fantasy, everything is bigger and more colorful, so I took the Wall and made it three times as long and 700 feet high, and made it out of ice." Mikal Gilmore, "George R.R. Martin: The Rolling Stone Interview," *Rolling Stone*, April 23, 2014.

100. Google "R+L+J" and you'll see how far back fans were right when theorizing about this one....

Chapter 5

1. See Chapter 3

2. This happens quite unusually, through the minor, one-shot comedic character of Jose Chung, invented by writer Darin Morgan for *The X-Files* episode "Jose Chung's 'From Outer Space.'" When the character was then used in *Millennium*'s "Jose Chung's 'Doomsday Defense,'" both series then become inextricably linked by canon, to the point following *Millennium*'s cancellation in 1999, *The X-Files* brings Frank Black in to work with agents Mulder and Scully in Season 7's "Millennium" as a means of giving the character some sense of closure.

3. Chip Johanessen, and Ken Horton, who were more involved in the first than second season, and struggled to reconcile both wildly different interpretations of the series into a cohesive whole in Season 3.

4. Who ended up suing Chris Carter after they claimed he did not given them due credit for the television series adaptation. Carter claims he changed everything from the comic book while Hudnall and Paquette begged to differ. Carter ended up winning the right to keep his solo "written by" credit. Emily Farache, "Harsh Lawsuit for 'Harsh Realm,'" *ENews*, Oct. 19, 1999.

5. *Harsh Realm* very much feels like an extension of *The X-Files* episodes "Kill Switch" and "First Person Shooter," in Seasons 5 and 7 respectively, which both saw the integration of technology, humanity and virtual realities as dangerous and corrupting. Both episodes were co-written by pioneering cyberpunk novelist William Gibson, though he had no involvement in *Harsh Realm*.

6. So named after 16th century English philosopher Thomas Hobbes, best

known for his 1651 work *Leviathan*, and as one of the founders of modern political philosophy.

7. "Interview: Chris Carter talks *X-Files*, maintaining mystery of Mulder, Scully," *660News*, April 28, 2015. https://www.660citynews.com/2015/04/28/interview-chris-carter-talks-x-files-maintaining-mystery-of-mulder-scully/.

8. Lesley Goldberg "Chris Carter on Why Amazon Scrapped *The After*—and What's Next," *The Hollywood Reporter*, Jan. 15, 2016.

9. After the cancellation of *Star Trek* in 1969, Roddenberry developed numerous projects including *Genesis II*—produced as a pilot in 1973, the story of a 20th-century man thrown forward in time, to a post-apocalyptic future, by an accident in suspended animation—*The Questor Tapes*, which aired in 1974 as a TV movie and starred Robert Foxworth as an android searching for his creator (very much prefiguring the character of Data in *Star Trek: The Next Generation*)—and *Spectre*, a 1977 TV movie about a demon-hunting criminologist. None of these became series and *Battleground: Earth*, the fourth idea he never had chance to produce, became after his death *Earth: Final Conflict*.

10. Original star Kevin Kilner, who played Boone, left after just one season.

11. Very much following the Mulder and Scully template popularized by *The X-Files* around the same time.

12. David Kushner, "Behind the Scenes with *Heroes* Creator Tim Kring and 'Hiro,' Masi Oka," *Wired*, April 23, 2007. https://www.wired.com/2007/04/magkring/.

13. A strike that affected everything from *Lost*, which resulted in a truncated 14 episode Season 4, to even James Bond movie *Quantum of Solace*. Indeed writer Paul Haggis completed his draft of the script just two hours before the strike began. Terrence Rafferty, "A License to Pursue the Inner Bond," *New York Times*, Dec. 9, 2007.

14. Scion of the time travel story in his years writing *Star Trek* series and movies.

15. Original series creator Marc Guggenheim stepped down as show runner in Oct. 2009, replaced by David S. Goyer, who himself stepped away just five months later. Joyce Eng, "*FlashForward* Changes Showrunners," *TV Guide*, Oct. 21, 2009.

16. Vlada Gelman, "Comic-Con: *The Event* Won't Leave Viewers Completely Lost," *Vulture*, July 24, 2010. https://www.vulture.com/2010/07/comic-con.html.

Chapter 6

1. CBS is now developing no fewer than four *Star Trek* series with the intention of having some iteration of *Star Trek* available at all times, recalling the 1990s heyday. *Star Trek* spent 18 years between 1987 and 2005 on television in some form. Nellie Andreeva, and Dominic Patten, "CBS All Access Bosses On More *Star Trek* Series, *The Twilight Zone* Status, Stephen King & More—TCA," *Deadline Hollywood*, Aug. 6, 2018. https://deadline.com/2018/08/patrick-stewart-star-trek-franchise-expansion-plans-cbs-all-access-executives-interview-tca-1202440492/.

2. Joseph Russell, How online streaming is changing TV storytelling, Den of Geek, Oct. 8, 2015.

3. Though by his own admission, Crichton never intended to originally: "That's the only way I could get the studio to let me direct. People think I'm good at it I guess." "Author of 'Terminal Man' Building Nonterminal Career: CRICHTON; GELMIS, JOSEPH. *Los Angeles Times* (1923–Current File), Jan. 4, 1974: d12.

4. Disneyland perhaps being the clearest example of this today.

5. Crichton's first movie also depicts Romanworld and Medievalworld, while the sequel is called and depicts *Futureworld*. The TV series has so far depicted Futureworld alongside Westworld, plus Shogunworld (set in feudal Japan) and Rajworld (set in colonial India).

6. *Westworld*: Chestnut, 1X02.

7. "Woke" is a term described by Amanda Hess as being "the inverse of "politically correct." If "P.C." is a taunt from the right, a way of calling out hypersensitivity in political discourse, then "woke" is a back-pat from the left, a way of affirming the sensitive. It means wanting to be considered correct, and wanting everyone to know just how correct you are."

Notes—Chapter 6

8. This is given there has been a repeated effort to ensure these characters interact as little as possible in order to allow each of their shows to stand on their own two feet as an entity. *The Defenders* series, which brings Daredevil, Jessica Jones, Luke Cage and Iron Fist together, does follow on from narratives and villains established in *Daredevil* and *Iron Fist*, but it is hard to really define these shows as having a unified mythology they are servicing.

9. Chris Evangelista, "'Castle Rock' is an Anthology with a Different Type of Stephen King Story Each Season [Comic-Con 2018]," slashfilm.com, July 20, 2018. https://www.slashfilm.com/castle-rock-anthology/.

10. Erik Amaya, "Tim Kring Talks *Heroes* History," *Comic Book Resources*, November 18, 2008. https://www.cbr.com/tim-kring-talks-heroes-history/.

11. Andrew Liptak, "Bryan Fuller Originally Envisioned *Star Trek: Discovery* as an Anthology Show, *The Verge*, July 29, 2017. https://www.theverge.com/2017/7/29/16062088/bryan-fuller-star-trek-discovery-anthology-show-cbs.

12. In the pilot episode of *Deep Space Nine*, "Emissary."

13. *Star Trek Deep Space Nine*: Trials and Tribble-ations, 5X12.

14. See Chapter 5—The Mytharcs That Never Were.

15. "[SPOILERS] George Confirms the Title of the First Prequel Show," Reddit, October 2018.

16. "*Game of Thrones* Spin-off Series in the Works, HBO Confirms," *The Guardian*, May 4, 2017. https://www.theguardian.com/tv-and-radio/2017/may/04/game-of-thrones-spinoff-series-hbo.

17. Lesley Goldberg, "Will Amazon's *Lord of the Rings* Series Be TV's Most Expensive Show of All Time?" *The Hollywood Reporter*, Nov. 15, 2017. https://www.hollywoodreporter.com/live-feed/will-amazons-lord-rings-series-be-tvs-expensive-show-all-time-1058129.

18. Mike Cecchini, Joseph Baxter, Kirsten Howard, "*Lord of the Rings* TV Series: Showrunners Selected," *Den of Geek*, July 30, 2018.

19. Gregory Paul Williams, *The Story of Hollywood: An Illustrated History* (Hollywood: BL Press, 2012), 87.

20. Most popularly known under the umbrella of the British label, Hammer Film Productions, who rose to prominence in the 1950s and 1960s, particularly with the *Dracula* series starring Christopher Lee.

21. None of these films, in their modern day incarnations, have remained canonical to the films made in the past—though given the recent *Rise*, *Dawn* and *War for the Planet of the Apes* trilogy take place in the near-future, it is possible they hold to the same continuity as the Charlton Heston original.

22. Though the *Police Academy* series has not released a film since 1994, both the *Rocky* and *Halloween* franchises have received canonical sequels as late as 2018.

23. 1980's *Superman II*, 1983's *Superman III*, and 1987's *Superman IV: The Quest for Peace*, though many people would like to pretend that one never happened!

24. Indeed the 1990s *Next Generation* movies are among the first examples of the forthcoming cross-pollination of cinema and TV. Seeing the *Defiant* from *Deep Space Nine* in *First Contact*, or mentions of the Dominion War from that series in *Insurrection*, or even an appearance by *Voyager*'s protagonist Kathryn Janeway in *Nemesis*—these are all examples of the *Star Trek* universe being unafraid to cross big and small screen to provide audiences with a cohesive sense of continuity.

25. Wolfgang Petersen, the German director of blockbusters such as *Air Force One*, planned with Warner Bros an adaptation in 2002 of the original *Batman vs Superman* comic. It sadly never came to fruition. "Superman represents sort of everything clear and bright and noble. He represents our hopes and ideals. Batman, on the other hand, represents the dark and obsessive and vengeful side." Ryan J. Downey, "*Batman vs Superman* Director Hints at What to Expect from Superhero Struggle," *MTV News*, July 10, 2002. http://www.mtv.com/news/1456016/batman-vs-superman-director-hints-at-what-to-expect-from-superhero-struggle/.

26. Essentially the reverse of the pre-credits sequence made famous primarily

Notes—Chapter 6

by the James Bond series; the post-credit sequences in MCU films frequently provide teasers for upcoming films, introduce characters we haven't yet seen, or provide some comic relief. This technique has been subsequently adapted by other filmmakers and franchises.

27. So named in the UK to avoid confusion with the 1960s TV series, *The Avengers*, and the 1998 film version of the same name.

28. "'My feeling was that I experimented and experienced what I wanted to,' Norton said. 'I really, really enjoyed it. And yet, I looked at the balance of time in life that one spends not only making those sorts of films but then especially putting them out, and the obligations that rightly come with that.'" Ryan Gajewski, "Edward Norton Offers New Explanation for Not Playing Hulk in *Avengers* Films," *The Hollywood Reporter*, Oct. 23, 2014. https://www.hollywoodreporter.com/heat-vision/edward-norton-talks-avengers-he-743265.

29. Favreau discusses in the commentary for *Iron Man 2* how the scene of Tony drunkenly carousing during a party in his armor at home, only to be interrupted by Col. James Rhodes, is the closest he came to adapting the "Demon in a Bottle" storyline in the film. Jon Favreau, *Iron Man 2*, Marvel Studios, DVD commentary.

30. Kevin K. Durand (2009). Buffy Meets the Academy: Essays on the Episodes and Scripts as Texts. p. 59.

31. The reveal that villainous Nazi organization H.Y.D.R.A. had infiltrated S.H.I.E.L.D in *The Winter Soldier* is played out on Agents of S.H.I.E.L.D as the team led by Clark Gregg's Agent Phil Coulson (who appeared in several films up to *The Avengers*) go after the remainder of H.Y.D.R.A. in a way the movies simply didn't have the time to do.

32. Perhaps the most memorable being references to the "Battle of New York," the climax of *The Avengers*, as the team take on Loki and the alien Chitauri, which appear in early episodes of *Daredevil*—though the series quickly attempts to move away from those connections.

33. An infamous Marvel story in which many of the heroes we have spent years following are revealed to be alien Skrulls in disguise all along.

34. Most notably the kitsch 1960s *Batman* series, played more for often psychedelic comedy than action, starring Adam West as the Caped Crusader.

35. Comics writer Mark Waid had a better adjective: joyless. "Look, I know everyone involved in *Man of Steel* went into it with the best of intentions. And trust me, there are not rivers or coastlines on this planet long enough to measure just how much I wanted to love this movie. If you don't know me, you can't imagine. And there were certainly things to like. But there was no triumph to it. None of Superman's victories in this movie are in any way the kind of stand-up-and-cheer events you'd think necessary in a movie with Superman in it. Did it succeed in what it sent out to do? I think probably so. But what it set out to do, as it turns out, leaves me cold. With the exception of the first-flight beat—the smile Superman gets when he first takes to the air—it's utterly joyless. From start to finish. Utterly. Joyless. And I just have no interest in relentless joyless from a guy who can fly." Mark Waid, "*Man of Steel*, Since You Asked." *Thrillbent*, June 14, 2013. http://thrillbent.com/blog/man-of-steel-since-you-asked/.

36. The last to that point being Bryan Singer's 2006 love letter to the Richard Donner originals, *Superman Returns*.

37. Sentiments echoed by legendary comics writer Grant Morrison: "I don't want to sound like some fuddy-duddy Silver Age apologist but I've noticed a lot recently of people saying Batman should kill the Joker and, yeah, Superman should kill, he should make the tough moral decisions we all have to make every day. I don't know about you, but the last moral decision I made didn't have anything to do with killing people. And I don't think many of us ever have to make the decision whether or not to kill. In fact, the more you think about it, unless you're in one of the Armed Forces, killing is illegal and immoral. Why would we want our superheroes to do that?" Brian Truitt, "Sunday Geekersation: Grant Morrison Switches Superheroes," *USA Today*, July 28, 2013. https://www.usatoday.com/story/life/2013/07/28/

Notes—Chapter 6

grant-morrison-sunday-conversation-batman-wonder-woman/2586739/.

38. "A grim whirlwind of effects-driven action" is the Rotten Tomatoes aggregator consensus. *Batman vs Superman: Dawn of Justice*, rotten tomatoes.com. https://www.rottentomatoes.com/m/batman_v_superman_dawn_of_justice.

39. It's therefore interesting that Snyder chose to cast Jesse Eisenberg, who memorably played the controversial Facebook founder in David Fincher 2010 biopic *The Social Network*.

40. Though the *Dawn of Justice* credits sequence cheats slightly by giving us a whistle-stop tour of the key events in Bruce Wayne's parents death.

41. Dave Tach, "*Avengers: Age of Ultron*'s Most Confusing Scene and the Gun That Almost Killed It, Explained," *Polygon*, May 11, 2015. https://www.polygon.com/2015/5/11/8585809/avengers-ultron-thor-cave-scene-explanation-cut-farmhouse.

42. Chiefly the tragic suicide of Snyder's teenage daughter which led to him quitting the production and, in one of the most ironic turns, Joss Whedon replacing him to complete the rest of the film.

43. Borys Kit, and Aaron Couch, "Universal's 'Monsterverse' in Peril as Top Producers Exit (Exclusive)," *The Hollywood Reporter*, Nov. 8, 2017. https://www.hollywoodreporter.com/heat-vision/alex-kurtzman-chris-morgan-exit-universal-monsterverse-1055854.

44. Matt Krantz, Mike Snider, Marco Della Cava and Bryan Alexander, "Disney Buys Lucasfilm for $4 Billion," *USA Today*, Oct. 30, 2012. https://www.usatoday.com/story/money/business/2012/10/30/disney-star-wars-lucasfilm/1669739/.

45. Disney head honcho Bob Iger has suggested they maybe jumped the gun a little bit on the volume of *Star Wars* films: "I made the timing decision, and as I look back, I think the mistake that I made—I take the blame—was a little too much, too fast. You can expect some slowdown, but that doesn't mean we're not going to make films. J.J. [Abrams] is busy making [Episode] IX. We have creative entities, including [*Game of Thrones* creators David] Benioff and [D.B.] Weiss, who are developing sagas of their own, which we haven't been specific about. And we are just at the point where we're going to start making decisions about what comes next after J.J.'s. But I think we're going to be a little bit more careful about volume and timing. And the buck stops here on that." Matthew Belloni, "Bob Iger Talks Disney's Streaming Service, *Roseanne*, James Gunn and a Coming *Star Wars* 'Slowdown,'" *The Hollywood Reporter*, Sept. 20, 2018. https://www.hollywoodreporter.com/news/bob-iger-disneys-streaming-service-james-gunn-star-wars-slowdown-1145493.

46. Lesley Goldberg, "*Star Wars*: Jon Favreau's TV Series Details Revealed," *The Hollywood Reporter*, Oct. 3, 2018. https://www.hollywoodreporter.com/live-feed/star-wars-jon-favreaus-tv-series-details-revealed-1149194.

47. Megan Farokhmanesh, "The Tragic End of Telltale Games," *The Verge*, Oct 4, 2018. https://www.theverge.com/2018/10/4/17934166/telltale-games-studio-closed-layoffs-end-the-walking-dead.

48. Mike Williams, "The Rise and Fall of Telltale Games," *U.S. Gamer*, Sept. 25, 2018. https://www.usgamer.net/articles/the-rise-and-fall-of-telltale-games.

49. They adapted the *Monkey Island* format into the episodic *Tales of Monkey Island*, structured in five episode "chapters" canonically continuing the adventures of hapless wannabe pirate Guybrush Threepwood.

50. Which was the case with the *Game of Thrones* game, as you become entangled in the machinations of the previously unheard of House Forrester across the first few seasons of the series, weaving in and out of scenarios and locations from the series.

51. His intended last being 2015's *Metal Gear Solid V: The Phantom Pain*.

52. Though it appears Netflix still intend to produce the game through a new developer. Matt Patches, "Netflix Still Intends to Produce *Stranger Things* Game Despite Telltale Collapse," *Polygon*, Sept. 24, 2018. https://www.polygon.com/2018/9/24/17896054/netflix-stranger-things-telltale-game-update.

53. Jamie Lovett, "'Star Trek Fleet Command' Writer Teases Post-'Beyond' Kelvin Timeline Stories," *Comic Book*

Notes—Chapter 6

Nov. 26, 2018. https://comicbook.com/startrek/2018/11/26/star-trek-fleet-command-kelvin-timeline-post-beyond-stories/.

54. The kind of tower blocks and high rises designed to represent "futuristic" living in the questionable social housing reforms of the 1960s and 1970s.

55. Ernest Cline, *Ready Player One* (New York: Arrow, 2012), 113.

Bibliography

Adcox, John. "Can Fantasy Be Myth? Mythopoeia and *The Lord of the Rings*." JohnAdcox.com. http://johnadcox.com/Tolkien.htm/.

Agresta, Michael. "How the Western Was Lost (and Why It Matters)." *The Atlantic*, July 24, 2013. https://www.theatlantic.com/entertainment/archive/2013/07/how-the-western-was-lost-and-why-it-matters/278057/.

Alexander, David. Star Trek *Creator: The Authorized Biography of Gene Roddenberry*. New York: Roc, 1995.

Amadeo, Kimberly. "Why Trickle-Down Economic Works in Theory But Not in Fact." *The Balance*, updated October 29, 2018. https://www.thebalance.com/trickle-down-economics-theory-effect-does-it-work-3305572.

Amaya, Erik. "Tim Kring Talks *Heroes* History, Comic Book Resources." Nov. 18, 2008. https://www.cbr.com/tim-kring-talks-heroes-history/.

Andreeva, Nellie, and and Dominic Patten. "CBS All Access Bosses On More *Star Trek* Series. *The Twilight Zone* Status, Stephen King & More—TCA, Deadline." Hollywood, Aug. 6, 2018. https://deadline.com/2018/08/patrick-stewart-star-trek-franchise-expansion-plans-cbs-all-access-executives-interview-tca-1202440492/.

Attwell, Wendy. *The X-Files*: Season Eleven Is All a Dream and Here's Why!" *Set The Tape*, July 23, 2018. https://setthetape.com/2018/07/23/the-x-files-season-eleven-is-all-a-dream-and-heres-why/.

Baxter, Joseph. "*Lord Of The Rings* TV Series: Showrunners Selected." *Den of Geek*, July 30, 2018.

Belloni, Matthew. Bob Iger Talks Disney's Streaming Service, *Roseanne*, James Gunn and a Coming '*Star Wars*' "Slowdown." The Hollywood Reporter, Sept. 20, 2018. https://www.hollywoodreporter.com/news/bob-iger-disneys-streaming-service-james-gunn-star-wars-slowdown-1145493.

Bernstein, David. "Cast Away." *Chicago Arts & Culture*, July 23, 2007.

Britt, Ryan. "Is This the Smoking Gun Proving *Deep Space Nine* Ripped Off *Babylon 5*?" Tor.com, Feb. 26, 2013. https://www.tor.com/2013/02/26/is-this-the-smoking-gun-proving-deep-space-nine-ripped-off-babylon-5/.

Brookhouse, Christopher. *Framing Hitchcock: Selected Essays from the Hitchcock Annual*. Detroit: Wayne State University Press, 2002.

Calloway, Tyler. "Marvel Vs. DC: Exposing the Fan War Myth." *Geeks*, 2017. https://vocal.media/geeks/marvel-vs-dc-exposing-the-fan-war-myth.

Campbell, Joseph. *The Hero with a Thousand Faces*. Princeton, NJ: Princeton University Press, 1948.

Caron, Nathalie. "*Star Trek* Producer Reveals the Reasons *Enterprise* Failed." *SyfyWire*, Dec. 14, 2012. https://www.syfy.com/syfywire/star_trek_producer_reveal.

Bibliography

Chamberlain, Adam, and Brian A. Dickson. *Back to Frank Black: A Return to Chris Carter's* Millennium. London: Fourth Horseman Press, 2012.

Chaney, Jen. "The Rise of the Messed-Up Parent on TV." *Vulture*, January 19, 2018. https://www.vulture.com/2018/01/the-rise-of-the-messed-up-parent-on-tv.html.

Chozick, Amy. "Clinton Scandal of '90s Resurfaces with Papers," *New York Times*, February 10, 2014.

Cline, Ernest. *Ready Player One*. New York: Arrow, 2012.

Clune, Michael. W. "When Neoliberalism Exploded." *Salon*, March 9, 2013.

Couch, Aaron. "Universal's 'Monsterverse' in Peril as Top Producers Exit (Exclusive)." *The Hollywood Reporter*, Nov. 8, 2017.

Cuny, Frederick C. "Humanitarian Assistance in the Post-Cold War Era." *Frontline*, July 1993.

Downey, Ryan. J. "'*Batman vs Superman*' Director Hints at What to Expect from Superhero Struggle." *MTV News*, July 10, 2002. http://www.mtv.com/news/1456016/batman-vs-superman-director-hints-at-what-to-expect-from-superhero-struggle/.

Durand, Kevin K. (editor). *Buffy Meets the Academy: Essays on the Episodes and Scripts as Texts*. Jefferson, NC: McFarland, 2009

Ellison, Harlan. *Harlan Ellison's Watching*. Los Angeles: Underwood-Miller, 1988.

Eng, Joyce. "*FlashForward* Changes Showrunners." *TV Guide*, Oct. 21, 2009.

Evangelista, Chris. "*Castle Rock* Is an Anthology with a Different Type of Stephen King Story Each Season [Comic-Con 2018], *Film*, July 20, 2018. https://www.slashfilm.com/castle-rock-anthology/.

Farache, Emily. "Harsh Lawsuit for *Harsh Realm*." *ENews*, October 19, 1999.

Farokhmanesh, Megan. "The Tragic End of Telltale Games." *The Verge*, October 4, 2018. https://www.theverge.com/2018/10/4/17934166/telltale-games-studio-closed-layoffs-end-the-walking-dead.

Friedlander, Michael. *At the Fringes of Science*. New York: Perseus, 1998.

Gajewski, Ryan. "Edward Norton Offers New Explanation for Not Playing Hulk in *Avengers* Films." *The Hollywood Reporter*, Oct. 23, 2014.

"*Game of Thrones* Spin-Off Series in the Works, HBO Confirms." *The Guardian*, May 4, 2017.

Gelman, Vlada. "Comic-Con: *The Event* Won't Leave Viewers Completely Lost." *Vulture*, July 24, 2010. https://www.vulture.com/2010/07/comic-con.html.

Gilmore, Mikal. "George R.R. Martin: The Rolling Stone Interview." *Rolling Stone*, April 23, 2014.

Goldberg, Lesley. "Chris Carter on Why Amazon Scrapped *The After*—and What's Next." The Hollywood Reporter, Jan. 15, 2016.

Goldberg, Lesley. "*Star Wars*: Jon Favreau's TV Series Details Revealed." *The Hollywood Reporter*, Oct. 3, 2018.

Goldberg, Lesley. "Will Amazon's '*Lord of the Rings*' Series Be TV's Most Expensive Show of All Time?" *The Hollywood Reporter*, Nov. 15, 2017

Goldfarb, Jeffrey. C. *The Cynical Society: The Culture of Politics and the Politics of Culture in American Life*. University of Chicago Press, 1991.

Gottlieb, Sidney. *Framing Hitchcock: Selected Essays from the Hitchcock Annual*. Detroit: Wayne State University Press, 2002.

Gregory, Chris. *Be Seeing You: Decoding* The Prisoner. Luton, England: University of Luton Press, 1997. Grünwedel, Albert. *Buddhist Art in India*. London: Quaritch, 1901.

Hess, Amanda. "Earning the Woke Badge." *The New York Times Magazine*, April 19, 2016.

Bibliography

Hooton, Christopher. "*Lost* Writer Admits They Just Made It Up as They Went Along." *The Independent*, Jan. 14, 2015.

House, Wes. "We Can't Ignore H.P. Lovecraft's White Supremacy: Lovecraftian Narratives of Race Persist in Contemporary Politics." *LitHub*, Sept. 26, 2017.

"How Was *The Lord of the Rings* influenced by World War One?" bbc.co.uk.

Howard, Kirsten. "*Lord of The Rings* TV Series: Showrunners Selected." *Den of Geek*, July 30, 2018

Hurwitz, Matt, and Chris Knowles. *The Complete* X-Files. London: Titan Books, revised 2016.

Jacobsen, Annie. *Operation Paperclip: The Secret Intelligence Program to Bring Nazi Scientists to America*. New York: Little, Brown & Co., 2014.

Joshi, S.T. *A Dreamer and a Visionary: H.P. Lovecraft in His Time*. Liverpool University Press, 2001.

Joshi, S.T. *H. P. Lovecraft: A Life*. West Warwick, RI: Necronomicon Press, 1996

Keveney, Bill. "The Many Aliases of J.J. Abrams." *USA Today*, Jan. 4, 2005.

Kit, Borys. "Universal's 'Monsterverse' in Peril as Top Producers Exit (Exclusive)." *The Hollywood Reporter*, Nov. 8, 2017.

Knight, Peter, Dr. *Conspiracy Culture: From Kennedy to* The X-Files. London: Routledge, 2001.

Krantz, Matt, Mike Snider, Marco Della Cava, and Bryan Alexander. "Disney buys Lucasfilm for $4 Billion." *USA Today*, Oct. 30, 2012. https://www.usatoday.com/story/money/business/2012/10/30/disney-star-wars-lucasfilm/1669739/.

Kushner, David. "Behind the Scenes with *Heroes* Creator Tim Kring and 'Hiro,' Masi Oka." *Wired*, April 23, 2007.

Lee, Peter. W (editor). *Exploring Picard's Galaxy: Essays on* Star Trek: The Next Generation. Jefferson, NC: McFarland, 2018.

Levitz, Paul. *75 Years of DC Comics: The Art of Modern Mythmaking*. Köln: Taschen, 2010.

Lewis, James. R. *The Gods Have Landed: New Religions from Other Worlds*. State University of New York Press, 1995.

Liptak, Andrew. "Bryan Fuller Originally Envisioned *Star Trek: Discovery* as an Anthology Show." *The Verge*, July 29, 2017.

Lofgren, Mike. "Anatomy of the Deep State." BillMoyers.com, Feb. 21, 2014.

Lovecraft, H. P. *The Complete Fiction of H. P. Lovecraft*. New York: Chartwell Books, 2016.

Lovett, Jamie. "'*Star Trek* Fleet Command' Writer Teases Post-*Beyond* Kelvin Timeline Stories." Comic Book, Nov. 26, 2018.

Malcom, Shawna. "*Lost* Boss Tackles Star Trek *Enterprise*." *TV Guide*, Aug. 11, 2006

Metcalf, Stephen. "Neoliberalism: The Idea That Swallowed the World." *The Guardian*, Aug. 18, 2017.

Mooney, Darren. *Opening* The X-Files: *A Critical History of the Original Series*. Jefferson, NC: McFarland, 2017.

Mooney, Darren. "'Talitha Cumi' (Review) / 'Gethsemane' (Review)." them0vieblog.com.

Neal. "TV Show Mythology." *Literal Minded*, Feb. 2, 2010.

Nevins, Jess. "A Brief History of the Crossover." *i09*, Aug. 23, 2011.

Newsweek Special Edition. "Gene Roddenberry's Wagon Train to *Star Trek*." *Newsweek*, March 3. 2016.

Overland, Brian. "Origins of Superman: Nietzsche and the Man of Steel." BrianOverland.com, 2013.

Bibliography

Pappas, Stephanie. "How Real Is the *Game of Thrones* Medieval World?" *Live Science*, April 3, 2014.

Pascale, Anthony. "Exclusive Interview: Ron Moore On Breaking Out of The Box." trekmovie.com, June 12, 2008.

Paskin, Willa. "The TV Club, 2015." *Slate*, Dec. 23, 2015.

Patches, Matt. "Netflix Still Intends to Produce *Stranger Things* Game Despite Telltale Collapse." *Polygon*, Sept. 24, 2018.

Patten, Dominic. "CBS All Access Bosses on More *Star Trek* Series, *The Twilight Zone* Status, Stephen King & More—TCA." *Deadline Hollywood*, Aug. 6, 2018.

Piller, Michael. "Fade In: The Making of *Star Trek: Insurrection*." 2003.

Pinch, Geraldine. *Magic in Ancient Egypt*. London: British Museum Press, 1994.

Rafferty, Terrence. "A License to Pursue the Inner Bond." *New York Times*, December 9, 2007.

Riley, Russell. L. *Bill Clinton: Impact and Legacy*. UVA Miller Center.

Rioux, Terry Lee. *From Sawdust to Stardust: The Biography of DeForest Kelley*. New York: Gallery Books, 2005.

Roddenberry, Gene. *The Making of Star Trek*. New York: Titan Books, 1991.

Roots, Kimberly. "*Alias* Oral History: Jennifer Garner, Series Creator J.J. Abrams and Cast Mark Spy Drama's 10th Anniversary." *TV Line*. May 4, 2016.

Russell, Joseph. "How Online Streaming Is Changing TV Storytelling." *Den of Geek*, October 8, 2015. https://www.denofgeek.com/tv/how-online-streaming-is-changing-tv-storytelling/.

Russell, Lynette, and Nathan Wolski. "Beyond the Final Frontier: *Star Trek*, the Borg and the Post-colonial." *Intensities: The Journal of Cult Media*, 1 (spring/summer 2001). https://intensitiescultmedia.com/2014/08/27/beyond-the-final-frontier/.

Simunic, Steven. "Why ABC's *Lost* Is Losing It." *The Daily Californian*, March 15, 2007.

Star Trek.com Staff. "Exclusive Interview: Part III, Nicholas Meyer on Today's Trek." September 24, 2014. https://www.startrek.com/article/exclusive-interview-part-iii-nicholas-meyer-on-todays-trek.

Star Trek.com Staff. "Manny Coto Talks *Enterprise* and *24*." April 27, 2014. https://www.startrek.com/article/manny-coto-talks-enterprise-and-24.

Stelter, Brian. "Fox TV's Gamble: Fewer Ads in a Break, but Costing More." *New York Times*, Feb. 12, 2009.

Tach, Dave. *Avengers: Age of Ultron*'s most confusing scene and the gun that almost killed it, explained, Polygon, May 11, 2015.

Till, Barry. *The 47 Ronin: A Story of Samurai Loyalty and Courage*. San Francisco: Pomegranate, 2005.

Tolkien, J.R.R. *Tree and Leaf; Mythopoeia; The Homecoming of Beorhtnoth Beorhthelm's Son*. New York: HarperCollins, 2001.

Tomasso, Vince. "Classical Antiquity and Western Identity in *Battlestar Galactica*." Tor.com, January 26, 2015. https://www.tor.com/2015/01/26/classical-antiquity-and-western-identity-in-battlestar-galactica/.

Truitt, Brian. "Sunday Geekersation: Grant Morrison Switches Superheroes." *USA Today*, July 28, 2013. https://www.usatoday.com/story/life/2013/07/28/grant-morrison-sunday-conversation-batman-wonder-woman/2586739/.

Van Der Werff, Todd, and Caroline Framke. "*Twin Peaks*, Decoded for Novices and Obsessives Alike." *Vox*, May 21, 2017. https://www.vox.com/culture/2017/5/19/15660502/twin-peaks-explained-showtime-david-lynch.

Vaz, Mark Cotta. "*Alias Declassified: The Official Companion*." New York: Bantam Books, 2002.

Bibliography

Waid, Mark. "*Man of Steel*, Since You Asked." *Thrillbent*, June 14, 2013. http://thrillbent.com/blog/man-of-steel-since-you-asked/.

White, Donald. W. *The American Century: The Rise and Decline of the United States as a World Power*, Chapter One, The *New York Times* on the Web, 1996.

Whitfield, Stephen. E. *The Making of* Star Trek. New York: Titan Books, 1991.

Williams, Gregory Paul. *The Story of Hollywood: An Illustrated History*. Hollywood: B.L. Press, 2012.

Williams, Mike. "The Rise and Fall of Telltale Games." *US Gamer*, Sept. 25, 2018. https://www.usgamer.net/articles/the-rise-and-fall-of-telltale-games.

Winters, Riley. "How It Ends: The Ancient Roots of Doomsday Prophecies and End of the World Beliefs." *Ancient Origins*, July 15, 2018. https://www.ancient-origins.net/history/ancient-roots-doomsday-prophecies-and-end-world-beliefs-002571.

Wohleber, Curt. "The Man Who Can Scare Stephen King," *American Heritage*, December 1995.

Wolski, Nathan. "Beyond the Final Frontier: *Star Trek*, the Borg and the Post-Colonial." *Intensities: The Journal of Cult Media* 1 (spring/summer 2001). https://intensitiescultmedia.com/2014/08/27/beyond-the-final-frontier/.

Wright, Matt. "Ira Steven Behr Reveals How He Really Wanted *Star Trek: Deep Space Nine* To End + More DS9 At STLV 2018," trekmovie.com, Aug. 21, 2018.

Zoglin, Richard. "A Bold Vision: How *Star Trek* First Made It to the Screen." *Time*, July 21, 2016.

Zoller Seitz, Matt. "The *St. Elsewhere* Finale at 30." *Vulture*, May 25, 2018. https://www.vulture.com/2018/05/the-st-elsewhere-finale-at-30.html.

Index

The A-Team (series) 19–20
ABC 132
Abrams, J.J. 44, 57, 72, 101, 109, 129, 132, 135, 156
Adcox, John 2
The Adventures of Superman 13
Aeschylus 3
Affleck, Ben 144
The After 123
Age of Enlightenment 117–118
Age of Reason 117
AIDS 98
Airwolf 20
Alcatraz 129–130
Alexander, Jaime 141
Alias 6, 17, 57–65, 72–73, 111, 119, 126, 130, 132, 156; "Before the Flood" 60, 63; "Countdown" 61–62; "The Descent" 63; "Firebomb" 59, 61; "Full Disclosure" 62–63; "In Dreams" 61; "Legacy" 65; "Page 47" 61; "Passage" 59; "The Prophecy" 59–60; "Q&A" 59–60; "Resurrection" 63; "Salvation" 59; "The Telling" 65; "30 Seconds" 62
Alice in Wonderland 46
Alien (franchise) 71–72, 118, 155
alien astronauts 70
All-Star Comics (DC) 12
Allah 56
Altman, Robert 19
Amazon 136, 139
The American Dream 96, 106
ancient aliens 70
Anderson, Gillian 20, 103–104
Angel (TV series) 135, 140, 143
Ant-Man (2015 film) 141
anti–Semitism 8–9
Aquaman (character) 145
Aquaman (2018 film)
ARG experience 45
The Army Game 15
Arrow 127, 135
"Arrowverse" 127, 135, 145; "Crisis on Earth X" 135
Assassin's Creed (film) 153

Assassin's Creed (franchise) 151–153
Assassin's Creed: Odyssey 152
Assassin's Creed: Origins 152–152
Assassin's Creed II 152
Assassin's Creed III
The Atom (character) 12
The Avengers (1960s TV series) 17
The Avengers (2012 film) 138–141, 144
Avengers: Age of Ultron 140–142, 146
Avengers: Endgame 139, 143
Avengers: Infinity War 139, 142, 146, 148

B-movie 14–15
"baby boomer" 15
Babylon-5 6, 20–21, 44–45, 56, 83, 88, 92, 118, 121, 124–126, 131–132, 149
backstory 6
Back to the Future (videogame) 150
Bad Robot (company) 129–130, 135
bagua 80
Barrett-Roddenberry, Majel 124
Batman (character) 12–13, 138, 143–144
The Batman (film) 147
Batman (films) 126, 138
Batman (1960s TV series) 15
Batman (videogame) 150
Batman Begins 144
Batman vs Superman: Dawn of Justice 11, 144
Battlestar Galactica 6, 56
Baum, L. Frank 14
BBC 132
The Beatles 15
Bellisario, Donald. P 20
Benioff, David 115, 118, 120, 149
Berman, Rick 89, 98
The Birth of a Nation 137
Black Panther (2018 film) 143
Blade (franchise) 138
Blade Runner 110
Bogart, Humphrey 14
Bonaparte, Napoleon 107
Bond, James (character) 4–5, 15–16, 153
Braga, Brannon 128

199

Index

Branagh, Kenneth 139
Braun, Wernher von 106
British Empire 106
Brooks, Avery 85, 89
Bruner, Kevin 150
Buffy the Vampire Slayer 3, 135, 140, 143
Burton, Tim 138
Bush, George W. 112

"The Call of Cthulhu" (H.P. Lovecraft) 9
Campbell, Joseph 4, 22–55, 71
Cannell, Stephen. J. 19
Captain America: Civil War 11, 141–142
Captain America: The First Avenger 139–140, 142
Captain America: The Winter Soldier 141–142
Captain Marvel (2019 film) 141, 143
Carey, Stan 1
Carpenter, John 11, 14
Carrie (1976 film) 135
Carter, Chris 1, 20–21, 23, 30–33, 65, 73, 104, 106–107, 109, 112–115, 121–124. 132, 151, 156
Castle Rock 135–136
Cavill, Henry 144
CBS All Access 101, 132
character 8
character arc 3–5
Chariots of the Gods? 70
Charlie's Angels (series) 19
chat room 45
cinema 14, 19
Cinescape (magazine) 1
Cline, Ernest 154
Clinton, Bill 83, 108
The Colbys 20
Cold War 53, 93–94, 98, 102, 106–107, 113, 151
colonialism 97–98
comics 11-
Conan Doyle, Arthur 10–11
Connery, Sean 155
Connors, Dan 150
Constantine, John (character) 13
Coppola, Francis Ford 19
counter-culture 13, 15, 18
Crichton, Michael 133–134
Crosby, Bing 137
Cruise, Tom 147
Cthulhu Mythos 7–11
culture 22
Cuse, Carlton 44, 49–50, 72–73, 78, 129, 132

Dante 123
Daredevil (character) 13
Daredevil (TV series) 127, 134

The Dark Knight 127
The Dark Knight Returns 13
The Dark Knight Rises 144
Dark Skies 125, 129
"Dark Universe" (franchise) 147
Davenport, Jack 128
The David Letterman Show 104
Day of the Tentacle 150
DC Comics 11–14, 19, 138, 143
DC Extended Universe 11, 143–147, 156
DC Films 144
"deep state" 113
del Toro, Guillermo 11
"Demon in a Bottle" (comic) 139
de Palma, Brian 135
Derleth, August 10
"Devious Weasel" 1
Disney 149
divine 22
The Divine Comedy 123
Dixon of Dock Green 15
The Doctor (character) 16
Dr. No 155
Doctor Strange (2016 film) 140, 143
Doctor Who 16; "An Unearthly Child" 16
Donner, Richard 138
Downey, Robert, Jr. 127
Dracula (franchise) 137
Duchovny, David 103
Duggan, Michael 42
Dune 10
"The Dunwich Horror" (H.P. Lovecraft) 9
Durand, Kevin 140

Earth: Final Conflict 124–125
Eccleston, Christopher 126
Ellison, Harlan 91
The Event 129; "I Haven't Told You Everything" 129
The Evil Dead 10

The Fall of a Nation 137
fan fiction 11
fandom 1, 11, 19, 45, 73
Favreau, Jon 139, 149
Feige, Kevin 138–139, 156
Fiennes, Joseph 128
Finger, Bill 14
Fisher, Ray 146
The Flash (character) 145
The Flash (film) 147
The Flash (TV series) 127, 135
Flash Gordon 147
Flashforward (novel) 128
Flashforward (TV series) 128
Forster, Robert 126
The 4400 130
Fox (network) 103, 132

200

Index

Fox, Gardner 12
Frankenstein (franchise) 137
Frankenstein, Victor (character) 110
free-market economics 96
Friedkin, William 19
Friedman, Brent V. 125
Fringe 90, 109–112, 127, 130; "Bound" 110; "Midnight" 111; "Pilot" 110
Frost, Mark 6, 20–21
The Fugitive 126
Fuller, Bryan 101, 135
fundamentalism 101–102
FX (network) 122

Gadot, Gal 145
Gaia 74
Gaiman, Neil 13
Game of Thrones 3, 6, 44, 56, 73, 90, 112, 115–121, 131–132, 136, 156; "The Dragon and the Wolf" 119; "Winter Is Coming" 118
A Game of Thrones (book) 116
Game of Thrones (videogame) 150
Garcia, Jorge 129
Garland, Judy 14
Gates, Bill 110
Geordie Shore 131
gothic 11
Goyer, David S. 128
Greeks 2, 4, 6–7, 12, 81
Green Lantern (character) 12
Griffith, D.W. 137
Grim Fandango 150
Guardians of the Galaxy (2013 film) 140–141, 143
Guardians of the Galaxy (videogame) 153

Halloween (franchise) 137
Hammer (film company) 15
Harris, Thomas 33
Harry Potter 6
Harsh Realm 122–123
HBO 3, 115, 136, 139
Henriksen, Lance 121
Herbert, Brian 10
Hercules 4
The Hero with a Thousand Faces 4, 22–55
Heroes 126, 135
Hollywood 14, 126
Homer 3
Homicide: Life on the Street 20)
Hoover, J. Edgar 125
Hope, Bob 137
Hopkins, Anthony 134
Howard, Robert. E 10
Hudnall, James D. 122
Hulu 135

I Love Lucy 15
The Incredible Hulk (2008 film) 139

Indiana Jones and the Fate of Atlantis 150
IDW Publishing 153
Illuminati 60
internet forum 1
Into the Wild 41
The Invaders 126
Invasion of the Body Snatchers (1950s movie) 14
Iron Man (film) 12, 138–139, 146
Iron Man 2 139
Isil 102
Italian Renaissance 117
It Came from Beneath the Sea 14
ITV 15
Ivanhoe 15

Jackson, Peter 3, 136
Jackson, Samuel L. 138
Jehovah 56
Jessica Jones (TV series) 127, 134
Jobs, Steve 110
Johannesen, Chip 39, 42
Johansson, Scarlett 139
Johnson, Mike 153
Johnson, Rian 149
Johnston, Joe 139
Jones, Alex 113
Joy-Nolan, Lisa 133–134
Jurassic Park (videogame) 150
Justice League (2017 film) 145–147

Kane, Bob 3
Katz, Evan 129
Keeping Up with the Kardashians 131
Kelly, Gene 14
Kennedy, John F. 125
Kennedy, Kathleen 149, 156
Kent, Clark (character) 13
King, Martin Luther, Jr. 4, 93
King, Stephen 8, 135
Kingston, Alex 128
Kirby, Jack 3, 13–14, 18
Kneale, Nigel 15, 19
Knight Rider 19–20
Kojima, Hideo 151
Kolchak: The Night Stalker 19
Kring, Tim 126–127
Kurtzman, Alex 109
Kurzel, Justin 153

Lamour, Dorothy 137
Law & Order 20
Lee, Stan 3, 14, 18
Legends of Tomorrow 135
Leonidas 4
Levitz, Paul 12
Lieber, Jeffrey 44

Index

Lindelof, Damon 44, 49–50, 72–73, 78, 129, 132
Long, Frank Bellknap 10
Lost 6, 17, 23, 44–55, 57, 64, 72–82, 109, 111, 115, 118–119, 121, 126–130, 148, 156; "Ab Aeterno" 77, 80; "Across the Sea" 74–77, 79–81; "All the Best Cowboys Have Daddy Issues" 47; "Because You Left" 53; "Cabin Fever" 51; "Dead Is Dead" 81; "Eggtown" 51; "The End" 54–55, 79, 82; "Exodus" 48; "House of the Rising Sun" 46; "The Hunting Party" 47–48; "I Do" 49, 77; "The Incident" 53, 76; "The Life and Death of Jeremy Bentham" 51; "Lighthouse" 76; "Live Together, Die Alone" 48, 81; "The Man from Tallahassee" 50; "Man of Science, Man of Faith" 47; "The New Man in Charge" 82; "Orientation" 53; "Pilot" 45; "Somewhere Nice Back Home" 51; "S.O.S." 78; "Stranger in a Strange Land" 48–49; "A Tale of Two Cities" 47; "There's No Place Like Home" 50, 79; "316" 52; "Through the Looking Glass" 50–51; "Walkabout" 45–46; "What They Died For" 77; "White Rabbit" 46–48
The Lord of the Rings (book) 2
The Lord of the Rings (TV series) 136
Lovecraft, H.P. 7–13, 15, 18–19
Lovecraftian 14, 74
Lucas, George 19, 147
LucasArts 150–151
LucasFilm 149
Luke Cage (TV series) 134
Lynch, David 6, 20–21

MacGuffin 10, 42, 65, 122
The Man from U.N.C.L.E. 17
Man of Steel (2014 film) 144
The Mandalorian 149
"Mandela Effect" 114
Manimal 20
Markstein, George 17
Martin, George R.R. 3, 115–116, 118–120
Marvel Cinematic Universe 3, 12, 126, 131, 134, 138–146, 156
Marvel Comics 11–14, 19, 153
Marvel Studios 138, 141
Marvel's Agents of S.H.I.E.L.D. 141
M.A.S.H. (series) 19
The Matrix 123
Mayer, Shelly 12
McDowell, Malcolm 126
McGoohan, Patrick 17–19
Mengele, Josef 107
message board 45
Metal Gear (franchise) 151
Metal Gear Solid: Guns of the Patriots 151

Metal Gear Solid: Snake Eater 151
Meyer, Nicholas 94
MGM 14
Middle-Earth 3
Miller, Ezra 146–147
Miller, Frank 13
Millennium (TV series) 23, 33–44, 57, 90, 121–123, 132, 135; "The Beginning and the End" 37; "Beware of the Dog" 38; "The Curse of Frank Black" 40; "Force Majeure" 37; "The Fourth Horseman" 42–43; "Goodbye Charlie" 38; "The Hand of St. Sebastian" 39; "The Innocents" 39; "Lamentation" 35–36; "Luminary" 41; "Midnight of the Century" 39–41; "Monster" 37–38; "Owls" 39–42; "Paper Dove" 34, 36; "Pilot" 33–34; "Powers, Principalities, Thrones and Dominions" 35, 40–41; "Roosters" 39–42; "A Single Blade of Grass" 39; "Siren" 40; "The Time Is Now" 42–43; "Weeds" 35; "The Well Worn Lock" 35; "Wide Open" 35
Mission Impossible III 782
Moffat, Steven 16
Molander, Troy 150
Momoa, Jason 146–147
Monaghan, Dominic 128
Monkey Island (franchise) 150
The Monomyth 4, 22–55, 86, 91
Mooney, Darren 67, 106
Moore, Alan 13
Moore, Roger 15
Moore, Ronald D. 6, 97, 99
Morgan, Darin 114
Morgan, Glen 36–37, 39, 42, 122
The Mummy (2018 film) 147
"mystery box" 58
myth 1–6, 8, 12
mythology 1–6, 12–14, 16, 18–19, 21, 28, 37, 58, 62, 69–70, 82–83, 87–90, 95, 104–105, 109, 113
mythopoesis 2–3, 7
mythos 7–12, 15, 19, 92

National Allied Publications 11
Native Americans 106–107
The Necronomicon 10
Neill, Sam 129
neoliberalism 96, 98
Netflix 11, 127, 134, 139, 141, 153
New England 8
"New Hollywood" 19
"new world order" 113
Nietzsche, Friedrich 12
9/11 59–60, 96, 100–101
Nintendo 151
Nixon, Richard 108, 147
Nolan, Christopher 126, 138, 144

Index

Nolan, Jonathan 133–134
Norton, Edward 139

Obama, Barack 113, 148–149
Oppenheimer, Robert 107
O'Quinn, Terry 35
Orci, Roberto 109
The Outer Limits 125
Overstreet, Robert 12

Paquette, Andrew 122
Piller, Michael 95–98
The Pink Panther (franchise) 137
Pinkner, Jeff 111
Planet of the Apes (franchise) 137
podcast 45
Police Academy (franchise) 137
post-truth 113
Prison Break 126
The Prisoner 16–18; "Arrival" 18; "Fall Out" 18; "Many Happy Returns" 17
Prometheus 71

Quantum Leap 20, 53
The Quatermass Experiment 15–16
Queen Elizabeth II 14

racism 9
Raimi, Sam 10–11, 138
Rawhide 15
Ready Player One (book) 154–155
Ready Player One (film) 154–155
Reagan, Ronald 96, 98
Red Dragon (book) 33
Reeve, Christopher 138
Reeves, George 13
Reeves, Matt 147
retcon 113
Rhode Island 7
Rice, Jeff 19
Road to… (franchise) 137
Robin (character) 15
rock & roll 15
Rocky (franchise) 137
Roddenberry, Gene 10, 18–19, 83, 91–93, 96–98, 100, 124
"Roddenberry's Box" 96–97
Rogue One: A Star Wars Story 149
Rolling Stone (magazine) 103
The Rolling Stones 15
Romans 2, 6
Ronin 102
Roosevelt, Franklin 106
Roswell incident 113, 125
Roundtree, Richard 126
Russell, Lynette 97

St. Elsewhere 89
Sam & Max (franchise) 150

Sandman (comic) 13
Sarnoff, Elisabeth 129
Sawyer, Robert J. 128
Schuster, Joe 14
Scorsese, Martin 19
Scott, Ridley 71–72
"Secret Invasion" (comic) 143
Sega 151
Serling, Rod 15, 19, 91
Shatner, William 84–85
Shaw, Sam 135
Shiban, John 105
Siegel, Jerry 14
The Simpsons 104
situation comedy 15
Smulders, Cobie 141
"snake in the mailbox" 50
Snipes, Wesley 138
Snyder, Zack 144
Solo: A Star Wars Story 149
A Song of Ice and Fire (novels) 3, 115–120, 136
Sons of Anarchy 112, 118, 121
Sophocles 3
Space: Above and Beyond 36
Spelling, Aaron 19
Spider-Man (films) 138
Spider-Man: Homecoming 146
Spielberg, Steven 19, 154
Spotnitz, Frank 31, 104
Star Trek (franchise) 10, 15, 82, 85, 90–91, 95–97, 101, 103, 115, 124–125, 135, 138, 147
Star Trek (post–2009 films) 101
Star Trek: Deep Space Nine 20, 57, 82–83, 85–89, 92, 94, 98–100, 102, 135; "Accession" 86; "The Changing Face of Evil" 100; "The Circle" 86; "Covenant" 88; "Destiny" 86; "Emissary" 86; "Far Behind the Stars" 89; "The Homecoming" 86; "Homefront" 100; "Image in the Sand" 87"; "Paradise Lost" 100; "Rapture" 87; "The Reckoning" 88–89; "The Siege" 86; "Tears of the Prophets" 89; "Waltz" 88; "What You Leave Behind" 87–88
Star Trek: Discovery 92, 101–103, 132, 135, 156; "Battle at the Binary Stars" 102
Star Trek: Enterprise 89, 92, 94–98, 100–102; "The Expanse" 100–101; "These Are the Voyages" 89
Star Trek: First Contact 95
Star Trek: Fleet Command 153
Star Trek: The Next Generation 73, 84, 87, 94–97, 99–101; "Conspiracy" 100; "Encounter at Farpoint" 95
Star Trek: The Original Series 82–84, 87, 92–94, 96, 101–102, 135; "Mirror, Mirror" 102; "Space Seed" 84; "The Squire of

203

Index

Gothos" 84; "The Return of the Archons" 84; "Where No Man Has Gone Before" 84
Star Trek: Voyager 82, 87, 92, 94, 99
Star Trek II: The Wrath of Khan 84
Star Trek III: The Search for Spock 94
Star Trek V: The Final Frontier 84
Star Trek VI: The Undiscovered Country 93–94, 96
Star Wars (franchise) 22, 32, 75, 77, 147–150
Star Wars: A New Hope 26, 148
Star Wars: Rebels 149
Star Wars: Resistance 149
Star Wars: Return of the Jedi 148
Star Wars: Revenge of the Sith 148
Star Wars: The Clone Wars 149
Star Wars: The Force Awakens 148
Star Wars: The Last Jedi 149
Star Wars: The Rise of Skywalker 149
Steven Behr, Ira 86, 88–89, 95, 99
Stewart, Patrick 85
Stokely, E.E. 2
story arc 3–5
Straczynski, J. Michael 6, 20–21, 65, 88, 125, 132
Stranger Things 11, 153
Supergirl (TV series) 127
Superman (character) 2–3, 12–13, 138, 143–144
Superman (1978 film) 138
Swamp Thing (comic) 13

Takei, George 126
Technicolor 14
Telltale Games 150, 153
"The Temple" (H.P. Lovecraft) 8
Ten Thirteen (company) 123
Terminator: The Sarah Connor Chronicles 112
"The Terrible Old Man" (H.P. Lovecraft) 8
terrorism 101
Tesla, Nicola 110
The Thing 14
The Thing from Another World 14
Thomason, Dustin 135
Thor (2011 film) 139
Thor: Ragnarok 146
Tolkien, J.R.R. 2, 120, 136–137
"The Tomb" (H.P. Lovecraft) 7
Tomb Raider 153
"trickle-down economics" 117
Trimble, Bjo 91–92
Trimble, John 91–92
Trump, Donald 103, 113, 148
TV drama 15
24 126–127
The Twilight Zone 15–16, 91
Twin Peaks 6, 20–21

Twin Peaks: Fire Walk with Me 21
2007 Writers Strike 127

Ubermensch 12
Ubisoft 151–152
utopia 96–97, 99–100

Verne, Jules 10–11
Vietnam War 147
viral marketing 45
von Daniken, Erich 70

Wagner, Richard 155
The Walking Dead (videogame) 150
Ward, Burt 15
"water cooler" 45
"Watergate" 147
Wauters, Nick 129
weird fiction 11
Weiss, D.B. 115, 118, 120, 149
Wells, H.G. 10
West, Adam 15
Western (genre) 14–15
Westworld 44, 56, 132–134
Whedon, Joss 139, 143, 146
Wheel of Dharma 80
Wheeler-Nicholson, Malcolm 11
Wiki 45
The Wizard of Oz (movie) 14
Wolfe, Robert Hewitt 99
Wolski, Nathan 97
Wonder Woman (character) 143
Wonder Woman (2017 film)
Wong, James 36–37, 39, 42, 122
World War II 14, 40, 99–100, 102, 106–107, 123
Wymam, J.H. 111

The X-Files 1, 4–6, 19–21, 23–33, 36, 39, 42, 44–45, 56–58, 62, 65–73, 75, 90–92, 103–115, 119, 121–126, 130, 132, 135, 141, 149, 156; "Anasazi" 25–27, 30–31, 104, 106–107; "Ascension" 66, 104; "The Beginning" 30, 70; "Beyond the Sea" 25, 67; "Biogenesis" 31, 69–71; "The Blessing Way" 25, 27, 104, 107; "Closure" 32; "Colony" 25, 29; "Conduit" 24; "Deep Throat" 66, 104; "Demons" 24, 28; "The End" 30, 70; "End Game" 24, 29; "The Erlenmeyer Flask" 26, 104; "Essence" 72; "Existence" 72; "Fallen Angel" 66; "Fearful Symmetry" 68; "Firewalker" 105; "Genderbender" 68; "Gethsemane" 29, 68–69; "Herrenvolk" 28–29, 67; "Hungry" 111; "Little Green Men" 23; "The Lost Art of Forehead Sweat" 114; "Musings of a Cigarette-Smoking Man" 28; "My Struggle" 113; "My Struggle II" 114; "My Struggle

204

Index

III" 114; "My Struggle IV" 32, 114; "Nisei" 27, 67, 107; "One Breath" 105; "One Son" 31, 70; "Paper Clip" 25–26, 104–105, 107–108; "Paper Hearts" 24; "Patient X" 66, 108; "The Pine Bluff Variant" 108; "Provenance" 72; "Providence" 72; "The Red and the Black" 30, 69; "Redux" 29–31, 68–69; "Redux II" 24, 28–30, 68–69; "Requiem" 70; "Revelations" 67; "731" 27, 106–108; "The Sixth Extinction" 69–71; "The Sixth Extinction II: Amor Fati" 28, 31–32, 69–71; "Squeeze" 111; "Talitha Cumi" 28, 66–68; "Tooms" 111; "The Truth" 32, 112–114; "Two Fathers" 31; "Unusual Suspects" 24

The X-Files: Fight the Future 29–30, 36
The X-Files: I Want to Believe 113–114

Z-Cars 15
Zabel, Bryce 125
Zuckerberg, Mark 145